SKIVVY NINE!

For my good friend, Ed Engle.

TW Beal AKA Wayne Babb

ISBN 1-59113-565-6

This manuscript has undergone a security classification review and was released (as amended) for publication by The Department of Defense Directorate for Security Review and The National Security Agency

Printed in the United States of America.

The events in this book are factual; however, all names, including that of the author, are fictitious.

Booklocker.com, Inc.
2004

SKIVVY NINE!

A Memior
by
Chief Master Sergeant T. Wyman Beal
United States Air Force, Retired

Dedicated to Frances and Bo, who did without a husband and dad for a year while I fought the Cold War on the Korean Peninsula.

TABLE OF CONTENTS

Introduction ix
Prologue xi
Chapter One IN THE BEGINNING........ 1
Chapter Two TESTING MY WINGS 10
Chapter Three THE IG'S COMING! THE IG'S COMING!........ 26
Chapter Four THEY'RE HERE! THEY'RE HERE!........ 43
Chapter Five THEY'RE GONE........ 67
Chapter Six THE AFTERMATH 77
Chapter Seven AND LIFE GOES ON........ 96
Chapter Eight THERE'S A NEW SHERIFF IN TOWN........ 114
Chapter Nine .....AND HE'S A BAD ASS 127
Chapter Ten TIGHTENING UP THE SCREWS 152
Chapter Eleven AND THE BATTLE LINES ARE DRAWN........ 182
Chapter Twelve IT DON'T GET MUCH WORSE THAN THIS........ 200
Chapter Thirteen ROCK BOTTOM 212
Chapter Fourteen THE IG'S COMING--*AGAIN!!* 230
Chapter Fifteen THEY'RE HERE! *AGAIN!!*........ 248
Chapter Sixteen IT WAS THE BEST OF TIMES 268
Chapter Seventeen THE WORM TURNS 294
Chapter Eighteen SLIDIN' ON OUT........ 301
GLOSSARY OF TERMS........ 307

Introduction

Korea--1952. The "police action" was at its height. A small, obscure Air Force organization far to the rear of the front lines quietly went about its business of gathering and disseminating intelligence information.

The unit was the 6969th Radio Squadron (Mobile). It had relocated up and down the peninsula many times as each side in the conflict gained or gave ground, but now it had been at one location for over three months since the lines of engagement had more or less stabilized. That was long enough for a small village of bars, pawn shops, eateries, and tailors to spring up from the muck and mire just outside the unit's compound.

The men of the 6969th frequented the village often, especially the bars. For it was in the bars that the lonely GIs could purchase not only rot-gut Korean whiskey and (surprisingly) state-side beer, but they could find what they thirsted for most--female companionship.

The women who plied their wares in the bars found the numerical designator of the 6969th amusing. Most were totally familiar with mutual oral sex but, like most orientals, viewed the practice as slightly risqué and a little off color. So it was only natural that when a member of the 6969th told one of the girls what unit he was in, that information would invariably produce a shy giggle and a tiny blush.

"Skivvy" is a slang word borrowed from the Japanese language that loosely translates to "slightly risqué and a little off color". The Japanese had occupied Korea for over 50 years before they were forced to leave by the outcome of World War II. But when they withdrew, they left behind tidbits of their language, especially the slang. Over time, this morsel of Japanese slang was attached to members of the 6969th; they became "skivvy boy-sans" and their unit "SKIVVY NINE".

The Korean War eventually ended, but SKIVVY NINE's presence in Korea did not. It moved many times before it took up residence at Osan Air Base where it is located today. And, over the years, the unit has had numerous numerical designators: 6923rd Radio Squadron Mobile, 6915th Security Group, Detachment 1 of the 6921st Security Wing, 6903rd Security Group, and its current designator, the 303rd Intelligence Squadron to name just a few. But the one thing that remained constant through all the moves and redesignations was its nickname--SKIVVY NINE.

This journal is a snapshot of one year in the long and distinguished history of SKIVVY NINE as seen through the eyes of its top ranking enlisted member--me. I was the Operations Superintendent of SKIVVY NINE and, in that capacity, I acted as the Operations Officer's right hand, was the ultimate supervisor and leader of the 250 enlisted people in the Operations Division, and advised the Unit Commander on all enlisted matters. It should have been the dream job of my entire Air Force career. It wasn't.

This story is real and so are the people in it. For obvious reasons, I've had to change their names (as well as my own) but that's all that's been changed. Everything else is just as I meticulously recorded it a day or two after the events happened while my memory was fresh.

For me, this was an incredible year; without a doubt, the best and worst year of my military career. It was a one million - two million experience: I wouldn't take a million dollars for it--I wouldn't do it again for two.

Prologue

THE LONG JOURNEY TO FIRST CLASS

I worked my way up the spiral stairs that led to the upper deck of the chartered Boeing 747. At the top of the stairs, I showed the flight attendant my boarding pass. She directed me to one of the seats in the cozy compartment. I slipped out of my uniform blouse, folded it neatly, and packed it in the overhead bin along with my briefcase. Then I sat, buckled in, and checked out my surroundings.

There were 10 leather-covered seats that resembled my recliner in front of the TV set back home. I pressed a button on the armrest and found that my seat *actually was* a recliner, complete with raised footrest. So this is how the "other half" lives, I thought.

I was still playing with the seat controls when the flight attendant leaned down and asked if I would like something to drink. I checked my watch--09:30 a.m.--coffee or bloody Mary? I opted for the latter. The flight attendant returned with a tray containing a fifth of Absolut Vodka, a carafe of tomato juice, sliced limes, celery stalks, Tabasco Sauce, Angostura bitters, salt, pepper, an empty glass and a bucket of ice. She set the goodies on the fold-out tray, smiled sweetly, and said "Enjoy". So this is how the "other half" lives, I thought.

I was just putting the finishing touches on my bloody Mary when a two-star General[1] took a seat across the aisle from me after completing his own blouse folding/briefcase stowing routine.

---

[1] See Glossary of Terms at the back of this memoir for a complete rundown on military rank.

"Mornin', Chief. Where you headed?" he smiled as he buckled his seat belt.

"Mornin', General. Headed for Korea. You?"

"Just a little temporary duty on Okinawa. First time in first class?"

Damn--I had been found out! I was an interloper in the realm of the high rollers, and the General could see right through me. I hid my discomfort and shot back, "How'd you know?"

He nodded toward the bloody Mary makings, and grinned. "I did the same thing the first time I rode up here just after I was promoted to Colonel. It was six o'clock in the morning, but I ordered a Singapore sling just because I could."

"Well you got to admit, General, it is the lap of luxury," I said. "I feel a little guilty--us enlisted men aren't used to this kind of treatment."

"Neither are us officers until we finally make Colonel. But it's OK, Chief. It takes a pretty special guy to do what you've done. You've reached the top of the enlisted ranks and you deserve this ride as much as the Colonels and us Generals. Now enjoy that bloody Mary. You've earned it."

The General unfolded a copy of The Washington Times and it was obvious our conversation was over. I took a sip of the best bloody Mary I had ever tasted, then leaned back in my personal recliner and closed my eyes as the plane began to taxi toward the end of the runway. When the big bird began its take off roll, my thoughts wandered back to how I had come to be here in the military version of first class.

♦♦♦♦♦♦♦♦♦♦

SKIVVY NINE!

When the recruiter asked me why I wanted to join his Air Force that afternoon back in 1961, I told him I had lived in Chattanooga, Tennessee my entire life. I could stay in Chattanooga, I said, get a job as a welder at one of the foundries, and live out my life right there. Then when I was old and gray and my grandkids asked where all I had been, I would have to look them right in the eye and say, "I've never been north of Knoxville or south of Atlanta." I didn't want that. I wanted to see what was on the other side of the mountains and ridges surrounding the city and I figured the Air Force was the only way for me to do it.

It was a well known fact that Air Force (or Army or Navy or Marine Corps) recruiters would tell you anything to get your name on the dotted line. I figured that's what was happening when the recruiter told me the results of the aptitude tests he had given me were good--good enough for me to qualify for just about any career field the Air Force had to offer. But if it was travel I wanted, he would get me into the intelligence field, specifically as a Radio Intercept Analyst or RIA. I asked him what an RIA did. He didn't know. Their job descriptions were classified, he said. But he did know that 90 percent of them were serving at oversea bases and, if I became one, the chances were 90 percent that I would be too. That was just what I wanted, I told the recruiter as I scribbled my signature on the paperwork that would send me off into the wild blue yonder.

Basic training at Lackland Air Force Base in San Antonio, Texas was a blur of marching, physical education, classroom work, obstacle courses, screaming Tactical Instructors, spit polishing boots, marksmanship training, more aptitude testing, learning to wear the uniform properly, midnight guard duty, and getting used to military life in general. But about half way through training, we were marched over to the personnel building for the most important interview we would have in our Air Force lives. It was called "Career Counseling".

As I stood in line waiting for my turn, I listened as the counselor spoke with each Airman Basic who sat at his desk. They discussed all the career fields the airman was qualified for, the openings available, the possibility for civilian application after the Air Force, location of technical schools, and on and on and on. And then at the end of each interview, the counselor and airman would agree mutually on what was best for both the airman and the Air Force, some paperwork would be signed, some stamps would thump, and everybody was happy.

When the man in front of me finished his interview at the career counselor's desk, I took a seat, not realizing that, for once, an Air Force recruiter had actually told the truth. I was about to get exactly what I had been promised back in that recruiting office.

I gave the counselor my personal information, then he looked through some papers in a folder with my name on it. Finally, he looked up and said, "You are going to be a Radio Intercept Analyst and receive six months of training at Goodfellow Air Force Base, Texas. When your training is completed, you will receive an overseas assignment. Any questions?"

"What's a Radio Intercept Analyst?"

"Can't Say?"

"Why?"

"It's classified. It doesn't matter anyway. You're gonna be one."

"That's it? I thought I was here to talk about possibilities."

"The aptitude tests you took in the recruiter's office and the tests you've taken here at Lackland indicate that you are perfectly suited to be a Radio Intercept Analyst."

SKIVVY NINE!

"But I think I might want to be an air traffic controller."

"You are going to be a Radio Intercept Analyst. NEXT!"

"But….."

"NEXT!"

The man behind me in line tapped me on the shoulder and motioned for me to vacate the chair. "Thanks," I said, not really meaning it.

When I left Lackland, I was promoted from Airman Basic to Airman Third Class (A3C), as was everyone who completed basic training.

The tech school at Goodfellow proved to be the most challenging experience of my life. I knew I was in deep trouble that first morning when a Senior Master Sergeant who looked as though he had no heart stood in front of my class and said that half of us wouldn't make it through the course. Even though we were supposedly the top 10 percent of recruits entering the Air Force, the course was so difficult that the attrition rate was almost 50 percent. Those who flunked out could look forward to the crappiest job the Senior Master Sergeant could find, he told us.

To make matters worse, the course was 26 weeks long, a test was administered every week, and if you flunked three of those tests, you were gone. I flunked two tests by the 17th week and lived in stark terror of failing another during the remaining nine weeks of the course. But I made it, barely squeaking through with a 72 percent average (69 was failing), and graduated at the very bottom of my class.

I thought at the time, and many times since, that I didn't belong at Goodfellow. I believe that either the battery of aptitude tests identifying me to be a Radio Intercept Analyst was either flawed, or I got incredibly lucky while taking the tests. Most of the students in the course were extremely smart and a few were brilliant. A very few bordered on genius. I was none of these. When I left Goodfellow, I was convinced I would never amount to anything in the Air Force, but I was promoted from A3C to Airman Second Class (A2C) as was everyone who graduated.

That oversea assignment I had been promised way back in the recruiter's office in Chattanooga turned out to be Misawa Air Base, Japan. Misawa was at the far northern end of the main Japanese island of Honshu where summers are short and mild and the winters are long with upwards of 100 inches of snow. But all that didn't matter to a testosterone-fueled 22-year-old who felt like a kid turned loose in a candy store every time he went in to the little town just outside the base. It was filled with dozens of cabarets, hundreds of bars, and thousands of women of questionable repute. I was determined to drink all the bars dry and bed every woman in sight. I was fairly successful in both endeavors.

On duty wasn't nearly as exciting. My first job was data input using an IBM 0-26 keypunch machine. It was a boring, mind numbing exercise that was necessary but I hated it. When I mastered that job, I was promoted to a quality control job where I checked the data other people had pumped into the system using the IBM 0-26. Miraculously, I was also promoted from A2C to Airman First Class (A1C).

When it came time for me to leave Misawa for another assignment, I found a new program had been implemented by the Air Force to entice people like me to volunteer for really bad duty stations. If you would volunteer for a "remote[2]" assignment, you would receive a temporary promotion to the next highest rank.

The ploy didn't work--at least not at Misawa. No one volunteered, so the Air Force volunteered for us. I received a remote assignment to Wakkanai Air Station, Japan, which was about 800 miles north of Misawa on the extreme northern tip of the island of Hokkaido, just 19 miles from the USSR.

Within a couple of months after I arrived at Wakkanai, I was promoted to the temporary rank of Staff Sergeant (SSgt). The Air Force called it a Spot Promotion, but I received the same pay, wore the same rank insignia, had the same privileges/perks, and, unfortunately, bore the same responsibilities as a *real* Staff Sergeant. In order to make my Spot Promotion permanent, all I had to do was reenlist in the Air Force at the end of my tour of duty. If I didn't reenlist, I would revert back to Airman First Class the day before I was discharged.

Shortly after becoming a Staff Sergeant, I was appointed Surveillance & Warning Center Supervisor (S&W Supe) on one of the operational flights[3]. The S&W Supe was in charge of all the other intelligence analysts and needed a working knowledge of all the jobs they did. He made the final decision on what intelligence was reported to higher headquarters and had heavy supervisory responsibilities. I was woefully unprepared for the job and failed miserably.

---

[2] Remote assignments were what the name implied--they were usually far removed from civilization. Facilities were often sub-standard and (the biggie) there was usually a lack of female "companionship". Since living conditions were harsh, remote assignments were only 12 months in length.

[3] Each unit is divided into four operational flights, designated Able, Baker, Charlie, and Dog. Three of the flights are on duty at any given time and one flight is off duty. Each flight had an officer in charge (Flight Commander) and an S&W Supe to run the show. See Appendix 1 for the Air Force echelon of command.

I blamed myself for my failures but, looking back, the idiots who foisted the job upon me were at fault. S&W Supes usually had 10-12 years experience and several assignments under their belt doing many of the jobs done by intelligence analysts. I had two years experience, all as a data input specialist. Due to my inexperience, I didn't have a clue and made many mistakes, some of which reverberated to the highest echelons of command.

Based on my bad experiences as an S&W Supe at Wakkanai, I decided an Air Force career was not for me. So when my enlistment was up, I opted not to reenlist and was discharged at Travis Air Force Base, California in January of 1965 and I went home to Chattanooga.

Almost a year to the day after I left Travis Air Force Base, I was there again on my way back to Japan. My return to civilian life hadn't worked out the way I had planned. I was back in uniform.

Good jobs weren't plentiful in Chattanooga but I finally ended up working at Velsicol Chemical Corporation as a "Utility Man", which was a fancy name for gofer. The starting wage was $2.10 per hour, which, for the time, was pretty good money. But the job involved hard labor and it required shift work. When I reported for duty on a midnight shift, the first task I had was standing thigh deep in a pit shoveling chemical residue into a wheelbarrow. At least they gave me hip boot waders to keep my clothes clean and a gas mask so I could withstand the fumes.

But everything wasn't negative. I had a job making $84 a week and I sometimes hit a hundred when I managed to squeeze in a little overtime. With all that money and no responsibility or debts, I was shitting in financial tall cotton. I was driving a brand new Ford Fairlane Sport Coupe, and I rented a furnished apartment to complete my carefree bachelor persona. In February, I met the lovely Miss Frances Parham, late of La Fayette, Georgia. By the end of the year, she would be my new bride.

By mid summer, I was seeing Miss Parham on a regular basis and that aspect of my life was good, but I was really getting fed up with my job and I began looking for a change in career direction. I was unsuccessful in my job hunt until one October afternoon when a commercial came blasting out of my car radio.

The voice on the radio said he was Technical Sergeant Chuck Jett of the Air Force Recruiting Office. He was looking for prior service people with intelligence experience. If I reenlisted, he said, I would do so at the rank held at discharge and I would have my choice of bases. Was I an intelligence specialist? Interested? Come on down, Chuck said, and he would take care of me. I did a U-turn in the middle of Rossville Boulevard and was in the Recruiting Office within 20 minutes.

TSgt Jett didn't have to recruit real hard—I had already made my decision. The first time I entered the Air Force it was to see the world, drink whiskey, and chase women. This time, it was to pursue a career. I intended to work my ass off, do the best I could, and go as far as I could.

After my visit to see TSgt Jett, I broke the news to Miss Parham. I was going back into the Air Force, I told her, and she could come along if she liked. It wasn't much of a marriage proposal, but it worked. We were married in November and I reenlisted in December. My first choice of bases was Kirknewton, Scotland but it was closing down. My second choice was Chicksands, England but it was overmanned with analysts. My third choice was Misawa and I got it. I was sent to Warner-Robbins AFB, Georgia to wait for a seat on a plane headed west.

Viet Nam was just getting cranked up good and every seat on every plane leaving Travis had an ass in it. So I was given a job in the assignments office for five weeks while I waited. That was good. It gave me time to get the new Mrs. Babb an ID card, passport, and all the other things that would make her a dependent wife. It also offered her the opportunity to learn a little about what she was getting in to and what she would have to do to join me later in Japan.

I finally got a flight out of Travis in the last week of January 1966. When I got back to Misawa, I was assigned right back to the office I had been assigned to before, only this time in the Air Defense Shop. It was a much better job that I enjoyed far more than the data entry duty and would be in it for the duration of my three year tour.

While I worked hard at my job, I also worked hard to make Staff Sergeant—again. I was hungry for the stripe. I had been an NCO and I liked it, so I wanted it back as soon as I could get it. I was rewarded for my efforts in March of 1968 when I was promoted the first time I was eligible.

In November of the same year, I received notification of my next duty assignment. I was given a choice between Anchorage, Alaska, Karamursel, Turkey, and San Vito dei Normanni, Italy. It was a no brainer—I took the San Vito assignment in a heartbeat.

When I arrived at San Vito in April 1969, I was assigned to Able Flight as the NCO In Charge of Data Preparation, much to my dismay. The old O-26 keypunch machines I knew so well at Misawa had been replaced by Teletype machines. They produced paper tape instead of IBM cards, but the input and output were the same, so the time I had spent in Data Prep at Misawa made learning the new job easy.

After 18 agony filled months in the Data Prep Shop, I was moved to the S&W Center, not as the S&W Supe, but as the reporter—Thank God! It was a pressure packed position; there was a lot of high profile reporting to be done and an extremely active airborne reconnaissance program over the Adriatic Sea. Many was the day I walked out of that place feeling like my head was filled with bumble bees. I must not have screwed up too badly—I was promoted to Tech Sergeant in April 1971; again, it was my first time eligible.

As the end of my tour neared, I decided to volunteer for instructor duty in the Analysis Tech School I had attended as a student at Goodfellow. I filled out the paperwork and fired it off, but before it had time to work its way through the system, I got an assignment to Viet Nam. I made a will, got Fran an unlimited power of attorney, adjusted my attitude, and I was ready to go. And then the Goodfellow assignment came screaming in and canceled out the Viet Nam assignment. I didn't know why the instructor duty took precedence over going to Viet Nam, but I didn't ask any questions. I just thanked my lucky stars and headed for Texas.

Teaching in the Analysis Tech School was the best job I've ever had. Even though I had to get up at 4:30 in the morning to make the six o'clock class start time, I actually bounded from the bed, sang in the shower, and would have run to the school house if I hadn't had a car. Well, maybe that's a stretch, but I did like my job.

About a year and a half into my tour, I was pulled out of the classroom that I loved so much to help write a "correspondence course". Since the course was the study volume for the promotion examination, the move was actually a step up in that it recognized my abilities as an analyst and an educator. I should have been flattered. I wasn't—I was pissed.

One day when I was feeling especially put out, I called the assignments people and told them I was ready for a change in scenery. After a quick check of their records, they realized I hadn't had my turn in the barrel in Southeast Asia. I could sit tight where I was, they said, and I probably wouldn't have to move for a year or two. But if I insisted on moving now, it would be to the war zone. I said I wanted to move.

They offered me flying status on RC-47s operating out of Tan San Niut Air Base near Saigon. I turned it down. Then it would have to be to the same assignment that had been canceled by the one to Goodfellow. That was the bad news. The good news was the unit had since been moved from Viet Nam to Thailand. I took it.

When I arrived at Ramasun Army Station, Thailand, I was assigned to Baker Flight as the senior reporter. As soon as I was properly trained, the S&W Supe left the Flight for another job in the unit and, even though it was a Master Sergeant position and I was only a Tech Sergeant, I became the S&W Supervisor. Rats!!

The mission at Ramasun was hot. The war in Viet Nam was winding down, but we were in direct support of what little war was left. We did preliminary analysis on almost everything we got, then forwarded it to the Air Situation Center on Monkey Mountain in Viet Nam. They used the information to prosecute the air war. We saw the results of our analysis within hours, sometimes minutes. Extremely rewarding job.

And, fortunately, my experience as an S&W Supe at Wakkanai was not repeated at Ramasun. This time, I had been around the block a couple of times, had seen a few things, had been a supervisor many times, and knew how to delegate responsibility and authority. With those attributes at my disposal, I made a fair-to-middling S&W Supe. But all that didn't matter when our new Operations Superintendent arrived.

The first thing the new Ops Supe did was fire me as S&W Supe, not because of performance problems, but because I was a Tech Sergeant working in a Master Sergeant slot. He replaced me with a Master Sergeant he brought in from another base specifically to take my place.

My troops damn near mutinied when *their* S&W Supe got fired. I gave them a strong talking to, reminding them that this *was* still the military, that the Ops Supe *was* a Senior Master Sergeant, that it *was* within his purview to relieve me of duty, that they *would* shape up—or else. When they left, I kicked a trash can real hard. He may have been a Senior Master Sergeant, and it may have been within his purview to do that, but I still hated his fucking guts. Things would be better at my next assignment; I was going back to my favorite job.

When I left Goodfellow for Thailand, I was participating in the "Guaranteed Reassignment Program". So after a year away from my beloved classroom, I was right back in it.

Shortly after I arrived back at Goodfellow, the Master Sergeant promotion list was released. For the first time in my career, I wasn't on a promotion list when I was eligible for promotion. I missed the score I needed for promotion by two points. The less than sterling performance report I received from the Ops Supe at Ramasun had the desired effect. He was probably proud of himself. I would have to wait another year for another try at it, but I did make Master the second time out.

Being promoted was the "good news" side of the story. The "bad news" was I had to leave the classroom. Management's theory was the students would be intimidated by all those stripes, couldn't relate to me, and therefore, couldn't learn. Although that was a crock of bullshit, I was yanked, kicking and screaming, from the classroom and appointed Manager of the Analysis Course. It was a not-shit job because the course didn't need managing. So for the first month, I sat around twiddling my thumbs and trying to figure out how to turn the non-job into a job. And then the non-job got turned into a job for me.

The Major General in charge of our command decided the course needed to be rewritten, top to bottom. That task would fall upon my poor undeserving head. Over the next 18 months, another Master Sergeant and I rewrote the Analysis Course *from scratch.* When it was finished, it was a 26 week monster that would produce good 202s.

While I rewrote the 202 course, I was also attending night classes at Angelo State University (ASU). It wasn't because I had a burning thirst for knowledge—it was because I needed an Associates Degree to enhance my promotion prospects. After receiving credit for all my Air Force schools, I still needed to attend five courses to get the AS Degree. It took 18 months, but I made it and I still consider it one of my proudest accomplishments.

And oh by the way, while I was rewriting the 202 course and attending ASU, I had an off-duty job as a freelance illustrator. But it wasn't a real hardship since I really enjoyed drawing and painting, I was having fun and getting paid for it. And the extra money paid for some really great vacations.

After over four fun-filled years at Goodfellow, I got itchy feet again, so I called the assignments people and asked what they had available for a Master Sergeant. One of the units on the list they gave me was on Crete, a Greek island in the middle of the Mediterranean Sea. I took it.

When I stepped off the Olympic Airways flight that took me from Athens to Crete, there were a group of men in uniform standing at the bottom of the ramp. I thought there must be a VIP on board. I looked back inside the aircraft, but there were only three little old Greek ladies and a couple of kids behind us. I shrugged it off and we went on down the ramp.

At the bottom, the Lt Col (who turned out to be the unit commander) stuck out his right hand for a shake, congratulated me by name, and handed me a set of Senior Master Sergeant stripes with the left hand. There were handshakes and pats on the back from the rest of the unit hierarchy. The promotion list had been released literally while I was somewhere over the Atlantic, and I was on it. Since it was my first time eligible, my chances of promotion were slim and none. I was amazed. WOW—what a way to begin a tour!

At work, I was assigned as an S&W Supe again, this time on Able Flight. It had been five years since my last stint in an S&W Center at Ramasun Station, so there was much to learn—changes to reporting instructions, upgraded equipment, an unfamiliar target area, a new jargon, working with women in the compound. Say what--women in the compound?

Women were recruited into the intel career fields in 1972 when the military draft was abolished. They had begun to filter into field sites by the time of my assignment to Thailand, but since that unit was in a "war zone", there were no women in it. Then it was back to Goodfellow where I taught them in the classroom. But all the compounds I had ever worked in were a man's world—until I arrived on Crete.

I thought back to the discussion I had had many years ago with one of the old timers at Wakkanai. Dependant women had just arrived on base and he was not a happy man. "It wasn't the six shooter that tamed the wild west," the old timer lamented, "it was 'respectable women'. Before they came, what you had were saloons and whore houses. After they came, you had churches and schoolhouses." The same was true inside the compound.

The atmosphere in the compound was totally different than anything I had experienced—much tamer, more civil. And then there were the problems. The women didn't present *more* problems than men, they just presented a *different set* of problems. The biggest dilemmas occurred when amour reared its ugly head. With boys being boys and girls being girls and biology working the way it does, they *would* get together. It was bad enough trying to keep them from making out behind an equipment rack on a mid shift, but when they broke up (and they always did), it was a nightmare trying to keep them from ripping each other's throats out when they were supposed to be working together. And while I tried to keep the testosterone and estrogen levels under control, there was a mission to cover.

The Middle East then was the same tinderbox it is now, so just about anything that happened in the area was reportable. It wasn't unusual for us to release twenty or more intelligence reports on a day shift, so tension was always high. And when we had an airborne reconnaissance aircraft in the area, the "tight sphincter" factor went way up. The Libyans had tried to shoot one of our recon aircraft down a couple of years before I arrived, but were unable to get him because of inept pilots. I spent every day watch scared to death they would try it again. And then there were the Israelis and Egyptians to worry about—I never knew what those crazy bastards might try to do. Put it all together and it was the hardest job I ever had.

I did a good enough job as an S&W Supe that I was "promoted" to Non-commissioned Officer in Charge (NCOIC) of the Analysis Branch. Since the position was a Chief slot and I was only a Senior, it was quite a step up for me. I spent the last 10 months of my tour there where the pace was laid back and I didn't have to endure shift work. Life was good.

But every good thing must eventually come to an end, and the Crete experience was no exception. Since I still longed to be in the classroom, I submitted a special duty request for the only schoolhouse in the Air Force that routinely employed Senior Master Sergeants in the classroom—The USAF Senior NCO Academy on Gunter Air Force Station in Montgomery, Alabama. I was accepted.

SKIVVY NINE!

I wasn't at the Senior NCO Academy a week when I realized I had made one of the biggest mistakes of my career. My main goal was to become a classroom instructor again and that goal had been met. But to do it, I had to work with fellow instructors who were a bunch of rebellious, egomaniacal, malcontented, prima donnas intent on spreading their venomous antimilitary message to the students they were supposedly preparing to be Chief Master Sergeants. As a result, the Academy was in a constant state of quarrelsome agitation and unrest.

Since its inception, the Senior NCO Academy had selected their instructors based on their academic credentials and not much else. If a volunteer had at least a Bachelor's Degree, he was pretty much in. As a result, every member of the faculty (but me) had a Bachelors, almost half had a Masters, and two had Doctorates. They were overeducated snobs with inflated self images who looked down their noses at me because I only had an Associate's Degree.

Another factor that contributed to the atmosphere at the Academy was the "rank compression" within the unit. There were around 60 people assigned to the Academy at any given time. Of those, over half were Senior Master Sergeants and all those Seniors were bucking for the two or three Chief stripes the unit got every year. Most of them ascribed to the old adage of the easiest way to make yourself look good is make the other guy look bad. The organization was rife with back stabbing, undercutting, and rumor mongering. As a result, morale was low and attitudes were shitty.

During my first year at the academy, a clean-up effort took place and many of the faculty and staff were reassigned or forced into retirement until we had just the right mixture of eggheads, middle of the roaders like me, and G.I. Joe wannabes. I was a satisfied dude with one major exception—I wasn't in the classroom any more. I was the chief of the Communication Skills Branch in the Curriculum Development Department. I left the classroom for a very selfish reason—I wanted to get promoted.

CMSgt T. Wyman Beal

My first time eligible for Chief, I had missed promotion badly. I was crushed, but my good friend, mentor, and vice commandant of the Academy, CMSgt Wayne Davis, took me aside and told me what I needed to do to get promoted. He talked for 10 minutes and I wrote for 10 minutes and when we finished, I had a list of things I had to do to become competitive. It would take me over ten months to check off every item on the list, but item one I did almost immediately—I came out of the classroom.

Although I had gone to the Academy specifically to be in the classroom, Davis told me that, in the history of the Academy, no classroom instructor had ever made Chief Master Sergeant. So, I could stay in the classroom and be happy, or come out and have a shot at Chief. What a choice!

Davis' counsel was sound--I was promoted to Chief Master Sergeant the next time I was eligible. I had reached the pinnacle of the enlisted ranks, but I was still unhappy at the Senior NCO Academy.

In the three years I had been there, the philosophy pendulum had swung from a far left wing paragon of academia, right through saneness, to a far right wing military stalag I called "Chickenshit U". There was a mandatory physical fitness program, inspections, Saturday morning work details, a demerit system, and periodic weigh-ins. There was even a requirement to run so many miles before students could graduate.

Life at the Senior NCO Academy was pretty miserable and I wanted out. I got on the phone to the assignments people begging to go back home to Electronic Security Command. There was only Chief's position open in the entire command. It was in the Inspector General's Office on Kelly Air Force Base in San Antonio, Texas. I took it.

SKIVVY NINE!

The IG Team consisted of 25 members about evenly divided between officer and enlisted grades. Its theme song was "On the Road Again" (by the venerable Willie Nelson) because we stayed on the road over half the time. Most of the bases we inspected were overseas and, to save travel time and money, we inspected two bases on one trip. That usually took 30 – 35 days. I got my first taste of the IG inspection routine a short time after joining the team. It went like this:

We always arrived at an overseas unit on Friday, supposedly to have Saturday and Sunday to settle into our quarters, orient ourselves to the base, and get over jet lag. Actually, it was to soak up some of the local culture and have a good time. Inspections began at 0800 on Monday morning with the unit presenting their "Welcome to Our Unit" briefing and the IG Team giving their "We're Here to Help You" briefing. After everyone registered their mental "bull shit", the inspection began.

At the end of the day, each inspector turned in his findings to his boss who presented the collective findings to the IG and Director of Inspections (the IG's number two) at the daily team meeting. Evenings were spent finding good places to eat and sampling the local night life. The rest of the week was repeat, repeat, repeat, and repeat. And then the weekend would come and it was more R&R.

Monday morning of the second week, each team member turned in a his portion of the inspection report to his boss, along with a rating for the office he inspected: Outstanding, Excellent, Satisfactory, Marginal, or Unsatisfactory. Then the department heads, the IG, and the DI got together, averaged everything out, and came up with an overall rating for the entire unit. After that, it was time to write the report and put the end-of-inspection briefing together. That took four days.

First thing Friday morning, the IG turned the finished report over to the unit commander in private, briefed him on the highlights in it, and revealed the unit's rating. Around mid morning, everyone in the unit gathered in the Base Theater where the DI and another team member delivered a formal briefing, complete with color slides. It was quite a production. When it was over, the Team either headed back to the States or on to the next unit to be inspected. Depending on the rating they got, the unit had one hellava party or a "cry in your beer" fest.

During my 14 months on the IG Team, I would repeat this routine at Mildenhall and Chicksands, England; Misawa, Japan and Hawaii; Okinawa and the Philippines; Anchorage and Fairbanks, Alaska; San Vito, Italy and Bad Aibling, Germany; and Augsburg and Berlin, Germany. In the States we did two week inspections at Ft. Meade, Maryland, Homestead/Key West, Florida, Offutt AFB, Nebraska, Goodfellow, and three units in the San Antonio area.

At the end of my stint on the IG Team, the Director of the Alert Center was retiring and I wanted the job when he left. Since he was a Lieutenant Colonel, it would be quite a feather in my cap to replace him. The I.G. gave me a strong recommendation, I got the job, I walked down the hall from the IG Office to the Alert Center to begin my new job.

In any other Air Force Major Command, the Alert Center would be called a Command Post. It was a 24-7 operation manned by four rotating flights of four people each. There was a small Day Shop with an NCOIC, a command post operations specialist, my secretary, and me. The place was impressive with giant wall maps, clocks showing the local time for major world capitals, several TV sets all tuned to a different news channel, a communications area with links to world-wide intelligence organizations, an area for preparing briefings, and a full blown kitchen. Since it was a showplace, all the fixtures were top-of-the-line, giving the joint that "plush" look and feeling.

SKIVVY NINE!

As the Director of the Alert Center, I had almost nothing to do except smile a lot and look good. Every morning at 8:00, I was standing tall by the Alert Center entrance dressed in a uniform with creases that could cut you, shoes you could see yourself in, wearing my ribbons and a tie. When the Commanding General arrived with his entourage for their morning intelligence briefing from my guys, I greeted him and escorted him to the briefing area. Then I stood off to one side waiting for him to ask for something or direct that something be done. He never did. When the General and his strap hangers left, my workday was pretty much done. I didn't like being Director of the Alert Center a lot.

When I had been in the job for about seven months, I got a call from the assignments people saying my name had popped up on their RADAR screen. I had been in the states almost six years (unheard of for an intel analyst) so I was hot for an overseas assignment. I didn't need an overseas assignment in my life at that moment. My wife had just hired on to a very good job and my son had just started high school, so I didn't want to uproot them. I weighed my options.

1) I could volunteer for an assignment, uproot them, and go overseas with family in tow on a *three* year tour; or..... 2) Volunteer for an assignment, go overseas without them on a *two* year tour; or..... 3) Don't volunteer for anything, wait for an assignment to hit, then submit my retirement papers; or..... 4) Volunteer for a *one* year remote assignment, leave them behind, and get a guarantee that I would return to San Antonio when the tour was over. I chose option four.

When I told the assignments people what I wanted to do, they told me I was a lucky man. There was only one overseas remote Chief slot in the entire command and it had just been vacated. It was at the 6903 Electric Security Group in Osan, Korea. I volunteered for the assignment on the spot.

The flight attendant tapping me on the shoulder brought me back to the present. What would I prefer for lunch, she wanted to know. Would it be filet mignon, Cornish game hen, pork pot roast, or a club sandwich with vegetable soup? Naturally, I went for the red meat.

When I finished the excellent meal, I retrieved my briefcase, took out my note book, and made the first entry in what would turn out to be a year-long project.

Tuesday, April 1st

Well, here I sit in the first class section of a big-ass Boeing 747. This old country boy has come a long way from the hills and mountains of Tennessee. I thought I knew what it was like to be a Chief--God knows I've enjoyed the perks and special treatment since I became one. But this first class thing is really something else.

For example, when I asked the flight attendant for a bloody Mary, she didn't bring me a glass of ice, a tiny bottle of vodka, and a can of Mr. T's Bloody Mary Mix. Noooooo! She brings me a fifth of Absolut Vodka, a carafe of tomato juice, sliced limes.........

Chapter One

IN THE BEGINNING.....

Wednesday, April 15th

There's a lot about this cattle drive they didn't tell me when I signed on. All I knew was I was about to become an Operations Superintendent. And not an Ops Supe at just any unit, but the Ops Supe of the 6903rd Electronic Security Group--the legendary SKIVVY NINE, the shit-hottest outfit in all of Electronic Security Command. It was a great job that any Chief Master Sergeant would want, and I got it. Well, I've been on the job a couple of weeks now, and I'm finding out it ain't all it's cracked up to be.

When I was a kid wearing one and two stripes, the Ops Supe was the old gray-haired guy that came around every Monday morning to make sure I had scrubbed and buffed the floors to his satisfaction. Sometimes he approved; sometimes he didn't. And when he didn't, I had to do it again. When I reached the point where I had people working for me, the Ops Supe was the fire breather I sent them to for a Major League ass chewing when they screwed up. When I entered the Senior NCO ranks, he was the ass-hole I had to push Airman Performance Reports (APR's) through to get them out of the unit.

I came here determined I would be more than that. I would be the *good* Ops Supe--dedicated to the mission, a role model for the enlisted force, champion of the underdog. But I'm finding there's a lot more to it than that, like covering my boss's ass.

His name is Major Kelly Weber. He's a good boss, but he's one of those "screw the paperwork--I've got a mission to run" type guys. That's all well and good, but when he's got 12 APR's and OER's

(Officer Efficiency Reports) that are 30-60 days overdue, the Commander tends to get a little pissed. Since he's having a little trouble managing his time, I've decided that I'll go through his in-basket every day and pick out the things that *have* to be done, stack them in a neat little pile in the middle of his desk, and *make* him do those things. If I don't, the Commander is bound to have his ass sooner or later.

Thursday, April 16th

Major Weber's inattention to paperwork has caught up with him before I had a chance to implement my "in-basket plan." Every piece of correspondence that comes into the office comes across my desk for screening, including the things that are addressed to "The DO[4]." Today, there was a sealed envelope in my in-basket addressed to the DO, so I opened it to see what it was. It was a note from Colonel Dale Meade, the Group Commander, that said if the major didn't take care of those overdue APR/OERs, he (Col Meade) was going to write him (Maj Weber) a letter of reprimand. That's pretty serious stuff.

The Major was out of the office "directing the mission" (as usual), so I tracked him down and showed him the note. He didn't seem too concerned--just read it and said, "I've got to get to that."

I said, "Major Weber, we need to go back to the office and talk."

---

[4] "DO" is an office symbol denoting "Director of Operations", more commonly referred to as the Ops Officer. Military people are creatures of jargon and routinely use office symbols in everyday conversation. It's also interesting to note that a person may be referred to by their office symbol. For example, a commander is often called "the CC", the executive officer is "the XO", and "the XP" is the plans and programs guy. You will see office symbols used throughout this memoir and a complete list of the ones used at SKIVVY NINE may be found in the Glossary of Terms.

When we got behind closed doors, I laid down the facts of life. I told him the mission was important, but the paperwork was important too, and if he didn't stay on top of it, he was going to end up with his ass in a sling.

He said that as long as he's in the office, he keeps getting interrupted (phones ringing, people coming in to see him, taking care of crisis situations) and he just never seems to get around to writing those pesky APRs and OERs. What he said was true. So I convinced him that, starting Monday morning, his office is going to be his room in the Bachelor Officer's Quarters (BOQ). And he's going to stay there 'till those APRs/OERs are written! I'll take care of the ringing phones, the crisis situations, and the constant stream of people coming into and out of the office to see him.

I know all this makes the guy sound like a real jerk, but he's not. Really, he's a super guy, probably the *best* Ops Officer I've ever run across. He knows the mission like the back of his eyelids, everybody in the unit (except Col Meade) loves him, and he's extremely intelligent. What I've got to do is point him in the right direction, help him set his priorities, and then make sure he does the important jobs first.

Thursday, April 23rd

Last Tuesday was miserable! It was "kick off" day for the base's quarterly exercise. We had to be at work by 6:00 A.M., so it was out of the rack at 5:00 A.M. to get ready. One problem--no electricity. Fortunately, I had a portable radio, so I had noise. Even more fortunately, I had some candles, so I had light. Suffered through a cold shower (no electricity; no hot water) and headed out for work.

It was raining--hard. It was cold--39 degrees. By the time I got to work, I was soaked from the knees down. A raincoat can only protect so much.

Once I got to work, I didn't come out 'till 6:00 o'clock that night. The building I work in is an underground bunker and is, supposedly, immune from chemical and conventional attack. So as long as I stayed inside, I didn't have to wear my "fear gear"--helmet, flak vest, web belt, canteen, gas mask, and other sundry protection from chemicals. But outside the bunker, the poor SOBs working on the flight line, Personnel Office, Finance, etc. have to wear that stuff from beginning to end of the exercise. If you get caught by an exercise monitor outside the bunker without your gear, or if you're wearing it improperly, you become a "casualty".

Becoming a casualty is not fun. The Security Police escort you to the gym and you spend the next 12 hours there, the first two wearing the gas mask. To make matters worse, there's no reading, no eating, no drinking, no smoking, no sleeping, no nothin'. So we're talking 12 *boring* hours.

Nineteen SKIVVY NINErs became casualties during the exercise. The reason I know the exact number is every time the SPs picked one up, they'd clear it through me before taking them to the gym. I had to make a determination if the casualties were *absolutely* mission essential. If they were, then the SPs would release them for work, but they had to return to the gym to finish out the sentence after duty hours. If they weren't, they went straight to jail. Under these conditions, you can understand why I stayed inside during the entire exercise. I wasn't about to become a "casualty".

Friday, April 24th

The exercise ended today at 4:00 P.M. After four days of playing war, the whole base was in a party atmosphere. The 03rd had a hamburger/hot dog cookout by the SKIVVY NINE Lounge. It was a beautiful, sunny afternoon with temps in the high 60's (warm by Osan standards) and a good time was had by all.

Saturday, April 25th

Ventured into "the 'Ville" for the first time last night. Well, not exactly the first time. But the other times were during the day for the purpose of shopping or just getting oriented. Last night was for the singular purpose of carousing--running the bars; drinking whiskey; raisin' hell.

The community outside Osan Air Base is not Osan. It's Song Tan. Osan is a quaint little farming village almost 10 miles from the base. (So why don't they call it Song Tan Air Base? I don't know; maybe it's just an Air Force thing.)

Song Tan in daylight and Song Tan at night are two different places. During the day, it's a dirty, smelly, unpleasant place to be. But the night hides the dirt, an alcohol saturated brain dulls the sense of smell, and the neon lights and loud music pouring from open doorways of bars gives the place a festive, party time atmosphere.

The occasion for my nocturnal venture onto the wild side was a "bean run[5]" Bean runs

---

[5] A SKIVVY NINE tradition (God only knows why/how these things got started) that honors new arrivals to the unit and those who are about to leave. New arrivals are green beans--fresh, unsoiled, innocent--while those leaving after a year of sampling Oriental culture are brown beans--shriveled, gnarled, used-up people who will never be the same again.

are semi-organized affairs. A flier is circulated a few days before the run announcing the event and containing a list of honorees (green and brown) along with a schedule indicating which bars the run will hit and the time it will hit them. The schedule is especially helpful for those who choose to drop in and out of the run or poor unfortunates who sometimes get separated from the group during the transit from one bar to another. They simply check the schedule, find the next bar on the list, go there, and rejoin the run when it arrives.

Although the bars on the schedule vary widely from one bean run to the next, there's an unwritten rule that says all runs must begin at O.B. Up[6] at 8:00 P.M. When I arrived at O.B. Up, not much was happening. A few guys and gals stood in a small wad by the bar, sipping on formaldehyde laced Korean beer and ignoring the bored looking Korean girl who gyrated aimlessly on the stage near-by. The rest of the joint was empty. They welcomed me with a "Yo Chief!," I purchased one of the rancid brews, and joined them in small talk and chit-chat.

So this was a bean run. Not much to it, so far as I could tell. At 8:25, there must have been some sort of signal, but damned if I know what it was. Talk stopped, bottles were drained, and everyone scurried out of O.B. Up and headed for Star Wars.

---

[6] Up/Down Bars: Up/Down bars in Song Tan are common. There's O.B. Up, a huge cabaret style room with topless dancers and acid rock, super loud music. O.B. Down is a cozy little bar in the basement where you can kick back and chill out to some soft country sounds without being accosted by young ladies in tight fitting dresses and breath fowled by kimchee demanding you buy them a drink. The phenomenon is repeated at My House Up/Down, only reversed--hard rock in the basement, Country & Western upstairs. And then there's Miss Penny's Up/Down, Texas Bar Up/Down, and on and on. I don't know why--it's a Korea thing.

At precisely 8:30, the bean run arrived at Star Wars and its number was doubled by runners waiting there. Beer was ordered all around, some dancing broke out, and frivolity began to take hold. This was starting to feel good. At 8:55, the O.B. Up routine was repeated, only this time on a larger scale. The mob filed out and headed for the Stereo Club.

The Stereo Club was jumping. The music fairly rattled the walls and the (count 'em) three dancers on the stage actually seemed to enjoy what they were doing. The dance floor was jammed with frenzied bodies, wriggling in the multicolored spotlights that illuminated them. I was hit up several times by working girls asking me to buy them a "juicy[7], but I graciously declined. They called me "Cheap Charley", but it didn't hurt much.

The bean run had reached full strength--about 50 people. Although some would be cut out of the herd by the expert manipulations of the working girls, our number would remain relatively constant the remainder of the evening. We might lose a few at the Stereo Club, but we'd pick up a few at the next place.

9:25--time to go! My House Down, Orient Express, the Silver Wings, the Club 88, and Ma Boogie's followed in quick succession. It was a party on the move. By the time we got to Ma Boogie's, the old gray haired Chief (that would be me) was pretty well shit-faced. But I wasn't alone. Everybody on the run was feeling no pain, but they weren't alone either. If you're a GI in Song Tan on Friday

---

[7] Colored water with no alcoholic content in a pretty glass. There's two good reasons why there's no alcohol in a juicy; a hustling "hostess" could consume as many as 15 to 20 of these things in an evening and alcohol costs money. Naturally, management doesn't want their hostesses falling down, knee-walking, slobbering drunk, but more importantly, they want a large profit margin. A juicy can cost anywhere from three to five dollars (or whatever a hostess can wheedle out of a drunked-up GI), it's a hundred percent colored water and, therefore, a hundred percent profit.

night at midnight, chances are you're so drunk you can't find your ass with RADAR. Last night was no exception.

There were two more bars on the bean run schedule after Ma Boogie's, but as the group left the place, I peeled off and began the long stumble back to the base. No one missed me; just another drop-out.

The main drag was packed with people just like me. They laughed, they cried, they whooped and hollered, they argued, they fought. Taxis and buses roared up and down the street, playing a deadly game of "dodge" with the revelers as they wandered from one side of the street to the other. I pressed forward against the crush, determined to get back to the base, back to my dorm, my room, and, most importantly, my bed.

I was making pretty good progress until I spotted Miss Lee's yaki-mandu stand. It is only one of many such contraptions parked along the curb of the main drag. They are stoves on wheels whose owners dispense all manners of grease permeated goodies to drunked-up GIs who roam the streets of Song Tan late at night. In the daylight, they disappear but, at night, they come out in droves.

Miss Lee's specialty is the soy burger. She bills them as hamburgers, but they are about 90 percent soy filler and 10 percent beef. I patiently waited my turn in front of the Golden Arches that decorated the canopy of her stand (Koreans have no compunction about breaking U.S. copyright laws), then placed my order and watched Miss Lee prepare the tasty morsel. Big globs of mayo and mustard on the bun; the "meat", a well done fried egg; shredded cabbage, sliced carrots, and radishes. Not exactly a Big Mac but, in my condition, it looked pretty darn good.

Miss Lee wrapped the fruits of her labor in aluminum foil and dropped it in a little plastic bag with handles. She handed me the bag, I gave her 1,000 Won, and resumed my trek toward the main gate of the base.

The taxi line started just inside the gate. It was long--real long--but it was three quarters of a mile to my dorm, and I wasn't about to walk (stumble) it. It would have been the old two steps forward, one step back routine, don't you know. It took 15 minutes to work my way to the front of the line and, while I waited, I swayed gently back and forth. But I didn't stand out; everybody swayed gently back and forth. A fella could probably get fairly sea sick just looking at that line.

Finally, I was next. The taxi swooped into the parking lot and screeched to a stop in front of me. I fumbled with the door handle but finally made it inside. When the driver asked me "where to", I was thankful my dorm number was 707--easy to remember. The driver floor-boarded the rickety old Buick Century, snapping my head back against the headrest and I clutched my Miss Lee Burger between my legs during the two minute ride to the dorm.

Inside, I snapped the cap on a Miller Lite (just what I needed), turned on the TV, sat down on the couch, and took the first bite of my midnight snack. The second bite never came. I woke up this morning with my face in the palm of my hand. It was kinda crowded in there because my face shared the space with the Miss Lee Burger. There was mustard, mayo, shredded cabbage, and congealed grease up my nostrils and in my eyebrows. My first night on the town--it was great!

Chapter Two

TESTING MY WINGS

<u>Sunday, May 3rd</u>

Chief Master Sergeant Kevin Novak was my predecessor as the Ops Supe of SKIVVY NINE. We had a full month overlap and, on the surface, that would seem to be a good deal--I would have plenty of time to learn the job from him. But when you try to put two Chiefs in one chair, that chair gets mighty crowded. Our relationship was no different. I wanted to take over and he didn't want to let go. To make matters worse, we both had our own ideas about how the unit should be run and those ideas were not always the same. One of our major differences was our philosophy on handling shift workers[8].

Kevin's attitude toward them was that they were no different than anyone else in the unit. "So they gotta work shifts--tough shit! Why should we make special allowances for them? I worked shift for years and no one made any special allowances for me." I agree a certain extent--shift work is a necessity and someone's got to do it. But if I can make life a little easier for them, I'll do everything I can to make it happen A good example is appointments scheduling. with him to a certain extent--shift work is a necessity and someone's

[8] Because of the nature of the business we're in, ESC has to have people on duty 24 hours a day. The 24 hours are divided into three eight hour shifts--Swings, Mids, and Day Watches. There are four Flights (Able, Baker, Charlie, and Dog) to cover the three shifts. The Flights rotate through the shifts, working four Swings, four Mids, and four Day Watches before going on "Break"--the shift worker's weekend. To see more on shift work, refer to the Glossary of Terms.

got to do it. But if I can make life a little easier for them, I'll do everything I can to make it happen. A good example is appointments scheduling.

A couple of months ago, the Mission Supervisors from all four flights approached Kevin on this issue. Normally, the Orderly Room schedules shift worker appointments and it's not unusual for a guy or gal to be scheduled for a routine dental exam at 10 o'clock in the morning after getting off a mid shift at 7:00 a.m. Not good. Or get scheduled for a records review in the middle of break (week end). Even worse. What the Mission Supe's wanted to do was be able to schedule their own people so they would be sure the appointments didn't screw over off duty time. Kevin didn't buy the proposal. His reasons were:

1. Mission Supes don't know how the appointment system works and they'd screw it up.
2. Scheduling appointments would take up time they should be devoting to other duties.
3. Catering to one segment of the unit would alienate other unit members.
4. The plan would put an undue administrative burden on the Orderly Room Staff.

I think Kevin's arguments are bogus. I just don't agree with him at all. But what-the-hey! The guy who takes my place isn't going to agree with everything I do either. Everybody's got a different way of doing things.

Thursday afternoon, the four Mission Supes showed up on my doorstep. They knew Kevin's last day was Wednesday and they wanted to see if the new guy would be any more receptive than the old guy. They told me what the problem was and what they wanted to do about it. I immediately agreed to approach the Orderly Room with the proposal.

The Orderly Room was not receptive. The man who could have made the decision is the unit's First Sergeant, Senior Master Sergeant Ron Duckworth. SMSgt Duckworth is serving for the first time with ESC and he has absolutely no appreciation for our people and the job they do. During our discussion (argument) on the merits of the scheduling proposal, he insisted on referring to the unit as "those people" and "you people" instead of "our people" or "my people". At one point, he referred to 202/5/7/8/9's[9] as "sniveling prima donna cry-babies". Needless to say, with an attitude like that, our discussion went nowhere.

Finally, Duchworth said, "If it were left up to me, the answer would be a flat 'No'. But it's Captain O'Rourk's Orderly Room, and if you can get him to go along, then so be it. But I don't think he'll go along."

Capt Paul O'Rourk is the Headquarters Section (better known as the Orderly Room) Commander. He's Duckworth's boss, and his office is right next door. The door was open during our entire conversation and he couldn't help but overhear it. So I got up and walked a few feet to his door and said, "Well?" He looked up from his paperwork, gave me a "thumbs up", and said, "Go for it." Starting Monday, the Mission Supes are in the appointment scheduling business.

♦♦♦♦♦♦♦♦♦♦

[9] Each military service has a method of identifying the job specialties of their enlisted force. With the Navy, it's the Navy Enlisted Code and the Army has the Military Occupational Specialty. In the Air Force, it's the Air Force Specialty Code. A full description of AFSCs may be found in the Glossary of Terms.

AFSCs have crept into the everyday language of military people. We identify ourselves and others by using (usually) the first three digits of the AFSC. "I'm a 202 and my friend here is a 209"

My first day on my own, a kid came into the office saying his Flight Commander was screwing over him and he needed my help. This guy had a shit-hot rock 'n roll band and
needed some time off from work so he could take the band to the theater-wide talent
competition at Yokota Air Base, Japan. The group has already won the local and Korea-
wide contests and if they win at Yokota, they'll go on to the big talent contest in the sky--All Air Force. For a young guy like this, that's pretty important stuff. Problem is, the Flight Commander wouldn't authorize the time off.

At first glance, it sounded like the kid had a valid bitch. But after talking to his boss, his Mission Supe, and the Flight Commander, I found that he had reported late to work four our of the last six day watches because he'd been up half the night practicing with the band. Also, the section he worked in was 80 percent manned and, if he were off playing his guitar somewhere, the mission would suffer. I came up with a compromise.

I recommended to the Flight Commander that, if the kid could find a buddy to work his shifts while he was gone, and if he didn't come to work late any more between then and the time of the theater-wide competition, he should be allowed to take leave and go to Yokota. The Flight Commander agreed and I went back to my office feeling pretty good.

Sunday, May 10th

The Ration Control Program was the backdrop for another little "set-to" between the First Sergeant and me Friday morning. The program is a major league pain in the ass and it works like this:

When you buy something on base, the purchase is recorded using a credit card-like device. Some (but not all) rationed items include coffee, mayonnaise, face cream (of all things), beer, booze, soda pop, and cigarettes and, when these things are purchased, the transaction is recorded. Additionally, the amount of money an individual can spend (even on unrationed items) in a month is monitored. Unaccompanied people (like myself) get a $750 per month allowance; family size determines how much an accompanied member can spend. What a person buys and how much it costs is fed into the big computer in the sky (Seoul, actually) and, once a month, it spits out a list of "naughty people" who have gone over on one or both categories. The list is sent to First Sergeants throughout Korea and they're supposed to take corrective action.

Previous SKIVVY NINE First Sergeants didn't take the list too seriously. As a matter of fact, the First Shirt just before Duckworth didn't even look at the list--when he got it, the threw it in the trash can. Last week, SMSgt Duckworth got a nasty phone call from some irate Colonel at Ration Control in Seoul. He said that the 6903rd hadn't submitted a report on what corrective action had been taken against violators in over 18 months. In his typical zeal to do things by the book, Duckworth decided to burn everybody on the April list. But he needed my help to do it.

He called and asked me to schedule everyone on the list (along with their supervisors) to come to his office for an ass chewing and Letter of Reprimand. I said I'd love to help, but I needed to see the list first. What I found was 99 percent of the violators were folks who had bought one extra carton of cigarettes, one case of beer too many, or gone $10-$15 dollars over their spending ceiling.

I asked SMSgt Duckowrth, "What's the purpose of the Ration Control Program? Is it to discourage smoking or inhibit the amount of beer and person consumes. Or is it to stop black marketeering?"

In an unusual attack of common sense, he said, "It's to keep people out of the black market, of course!"

I said, "OK, lets go through the list and identify those folks that obviously are buying more goods than they could possibly use. Then you can bring them in and burn their asses to a crisp and I'll light the fire. But the other people on the list shouldn't be called in." I was amazed when he agreed to the arrangement without an argument.

As we went through the list, we found a couple of guys that had gone $300 or more over their money limit--obviously candidates for a closer look. Another guy had gone 22 cases over his beer ration. In the end, there were six people in the entire unit that looked really suspicious. So I took the shift schedule and set up appointments with the First Sergeant so they could explain why they had busted ration control. The other 30-odd individuals on the list won't get so much as a phone call. SMSgt Duchworth was happy, I was happy, and when he gets the report that six SKIVVY NINErs were hung from the highest yardarm for violating ration control, the Colonel in Seoul will be happy.

Wednesday, May 13th

Found out something interesting about Maj Weber yesterday. I knew he was a fast burner (promoted to major early in his career) but I didn't know why. I also knew his last assignment was (in his words) "in the D.C. area", but I didn't know where.

We had gone to lunch at the Golf Course Club House and, on the way back to work, we stopped by his quarters to pick up some paperwork. I went in with him and, while he was in the bedroom gathering up his stuff, I was snooping around his living room. The place was real "junky" with books and papers and computer equipment all over the place. But there was one piece of paper that really caught my eye.

It was an 8 x 10 color photograph with a handwritten note on it that said, "Kelly; Best of luck in future endeavors. Ronald Reagan."

The picture itself showed Big Ronnie shaking hands with the Major. Naturally, I had to ask how he came by a flick like that and he said he came to the 03rd from the National Security Council where he was an intelligence analyst. As a matter of fact, the endorsement on his last OER was written by Admiral John Poindexter, the former director of the NSC. Needless to say, I was impressed. But the Major played the whole thing down as just another job. "Hell, I was just lucky to get out of there before the shit hit the fan over that Iran-Contra thing." I tried to pump him for more information, but he wasn't playing. Interesting man I work for.

♦♦♦♦♦♦♦♦♦♦♦

Got to bed early last night--word was out that we were having another exercise (unit, not base) kicking off at 4:00 a.m. I set my alarm for three o'clock so I would be able to shower and do my "twa-lett" before the exercise started. I finished at 3:45 and figured there would be a knock on my door just any minute and there would be "the runner" telling me to report to work immediately. "The runner" finally showed up at 5:20!

There were two reasons I was so late getting notified. First, the word I got on the starting time was bogus; it didn't begin until 4:30. Second, the Flight Commander who initiated the recall used an old roster, not the brandy-ass new one published just last Monday that had the notation at the top in big bold letters stating, "In addition to calling the CC, CD, and DO, dispatch a runner to Dorm 707, Room 120, to notify CMSgt Beal, the Operations Superintendent."

I probably would have still been waiting for that runner, but when Maj Weber got to work and saw I still wasn't there, he sent a runner for me and then had a large chunk of a Flight Commander's ass. By the time I dressed and walked to work, we were way over an hour into the exercise and I was definitely behind the power curve. I never did recover and my part of the exercise was a disaster.

The exercise went about as smooth as a shot glass full of thumbtacks; nobody did *anything* right. At the lessons learned meeting immediately after the exercise, Col Meade said he wants to exercise twice a week until we get it right. The reason for all this concern is we were notified last week that the Inspector General is paying us a visit starting June 15th. This time, I'll be able to see what an inspection looks and feels like from the other end of the stick.[10]

The unit's stuff is really ragged in a lot of areas--our Operating Instructions and unit regulations are in a jam; hardly anyone in the unit stamps classifications on papers and documents they write; our exercise ability is next to zero; all the things that the IG looks at are in a world of hurt.

The overriding attitude of the average SKIVVY NINEr is, "If it don't involve killin' commies, it ain't worth doin'!" That's a great attitude if I'm in a fox hole with these guys, but when the IG's coming to town, it's the kind of attitude that can kill a unit. I saw that attitude several times when I was on the Team--good units going down the tubes because they have a wartime mentality in a peacetime environment. So we've got a lot of getting ready to do. If we don't get it done, I can see a MARGINAL rating from the IG in our future.

---

[10] For almost two years, I was a member of the ESC IG Team and I've seen how it ticks from the inside. Just like any other military organization, the IG Team is staffed with good guys and bad. The big difference is IG Team members possess *extreme* power, so the things they do (or don't do) have a tremendous impact on entire units and individuals they inspect. An IG Team member with a superiority complex can cause BIG harm.

To make sure the Operations Division is ready, the Major and I have agreed that we need to work every Saturday morning from 8:00 to 12:00 until the IG Team arrives. The troops don't like it even a little bit, but…..

Sunday, May 24th

Major Weber was back in San Antonio at ESC Headquarters all last week attending the World Wide Operations Officer's Conference. I was a little apprehensive about minding the store while he was gone, but I made it through the week just fine, thank you. No major (excuse the pun--none intended) operational problems, but I did have three headaches with some folks in the unit.

HEADACHE NUMBER ONE: Capt Raymond Smith. Capt Smith is filling the newly created Assistant Operations Officer position, but he don't have a clue about operations. It's not his fault--he's not an Intelligence Officer by trade. He's actually an F-4 "back seater" (Electronics Countermeasures Officer).

Until a little over two weeks ago, Capt Smith was heading up the Tactics Analysis Branch. He wasn't really needed there, so Maj Weber decided he wanted someone to help out with the day-to-day administrivia, he created the Assistant Ops Officer position, and assigned the Captain to fill it.

Before he left for the Ops Officer Conference, the Major got Capt Smith and me together and told us that, while he was gone, any operational issues would be handled by the Ops Supe. As the Assistant Ops Officer, the Captain would rubber stamp my decisions, but the bottom line was, "The Ops Supe is in charge."

Later that day, I brought up the matter of transportation with Maj Weber. I usually have full use of the Major's pick-up truck during duty hours, but at the end of the day, he takes it to his quarters. If he's called out in the middle of the night for some operational emergency, he needs wheels so he can get to work in a hurry. I told him while he was gone, I'd be taking the truck to my quarters for the same reason. It's a 10 minute walk from my dorm to work and, in an emergency, that's too long. The Major agreed and told me to take the truck. I did.

I was in before Capt Smith the next morning. When he came in, he walked directly to the front of my desk and said, "Did you take the truck home last night?"

I said, "Yes Sir, I did."

He leaned across my desk and put his finger in my face and said, "Don't you *ever* do that again!" And then he turned and stomped out of my office.

I was flabbergasted, stupefied, befuddled, and *super pissed*! He was gone for about 10 minutes, which was good; gave me time to cool off a little and compose my thoughts. When he came back, I closed the door so the admin folks outside my office couldn't hear. They didn't need to hear what I was about to say.

I went to the front of his (actually Maj Weber's) desk, leaned across it, and said, "Captain, I have two problems with what you just did. First is the way you talked to me. I haven't had anybody talk to me in that tone of voice since I was a two striper. I didn't like it then and I won't stand for it now. Even if I *was* a two striper, that's no way to talk to *anyone*. But I'm not a two striper--I'm a Chief Master Sergeant in the United States Air Force and you damn well *will* treat me like one. Don't you *ever* talk to me in that tone of voice again. Got it?"

He opened his mouth to say something, but I held up my hand to stop him. "You can talk when I'm finished, and I'm not finished. The second problem I have was your order for me not to take the truck home at night. When the Major left, he told me to do that so I could get out here in a hurry in case there was an emergency. Now, if you want to countermand his instructions to me, that's fine. I realize full well that 'you officer--me enlisted' and that you have the authority to order me not to take the truck. Well, I follow orders real good, Sir, and I won't drive that truck to my dorm again if you insist. But, Sir, I strongly recommend you reverse your order. Now I'm finished. Your turn."

I went back to my desk, sat down, and waited for what I thought would surely be some harsh words on insubordination. Instead, the Captain just sat there for a long time, looking at me like he couldn't believe what had just transpired. Finally, he began to speak.

He said he didn't know that the Major had authorized me to take the truck overnight. He went on that personal use of government vehicles was "rampant" (his word) in the unit and that he was really concerned about it. When he saw me take the truck, he thought it was just so I wouldn't have to walk to and from work. He said senior people had to set the example and if the troops saw me driving the truck for my personal convenience, they would think it was OK for them to do the same. Then he told me I had his permission to take the truck to my dorm at night. I thanked him and went back to doing paperwork. End of discussion--end of incident.

<u>HEADACHE NUMBER TWO</u>: CMSgt Bruce Lewis. Bruce is the only other Chief in SKIVVY NINE and is my counterpart in Logistics and Maintenance (LG). He's a nice enough guy, but a real stickler for regulations--a real by-the-book kind of fella. His insistence on going by the book put us at odds last week.

A couple of weeks ago, Maj Phil Reardon (the Deputy Commander) went to the Seventh Air Force staff meeting representing Col Meade who was away from the unit at the time. During the staff meeting, there was an announcement that the Air Force Uniform Board had authorized the wear of Battle Dress

Uniforms (BDUs)[11] by all Air Force personnel. Maj Reardon brought the word back and made an announcement at our Commander's staff meeting and said, "Tell your people if they got 'em, wear 'em." I, in turn, made the announcement at the Ops Officer's staff meeting and the word spread like wildfire.

Bruce Lewis came to see me later that afternoon and said he thought Maj Reardon might have jumped the gun on the BDU issue. He said that, although the uniform Board had authorized them, Air Force Regulation 35-10 hadn't been updated yet and, until it was, BDUs weren't really legal.

I acknowledged that what he said may be technically correct, but there was a message from the Air Staff saying BDUs could be worn and our Deputy Commander had interpreted that to mean right now. And since he had made that interpretation, I had to support him. Besides--so what if we're a couple of months early? The regulation will change eventually and, in the meantime, allowing the troops to wear BDUs early might give morale a little boost. Bruce didn't agree with me, but he didn't press the issue further and left. I thought the case was closed. I was wrong.

During the next couple of days, there was a buying frenzy on BDUs. Since Air Force Clothing Sales here at Osan didn't have them in stock (after all, they're not authorized yet), SKIVVY NINErs kept the road hot between here and Camp Humphries (an Army base about 25 minutes from Osan) where BDUs are plentiful.

Within a week, at least 100 people in the Operations Division were wearing BDUs. Meanwhile, back in LG, Bruce had put out

---

[11] This is an "every day" or work uniform recently authorized for wear by Air Force people. The Army has been wearing them for years. Material used to make BDUs is a camouflage pattern, so they are sometimes called "cammys". They're slouchy and baggy and they replace the traditional Air Force fatigue uniform that is a nice shade of green, form fitting, and (in my opinion) much better looking.

the word that his people were not to wear BDUs until AFR 35-10 had been changed. So what we had was a situation where two-thirds of the unit (DO) could wear BDUs and a third (LG) couldn't. Not good.

Pretty soon, word on what was happening got back to Maj Reardon and he was not a happy camper. He called Capt Ed Jacoby (Bruce's boss) into his office and told him to tell his Chief to back off--the decision had been made to wear the new uniform and, whether it was the right decision or not, he expected his senior people to support him. I thought the matter was closed. It wasn't.

Monday morning, I got a call from CMSgt Joel Tennant, the 51st Tactical Fighter Wing Senior Enlisted Advisor[12]. The 51st TFW is our host unit on Osan Air Base and we have to pretty much play by their rules. He said Chief Lewis had been to see him with some disturbing news--6903rd people were wearing BDUs in gross violation of Air Force Regulation 35-10.

I recapped the whole story of what had transpired to Joel and told him that, since my Deputy Commander had authorized them and so many of my people had them, I wasn't going to ask Maj Reardon to reverse his decision. Chief Tennant said that was unfortunate, because he intended to issue instructions to his Security Police to start randomly stopping people wearing BDUs and asking them what unit they were in. Any SKIVVY NINEr found wearing them would be issued a uniform violation citation. Well now--*that* got my attention.

Soon as I got off the phone with Tennant, I beat feet to Major Reardon's office and broke the news to him. He came unglued! He wanted to have Lewis into his office for a large chunk of his ass, but Bruce wasn't in his office when the Major called. He was busy out-processing--he leaves Osan in less than a week! That was good,

---

[12] See Glossary of Terms for full profile of SEAs.

because it gave Major Reardon a chance to cool off and us to figure out what we needed do to get out of this mess.

What we decided was: call Colonel Lou Hopkins (the big Kahuna of things like uniform wear at Headquarters ESC) and get him to issue a change to the ESC Supplement to AFR 35-10 authorizing all ESC people to wear BDU's. Col Hopkins bought the idea and said the change would be forthcoming ASAP. I called Joel Tennant back and told him what we had done and asked him to call off his Security Police. He wasn't a happy camper, but there wasn't a whole hellava lot he could do about it. I thought the matter was closed--and it was.

HEADACHE NUMBER THREE: Captain Paul O'Rourk. As I've pointed out earlier, Capt O'Rourk is the commander of the Orderly Room. It's his first time in ESC and he, like the First Sergeant, has absolutely no appreciation for our people and their problems.

About three weeks ago, the Orderly Room announced physical fitness testing would be conducted on the 19th and 20th of May at 7:00 a.m. and 3:00 p.m. SMSgt Duckworth coordinated the times with me and I said everything looked OK. Shift workers get off day watches at 2:00 p.m. and would have an hour to get ready for testing at 3:00.

A couple of weeks later, the Korean Government unexpectedly decided to go to daylight savings time. Korea is one of the few industrialized countries in the world that had never observed daylight savings time. For reasons I won't explain here because of classification reasons, we had to change the duty hours for shift workers to fit the daylight savings time thing. Instead of having the Day-Swing shift change at 2:00, we had to change to 3:00. I guess I should have called the Orderly Room to get them to change the physical fitness testing times, but with all the other things I've got crashing around inside my cranial cavity, I just plain forgot.

At the Ops Officer's staff meeting on the15th, I reminded everyone about the date/time for the testing. Capt Ellen Ringer (Ops Production Branch Chief) told me that Baker Flight was working day watches both days of testing and I needed to get the Orderly Room to change the afternoon time to 4:00 p.m. on one of the dates. I didn't think there would be any problem with that; it would be a simple matter to roll the time back an hour and there was still plenty of time for the Orderly Room to get the word out on the change. Wrong again (woe is me).

I ran into Capt O'Rourk in Col Meade's office that afternoon. I told him Operations had a little problem with the testing times and wold like to roll the afternoon time back an hour on one of the test dates. He **EXPLODED**! "You people have known about the testing times for over three weeks. We coordinated everything through you and you said everything was OK. Now you come to me at this late date and want a change? Well, you're not going to get it! Any of your people that don't show up at the established times will be rescheduled to do their physical fitness training on a day of break. End of discussion!"

Instead of breaking the little bastard in two like I wanted to, I said, "Thank you for your time and consideration, Sir. I understand you perfectly." Then I went back to my office and let my blood pressure subside.

When my stomach stopped churning, I went back to the Command Section to see Maj Reardon. Capt O'Rourk was still there bullshitting with one of the Admin folks who work there. I went into Maj Reardon's office and told him about my discussion with the Captain. (I guess by this time, the picture starts to develop that Maj Reardon is a pretty decent troop and we're kinda tight. *Good* guy!)

After he heard my story, he called the Captain in and told him that the 3:00 testing time would not change. However, Baker Flight would not be available for testing until 4:00. The Captain and his Orderly Room staff would provide special testing for Baker Flight at that time--case closed--period. And yet another happy ending.

♦♦♦♦♦♦♦♦♦♦♦

And that was the week that was. To the casual observer, it would appear that I'm having an overabundance of problems, but really, I love every minute of it. Ninety-nine percent of the folk I deal with are fantastic, but the one percent ass hole population really gives me a pain in the buns. I'm just glad I'm finally in a position where I don't have to put up with bullshit laying down. And if I can help the troops out along the way, that's just icing on the cake.

Chapter Three

THE IG'S COMING! THE IG'S COMING!

Wednesday, May 27th

It's 5:00 a.m. and I'm sitting here waiting for a knock on my door. I have it from a relatively good source that we're having a unit exercise this morning but, so far, nothin's shakin'. I got up at 4:00 and did my morning routine thinking that the recall would probably kick off around 4:30 and, by the time they dispatched a runner for me, I'd be ready just about the time he got here.

We've been having an exercise/recall a week for ever since Col Meade found out we're scheduled for a visit from the IG Team. And we have good reason to practice--our recall procedures suck! The last two times, it's taken 30-plus minutes for the runner to come for me. The first time, the Flight commander who initiated the recall used an old roster that didn't have my name on it. The next time, the runner swore he couldn't find my dorm. By the time they sent out another runner who *could* find my dorm, I got dressed, and walked to work, it was 55 minutes into the exercise. I don't know what the problem is this morning, but I've *got* to get it fixed. The IG will be here in a month and if I don't have it fixed, they're gonna eat our shorts.

Well, I've waited long enough. Guess I'll just hoof it on out to work and find out why the runner didn't show up when I get there. I'll finish this entry when I get home tonight.

♦♦♦♦♦♦♦♦♦♦♦

SKIVVY NINE!

BAD NEWS: It's 5:45 p.m., 12 hours from when I made my last entry. Long day--and we never *did* have a recall!

GOOD NEWS: Maj Weber was back to work yesterday. Said he really enjoyed his trip back to San Antonio. He got back in-country late Saturday night and Sunday morning he went to Seoul and bought himself a car. That's good news for me, because it means he won't have to drive the truck to his quarters at night, which means I can.

He came up with the idea for me to take the truck at night on his own. "Chief, this business of having to send a runner for you, then you walking to work in response to a recall is ridiculous. We can't live with a 45 minute to one hour response time for our Ops Supe. I want you to get a pager [beeper] and start driving the truck everywhere you go. Then when we have an exercise or a real world situation, for that matter, you can be in here as fast as I am. How does that set with you?"

All I could say was, "SIERRA HOTEL! *Throw* me in that briar patch!"

The Major chuckled and said, "I took care of the wheels. You take care of the beeper."

Once I have both transportation and a way to be notified quickly, that should solve the slow response times I've been having. We'll see.

BAD NEWS: When I finally got to work this morning, I had a little heart-to-heart talk with SMSgt Ozzie Harpster. Ozzie was my source that said there would be a recall this morning. You'd think he'd know--after all, he's the Emergency Evaluation Team Chief. Those folks always know when a recall/exercise is coming. In Ozzie's defense, the recall really was scheduled for this morning, but Col Meade got cold feet at the last minute and called it off, saying, "We're not ready yet." Well, Gawd Dammit, if we don't practice, we're never going to be ready.

Sunday, May 31st

This past week was really hectic; earned every dime of my pay check. The unit had a Senior Enlisted Advisor (SEA) until March 1st of this year when the position was deleted. ESC had been "cheating" for years by having SEAs at the Group level, but Big Air Force finally put its foot down and ESC had to do away with SEAs below the wing level. When the SEA position went away at SKIVVY NINE, the duties and responsibilities, unfortunately, didn't. So Kevin Novak bellied up to the bar and volunteered to hold down both the Ops Supe and SEA positions. I'm sure the fact that he was leaving in a couple of months didn't have anything to do with his volunteering. Bullshit. Well, anyway, by the time I showed up, the precedent was set so there's no backing out now.

What all this means is, in addition to doing my Ops Supe thing, I have to handle people's personal problems, ramrod the recognition programs (promotion ceremonies, annual dining out, awards breakfasts, chair Airman/NCO/Senior NCO of the Quarter boards, run the Professional Performer Program, and on and on and on), advise the Commander on enlisted issues, and the BIGGIE, work with the Consolidated Base Personnel Office (CBPO) to resolve problems with assignments, orders, port calls, and other administrivia. I've been in the Air Force over 25 years and stationed at bases all over the world and this CBPO is absolutely the worst I've seen anywhere.

The people down there are not only incompetent, they're downright surly and nasty. After Johnny Two-Striper has been given the run-around and farted off long enough, he ends up in front of my desk asking for help. Last week, I was in CBPO at least an hour a day every day. So between CBPO and internal unit problems, it all starts to get to me after a while.

One of the more sensitive problems I worked last week was what I call the "microwave oven fiasco". Shift workers usually don't get to go to chow, so they order box bennies[13] from the dining hall and send a couple of guys to pick them up at meal time.

The lunches are prepared two or three hours in advance and, by the time the food reaches the shift worker, it's cold with congealed grease all over it. Until December last year, there was a microwave oven available to reheat the food. But the microwave broke down and my supply NCO has been trying to replace it through supply channels for the past five months with no luck. He finally shoved all the paperwork through last week and the supply people said we would be getting a new microwave--in only six months! When they heard this distressing news, the Mission Supes got together and came to see if I could possibly do something about the situation.

I had the SKIVVY NINE Lounge manager call an emergency meeting of the Lounge Committee and presented the problem to them. They voted unanimously to buy the microwave from the Base Exchange (BX) using Lounge treasury funds and give it to the Shift Workers.

The next day, Col Meade went to the Lounge manager requesting $500 to buy prizes and refreshments for the unit's annual golf tournament. The Morale, Welfare, and Recreation (MWR) Division was originally supposed to foot the bill but, for whatever reason, they reneged. The Lounge manager told Col Meade that the treasury didn't have enough money to buy the microwave, pay for

---

[13] Bennie: short form of "benefit". The troops, with their tongues *buried* in their cheeks, refer to box lunches as one of the many benefits supplied by the military.

the golf tournament, and maintain operating capitol. The Colonel said the microwave would have to wait; he had to have the money for the golf tourney *now*.

Word of that got out within an hour and, when the troops heard about it, they were *PISSED*! All that happened late last Friday, and the situation festered over the three-day weekend. Tuesday morning, I went to see Col Meade and told him his stuff was pretty ragged on this one and asked him to reverse his decision. He said two months of planning had gone into the tournament and it was too late to call it off (it was scheduled the following Wednesday). I told him moral was lower than snake shit in a wagon track already and his decision wouldn't help matters at all. Even when I played my trump card--It's not good to have unhappy troops with the IG coming--he wouldn't back off.

I talked the situation over with Maj Weber and we decided it would be a good thing to take up a collection from all the officers and the two Chiefs and buy the microwave. I went to the BX and priced the best microwaves they had and divided the number of officers and Chiefs into the price to determine our contributions. It came to $13 each. Not bad.

I made the rounds and collected the money (including Col Meade), but when I got to the LG Supe, he wouldn't cough up. I knew Bruce Lewis was an ass hole, but this really nailed it. Maj Weber and I each tossed in six bucks extra and I went to the BX and bought the damn thing. That night on swing shift, the troops were warming their box bennies and making popcorn. I felt good.

♦♦♦♦♦♦♦♦♦♦♦

One of the things the IG always looks at closely is "amount of supplies on hand." It's a write-up if you don't have enough, and it's an even bigger write-up if you have too much. Yesterday, my Supply NCO broke the news to me that we have too much six-ply paper. We're authorized 40 boxes; we have 73. CMSgt Ted Doyle (the IG Supply Inspector) would have a field day with that one.

I told SSgt Jim LaMora (my Supply NCO) to find a place to hide the stuff until the IG Team is gone. He suggested several places, but they were all places Doyle always looks for unauthorized supplies. Finally, Jim suggested that he take the extra paper to his house off base. Sounded good to me, so I told him to get it done one day next week.

After I finished up at work, I went to the Korean Air Force picnic. It's an annual event and they invite SKIVVY NINE's key people to attend. They invited me, so I went. I was sitting under a tree with Col Meade, drinking a beer and watching the Koreans play soccer, when I told him about the excess paper situation and what we were doing about it. His reaction was, "You can't *do* that!"

I thought he was going to give me some kind of horse pucky about the ethics of hiding stuff from the IG (he's that kind of guy--straight arrow all the way.) But he didn't. In fact, he had a good reason for not storing the stuff at Jim's house. His reasoning: "What if the Security Police stop SSgt LaMora at the gate and discover that he's taking Government property off base? They'd arrest him on blackmarketing charges, he'd say we ordered him to do it, and then we're all in trouble."

Hmmmm--hadn't thought about that. So I asked him what he suggested. "We'll hide the stuff at my house on base."

I gave the Colonel a "high five" and told him I'd take care of it. I guess he's not an asshole all the time. But Capt O'Rourk is.

♦♦♦♦♦♦♦♦♦♦

The good Captain reared his ugly head again during last Thursday's Commander's Staff Meeting. When it came time for his input, he said the Ops Division had 40 no-shows at last week's physical fitness testing. He then went on to casually announce that each one of them would receive a Letter of Reprimand (signed by himself) for violation of Article 86 of the Uniform Code of Military Justice (failure to be at the appointed place at the appointed time).

Needless to say, I was somewhat taken aback by this revelation. I asked Capt O'Rourk if he had contacted any of the delinquents to see if they perhaps had valid reasons for not being at the appointed place at the appointed time. He said there was no need for that--there was *no* valid excuse for missing the formation.

Realizing that I was making zero headway with the Captain, I took my case to Col Meade, who seemed oblivious to the fact that his staff meeting was on the verge of becoming a pissing contest. I told him that if LORs were to be written, the distasteful task should fall to the supervisor, not the Commander of the Orderly Room. "It was *my* formation they missed," Capt O'Rourk whined, "so *I* should get to write the LORs."

I countered that supervisor-subordinate feedback (both positive and negative) was an inherent responsibility of the supervisor and should not be shrugged off to anyone. Col Meade agreed. Once I had him in the boat on who should take action, I went on with the second part of my proposal.

Instead of issuing "blanket" LORs on all 40 people, each case would be looked at individually, with LORs being written when warranted. If supervisors determined an LOR wasn't needed, they would write a memo for record to the Orderly Room explaining why an LOR wasn't accomplished. All LORs and MFRs would come to me for consolidation and I would deliver them to the Orderly Room within one week.

This dose of common sense and fair play brought a groan of disapproval from Capt O'Rourk and his lackey, SMSgt Duckworth. Spineless supervisors wouldn't have the guts to "do the right thing"; no-shows would get off scot-free; justice would not be served, Fortunately, Col Meade would have none of the Captain's argument. Now, all I have to do is make sure the innocent aren't punished and the guilty get nailed to the wall.

Wednesday, June 3rd

Everyone is getting geared up for Saturday's big event, SKIVVY NINE's Annual Spring Fling. We've got the base picnic area reserved and, after an IG Saturday morning, everyone will fall out for a big party. I've been trying to hype it up as a "get ready for the IG party". Hope it works.

I painted up three signs advertising the event, volunteered to man the grill cooking dogs and burgers for a couple of hours, and got my arm twisted into judging the punch making and ugly shorts contests. According to the old-timers, this thing is always a "barn burner". I hope this one is no exception; God knows we need the diversion.

♦♦♦♦♦♦♦♦♦♦

UPDATE: All the people who missed physical fitness testing have been interviewed and a total of four out of 40 have been given Letters of Reprimand. Some of the "excuses" for missing were:

1. A girl whose foot was run over by a taxi the day before testing had (not surprisingly) a medical excuse.
2. Twenty-one of the 40 no-shows were on leave or away at other bases on temporary duty when the testing was conducted.
3. Two had physical profile changes exempting them from participating in all physical fitness events.
4. Two had doctor's notes excusing them from testing.

Most of the remaining people had actually attended one of the sessions, but Orderly Room personnel had failed to record their attendance. As a matter of fact, four of them were at the same session as me, and I personally vouched for them in their memos for record.

The most bizarre "excuse" was a girl who had been on stand-by for an OB-GYN exam and got a call from the hospital on her way out the door for the testing. She was between a rock and a hard place; she had been waiting almost a month to get into the OB-GYN Clinic and she figured there would be a make-up session so she opted for the medical examination. Fortunately for her, she cleared her decision through her Mission Supe who OK'd it.

Tomorrow, I'm taking the LORs to Capt O'Rourk along with the MFRs. I've got a feeling there's going to be a real tussle on this one, but I plan to take it all the way to the wall if necessary.

♦♦♦♦♦♦♦♦♦♦

I've found another way (in addition to having him stay home to write APRs and OERs) to get the Major out from under the paperwork avalanche. I've mastered both his signature and his initials. There's a ton of stuff that comes across my desk every day that he's supposed to see, but *really* doesn't need to see. I talked it over with him and got his approval to screen his correspondence and, if I decide he doesn't need to see it, I'll sign or initial it. Illegal as hell, but I'm going to keep this boy out of trouble if it kills us both.

♦♦♦♦♦♦♦♦♦♦

I'm really enjoying bringing the truck to the dorm with me at night. That walk to/from work was really a bummer. But I'm running into major obstacles trying to get a beeper. The beeper keepers in LG are giving me 99 reasons why it can't be done. But I'm going to keep pressing 'till I make it happen.,

Meanwhile, the "runner system" is starting to come around. We had another unit recall this morning that kicked of at 6:00 a.m. The runner arrived at my door at 6:09, took me one minute to get dressed, and three minutes to drive to work. Thirteen minutes response time. Not bad. The time would have been at least 25-30 minutes on foot. If I can get the beeper, that will take away the time it takes the runner to get to me and I can probably cut the time down to 8-10 minutes.

Sunday, June 7th

Went in yesterday morning for another IG Saturday and put the final touches on my stuff and made sure everyone else did the same. Looks like we're ready as we're gonna get. We better be--the bad boys will be here next Saturday.

Knocked off work around 11:45 and strolled on down to the pavilion where the Spring Fling was being held. The weather was absolutely fabulous, an oddity for Osan. Everybody, including me, had a great time. A lot of steam was released and everyone seemed to be genuinely psyched up for the inspection when the fun and festivities was over.

♦♦♦♦♦♦♦♦♦♦

Friday afternoon, we had our final exercise in preparation for the IG's visit. Like I've said before, we *need* to exercise--that's one of our weakest areas--but on Friday afternoon? Every time I think Col Meade is coming around, he shoots himself in the foot with the troops. They don't mind exercising; it's a pain in the ass, but they know there's a real need for it. But they want it to be done the *right* way.

The Colonel had this exercise kick off at 1:00 p.m. and everybody scurried around and got their stuff together. Then all of a sudden at two o'clock, Col Meade puts the exercise on hold and told everyone to remain in place. Then he left the Unit Control Center (UCC), went down to the flight line to congratulate a couple of maintenance troops for getting promoted to Tech Sergeant, went to an hour-long meeting at 7th Air Force Headquarters, then went back to his office to do some paperwork. During all that, the whole damned unit was sitting around on its collective ass in suspended animation twiddling it's collective thumbs.

At 4:00 p.m., Col Meade returned to the UCC and resumed the exercise. It lasted until nine-thirty. At one point in the exercise, a two-striper acting as a runner for me and my staff in the Operations Sub-Control Center asked, "Chief, why did the Colonel do the exercise this way?" I told him I didn't know and didn't comment further.

The two-stripe airman sighed and said, "Boy, morale in the unit has really been going up the last couple of months. I guess the Colonel figured he'd better do something about it." I didn't say anything, but I thought, "No, that's not it, Son. He's just a dumb son-of-a-bitch that just don't know any better."

I'm going to see the Colonel tomorrow morning and tell him about the incident. I don't think he really realizes when he's screwing up. As his de facto SEA, I think I owe it to him to let him know when I think he's screwed up. And I think he owes it to me to have a little talk before he does something as radical as a split shift, eight hour exercise on Friday afternoon.

♦♦♦♦♦♦♦♦♦♦

Last Thursday, I got a call from Maj Walt Gross, the Ops Officer at the 6949th Electronic Security Squadron at Offutt Air

Force Base, Nebraska. Sgt Joel Prestel used to be at the 49th but arrived here during the first week in May.

The Major told me that Joel was in some serious financial trouble and needed to get in touch with the President of the Offutt Credit Union ASAP. Seems Joel's brother-in-law had somehow gotten hold of his wife's Automatic Teller Machine card and, in less that a week, the ass-hole had withdrawn all Joel's money plus over $6,000 in overdrafts. In addition to that, the Credit Union had hit him with $1,200 in overdraft charges.

Maj Gross said the Omaha police had been called in on the case, so Joel needed to call the Credit Union president in one hellava hurry so the prez could tell him what he needed to do to get out from under this thing. I put runners out in all directions, but it took over three hours to track Joel down. But we got lucky when he just happened to stop by the Orderly Room to pick up an authorization letter to buy some stereo gear and they told him to report to me immediately.

When Joel got to my office, I broke the news to him and the boy turned white as a sheet. Can't say I blame him. I got on the phone to the ESC Alert Center back in San Antonio and requested a phone patch through them to the Offutt Credit Union president.

The Credit Union guy had a whole string of instructions, one of which was to stop Joel's paychecks from going to the Credit Union immediately. Any money coming in would be automatically applied against the deficit, leaving poor Joel destitute. Normally, stopping a direct deposit to a bank takes two or three weeks, but we didn't have that kind of time. It had to be done by the 15th payday (this was the 4th) or Joel would lose that money.

I called Chief Sean Miller at the Finance Office, gave him the whole sordid story, and asked if he could work some magic. Glad to! He said he would make sure the whole thing got done in two or three days (not weeks).

The next order of business was the fact that Joel only had a couple of dollars in his pocket to tide him over 'til the 15th. Plus, he didn't know if his wife had any money. The Alert Center got a phone patch through to her and, sure enough, she was broke too. I got in touch with both the Air Force Aid Society and Red Cross representative and they agreed that this situation warranted their financial help. That news gave Joel a lot of peace of mind.

Since clearing this mess up was going to require several long distance phone calls between here and Omaha (and God knows Joel couldn't afford that), I got the Alert Center back on the phone and told them to give Joel unlimited access to the phone lines until he straightens everything out. I'm starting to realize that the Ops Supe isn't just the old gray haired fart that makes sure the floors are clean.

♦♦♦♦♦♦♦♦♦♦

GOOD NEWS: I finally got my beeper! I went to Capt Jacoby Friday morning and told him what his beeper keepers had been telling me--that it would take six or seven months to bet me a pager. He wasn't too sympathetic; basically, "Tough shit, Chief. You'll just have to wait like anybody else."

Since getting the paperwork through the Communications Group seemed to be the major hold-up, I went to see Chief Dan Heffner, the Comm Group Ops Supe. I told him my sad story, figuring the best he could do was speed up the paperwork. Instead, he turned to the Staff Sergeant at the next desk and said, "Give the Chief a pager." He did. Simple as that.

The beeper I got is a Comm Group spare and, if they need it, I have to give it back. But Heffner told me that probably wouldn't happen--they have over 20 spares. Meanwhile, the 03rd beeper keepers will put in the paperwork and get me my own pager. When it comes in, I'll give this one back to the Comm Group. Gawd! Am I glad the "Chief's Fraternity" is alive and well.

Wednesday, June 10th

What a day! What a week! Here it is Wednesday, and I have no idea where Monday and Tuesday went. Since I've been here, I've been using a "To Do List"; the things I have to get done before the day is over. When it comes going home time, the list is usually longer than it was when I started working on it. I'm glad that's the way it is though. At least I'm not sitting around twiddling my thumbs and counting the fly specks on the ceiling. Makes time go by faster.

Got my first beeper call Sunday night. Seems Capt Ringler's (Chief of Ops Production) people had called in a work order to Logistics and Maintenance to get some equipment fixed. The item was logged out Thursday, here it was Sunday, and it still wasn't fixed. Capt Ringler called the maintenance folks, chewed ass, and told them to get the equipment fixed *NOW*! The maintenance folks got their panties all in a twist and called their boss (Capt Jacoby) and "told on" Capt Ringler. Capt Jacoby, in turn, completed the loop by calling Capt Ringler and chewing her ass out for chewing his people's ass out. At this point, Capt Ringler would normally have called Maj Weber to "tell on" Capt Jacoby. But Maj Weber was in Seoul attending Maj Che's (Korean Ops Officer) wedding. So who's left to call? The old gray-haired Chief, that's who.

After I got the call, I went out to Operations to talk with Capt Ringler for her side of the story, then spent the next couple of hours trying to track down Capt Jacoby to get his side of the story. Finally located him in his quarters and found that the broken equipment didn't belong to the 6903rd, which meant his people weren't responsible for fixing it in the first place. It really belonged to the Comm Group and their people had been working on it since early

Friday morning. In fact, they were working feverishly on the equipment even as we spoke.

Got back with Capt Ringler and told her what was *really* happening. By Monday morning, the Comm Group had worked their magic, the equipment was up and running, and everything was back to normal. I didn't know refereeing pissing contests between Captains was part of this job.

♦♦♦♦♦♦♦♦♦♦

Had a long talk with Col Meade Monday morning. I brought up the Friday afternoon exercise fiasco and told him he had really screwed up with the troops by breaking it up the way he did. I told him there was a right way and wrong way to handle unpopular/distasteful things like exercises but, if he would work with me, I would help him handle these things the best way possible. The exercise was the perfect example.

I told the Colonel that, if he went to the lowest ranking person in the unit and asked him what he thought about exercises, he'd say, "They suck!" But then if you asked the same guy if they were necessary, he'd say yes. So here's a situation that's unpopular/distasteful, but the troops know it's necessary, so they'll accept it if it's handled right. The Colonel agreed and said he'd consult me on future situations of this nature

I thought I was on a roll, so I decided to bring up the subject of administrative support manning. The unit as a whole is authorized 22 admin support types and we're six short for a total of 16 on board. That doesn't seem too bad at first glance but, as I pointed out to the Colonel, the shortage isn't spread throughout the entire unit. All six shortages are in Operations. MSgt Joe Del Ricco (my NCOIC of Admin Support) is making the best of a bad situation, but it looks like he's fighting a losing battle.

Every other division in SKIVVY NINE is 100 percent manned in admin people and the Command Section is 200 percent manned (they're authorized one and they've got two). I looked Col Meade straight in the eye and said, "Colonel, we need to realign our admin resources. Furthermore, I want one of your admin people to come and work in Operations." He looked me straight in the eye and said, "No". Oh well, so much for progress.

As I was leaving Col Meade's office, he followed me to the door and I could tell he had something on his mind. He said, "Hmmmm..... ah..... uuhhhhh. I don't know how to say this without sounding condescending. Uhhh...I guess the best way to say it is to just come out and say it. Ahhh...I like they way you're doing your job." I wanted to say, "Jesus, Colonel, you don't even know how to give a compliment." But I didn't. Instead, I said, "Thanks."

♦♦♦♦♦♦♦♦♦♦

Started out my day this morning by attending a breakfast in honor of Chief Master Sergeant of the Air Force John Ballenger. He covered a lot of areas in his little after-breakfast talk, but the one that really made my day was in the area of uniforms.

Chief Ballenger said about six months ago, he had approached the Air Force Uniform board with a proposal to make Battle Dress Uniforms the official fatigue uniform of the Air Force. They said the proposal would have to be "staffed", then a two year test would have to be conducted and, if the test turned out OK, bids would be let on a contract to make the uniforms. And then there would be the time it takes to manufacture the clothes, not to mention the time it takes for the supply system to be retooled to handle the new uniform item. If everything went just exactly right, BDUs should become the official fatigue uniform in about three to five years.

During a flight to Europe a couple of months ago, General Leonard Webb, the Chief of Staff of the Air Force, asked John if he thought BDUs were a good idea. His answer was yes. General Webb said, "I like the idea, too." Then after giving it a little thought, the General said, "If you like 'em, and I like 'em, and we're the two guys who run this damn Air Force, then why the hell do we need a test. When we get back, tell the Uniform Board to put out a message authorizing the wear of BDUs!" And he did.

John said that ever since that message hit the street, there had been mass confusion. Did the Uniform Board message really constitute authority to Wear BDUs, or did units have to wait for a formal change to Air Force Reg 35-10? (Sound familiar?)

The CMSAF went on to say that as far as General Webb was concerned, he had made a decision and, just because some Tech Sergeant at the Military Personnel Center hadn't gotten around to putting out a message that made that decision official, units shouldn't hesitate to implement that decision. Then John gave the official word on the wear of BDUs: "These are the words of the Chief Master Sergeant of the Air Force representing the Chief of Staff of the Air Force. Watch my lips: effective this date, 10 June, you and your people are authorized to wear BDUs. If you've got 'em, wear 'em. If you've already been wearing them before this announcement, good on you. That shows a lot of initiative."

It was all I could do to keep from coming out of my seat with a loud, long Rebel Yell. Hot damn! That made me feel good. Joel Tennant (the 51st Tac Fighter Wing SEA) looked like he was about to swallow his face. I would have given anything if Bruce Lewis could have been there, but the son-of-a-bitch is already gone. Chalk up one for the good guys!

Chapter Four

THEY'RE HERE! THEY'RE HERE!

Sunday, June 14th

Well, the fun started yesterday with the arrival of the I.G. Team. The 6903rd Electronic Security Group will be under their magnifying glass for the next week and, Gawd, I hope the rest of the inspection goes smoother than the way it started out.

When the I.G. Team swoops in for an inspection, the inspected unit does everything they can to make the Team's stay as pleasant as possible. For starters, the inspected unit always has a group of "baggage handlers" meet the Team's plane, gather up their luggage, and transport it to their quarters where it will be waiting when the members get to their room. Nice touch.

Friday morning, I got the group responsible for performing this detail together. I told them that, although it seemed like a not-shit detail, they were a very important part of a successful inspection. They would be the first SKIVVY NINErs the I.G. Team would see and would be the basis for their first impression of the entire unit. The bottom line was: they had to look sharp and they had to be courteous.

At around 10:00 o'clock Saturday morning, I got a beeper call to report to Col Meade at the SKIVVY NINE Lounge. When I got there, he was in a tizzy. He said the baggage handlers were a disaster and wanted me to fix the problem immediately. I went outside where they were gaggled up and took a look-see. Seven of them were pictures of perfection--model Airmen all. Billy Nagle was an absolute shambles.

I would have replaced Billy on the spot, but finding a replacement on a Saturday morning with only two hours left until the I.G. arrived would be impossible. I took him to my dorm room so my houseboy could iron his uniform and Billy could shine his shoes. After his uniform was in shape, I told him to hot-foot it over to the barber shop to get shorn, but he said he didn't have any money (it was, after all, two days before payday). So I gave him three dollars to get the job done and a ride to the barber shop. He made it back to the Lounge just in time to greet the team looking sharp.

Aaah, Billy Nagle--one of my perennial problem children. Billy has had continual problems since he arrived here from tech school. He was a 19-year-old kid away from home for the first time and really not very mature. He got a place off base and in the first five months he was here, he fell in love and got engaged to five different Korean lovelies. He was constantly late for work and his training progression was way below standards. He flunked his first proficiency evaluation and was placed in intensive remedial training. And then he flunked again.

Billy had to go before a Special Review Board to be evaluated as to whether he was "trainable". During the proceedings, it became apparent that his problems were caused by his living in the 'ville, partying every night until two or three o'clock in the morning, and coming to work so tired and hung over that he couldn't concentrate. At the conclusion of the review, Maj Weber gave Billy a lawful order to move back into the dorm to "remove him from the temptations to be found in the 'ville." Having solved the problem, the panel voted to allow Billy to continue in training.

He did pretty well at getting to work on time and his training progression was satisfactory for the next few weeks. Then right after I got here, Col Meade was conducting a tour of the unit for a VIP visitor. When they walked down the aisle Billy worked on, there was the ass hole kicked back from his position with his head on the back of his chair sound asleep. Col Meade had a conniption fit.

Turns out Billy was back up to his old ways and we hit him with an Article 15 for sleeping on duty. On top of that, Maj Weber had his clearance revoked while he underwent psychiatric evaluation. The reason for the eval? The Major figured anyone stupid enough to move back off base despite his lawful order was either addicted to booze and broads or had to be a little whack-o.

Billy went on casual status[14] while the evaluation was being performed, When it was over, the medicos decided there was nothing wrong inside his cranial cavity. We had no reason to withhold his clearance and had to let him back into the compound. B.O. O'Banion (Billy's ex-boss) said he didn't want the dirtbag back, so I put him to work with SSgt Jim LaMora, my Supply NCO, to help him get ready for the I.G. visit. He did OK as long as Jim told him exactly what to do, when to do it, and how to do it. That's how Billy made it onto the baggage handling team--I gave Jim the task of rounding up "volunteers" for the detail and, since Billy worked for him, he was a natural choice. I've got to talk to Jim about his judgement.

♦♦♦♦♦♦♦♦♦♦

And speaking of problem children, Senior Airman Walker Staggs--a name that makes my eyes glaze over when I hear it--comes immediately to mind. This young gentleman has been a royal pain in my ass for almost a month, but I guess it's guys like him that are the reason they pay Ops Supes the big bucks.

---

[14] When a person is unable to perform their normal duties for any reason, they are placed on "casual status" where they perform "casual" duties--menial tasks such as mowing lawns, painting rocks, picking up trash, cleaning latrines, mopping floors, etc. The majority of people on casual status in ESC are there because their clearances have been revoked or withheld for any reason.

First, SrA Staggs was scheduled for drug testing (peeing in a bottle) a couple of weeks ago and didn't show up. His supervisor wrote a Letter of Reprimand on Staggs for "failure to go." He came whining to me about how innocent he was, but his story didn't hold water, so I told him I couldn't help.

Having failed with me, Staggs went to his Flight Commander (a real bleeding heart liberal) with his tale of woe, and the Flight Commander bought it. He put pressure on the supervisor to pull the letter back, so the supervisor came to me looking to get the Flight Commander off his back. Before you could say "pissing contest", the Flight Commander's supervisor (Capt Ringler) and Capt O'Rourk were involved, both pushing the supervisor to let the Letter of Reprimand stand. I advised Capt Ringler to give the Flight Commander a lawful order to back off so the supervisor could do what needed to be done. She did and he did.

Last Wednesday morning, the Staggs saga continued when he and his brand new bride, Kathy, showed up on my doorstep. She's squalling and slinging snot because her supervisor was doing her wrong. Seems they were scheduled to go on leave to the States, and the plane was departing that very afternoon. The big problem was she had taken her proficiency exam earlier that morning and blew it down her leg.

Maj Weber's policy when someone flunks a proficiency test is they can't take leave until they re-take and pass the test. In Kathy's case, she had originally taken the test Monday and flunked it, then turned right around and took it again Wednesday and flunked it again. Second failures have to wait 60 days before a retest is administered and she couldn't wait that long to take leave. They just had to get back to San Antonio to take care of some personal business caused by Staggs' recent divorce from his first wife.

SKIVVY NINE!

My initial reaction was this was just another "Staggs-ism" and that they were wasting my time because I wasn't about to help them out. The Major's policy was policy and if we allow exceptions to it, everyone is going to want to be an exception. But as Kathy told her story, she brought two things to light that made me change my mind.

First, she had a signed leave form in her possession and, technically, had been on leave since one minute after midnight Wednesday morning. Kathy's supervisor had allowed her to go on leave that day, betting on the come that she would pass the proficiency retest. He lost.

Once the deed was done and she was on leave, by regulation, the only reason to recall her from leave would be for "dire and immediate operational necessity". I didn't know what the legal ramifications of calling her off leave were, but I didn't think her failure of the retest constituted "dire and immediate operational necessity."

Second, Kathy said she could name names and show written proof that all Mission Supervisors on all flights weren't applying the Major's policy uniformly across the board. Two of the Mission Supes (her's included) were applying the policy to the letter; no passee test, no takee leave. The other two were letting people go on leave whether they passed or not. At first, I thought there wasn't much of a problem; The Major would simply kick ass on a couple of the Mission Supes and the problem would be over. I was wrong.

When the Major implemented the policy, it was verbal--he didn't write anything down. The two Mission Supes that were allowing their people leave were new and, since there were no written instructions to tell them differently, they probably didn't know they were wrong-doing.

With all the facts together, I advised the Major to allow Kathy Staggs to go on leave. She had us on a technicality. Knowing the kind of people we were dealing with, I had no doubt that they would go straight to the I.G. when they came to town if we didn't let her go. I also knew our dirty laundry couldn't stand close scrutiny from the I.G. So they caught the great Freedom Bird that afternoon and are on leave even as I write.

♦♦♦♦♦♦♦♦♦♦♦

But the "Staggs Story" continued even after they were gone. Last Tuesday, Capt Ringler called me with some disturbing news. She had one of the troops take her pick-up in for its six weeks check-up and oil change. The Noncommissioned Officer in Charge of the Motor Pool called her and said her truck had been the victim of vehicle abuse. It had dents and scratches all over it. He also said there were places on the vehicle with imprints of the bottom of a shoe; someone had kicked the living shit out of it. To top off the gory deed, there were scratches down to the metal the length of the truck that looked as though they had been inflicted by a nail, knife, or some other pointed instrument. In short, the truck was trashed.

Capt Ringler went to the Motor Pool for a look-see and, sure enough, what the NCOIC told her was true. Since her dorm is less than a two minute walk from work, Capt Ringler rarely uses the pick-up. Instead, she leaves it at work for the shift workers to use for box bennie pick-up and other errands. Therefore, there are a *lot* of drivers on a given day, and any of them could have trashed the truck.

The Motor Pool NCOIC said, since the damage was malicious, the unit would have to pick up the tab for fixing it to the tune of between $500 and $700. Capt Ringler and I agreed that we needed to find the scumbag that done the deed and let him/her pay for the repairs. To make that happen, she asked me to help her conduct an "investigation" and I would have, but I was tied up with the Staggs leave fiasco all morning Wednesday, so the Captain had to go it on her own.

She started at the point in time where she had personal knowledge of the condition of the truck. That was Monday morning when she had inspected it herself. At that time, the truck was in perfect condition. The damage was discovered Tuesday afternoon, so it was a simple matter of determining who the drivers were between Monday morning and Tuesday afternoon. The next stop was the Mission Supe's Vehicle Sign-out Log.

She pulled all the names from the log who had driven the truck since she inspected it and contacted each individual. They all swore the truck was in good condition at the time they drove it. She had no reason not to believe them--they were all pretty straight shooters with good records. But, although it's required by regulation, they probably didn't give the truck a good, long look before they drove it

The big breakthrough came when she talked to four Maintenance troops who had driven the truck at 10 a.m. Tuesday morning. The significance of the driver being a maintenance dude is the fact that, unlike Operations weenies, they *ALWAYS* inspect a vehicle thoroughly before they drive it. And even better, there were four of them to corroborate the story. All four swore there was nothing wrong with the truck, They turned the keys in to the Mission Supe at 10:45 a.m. and the Motor Pool NCOIC reported the damage at two o'clock. That meant there was a three hour and forty five minute window when the truck was done in. All Capt Ringler had to do now was determine who had access to it during that timeframe.

The Able Flight Mission Supe had detailed one of his people to fetch the box bennies at 11:30 and the same guy to take the truck in for its check-up at 1:30. He was the only person to drive the vehicle after the Maintenance troops inspected it. The driver was Senior Airman Walker Staggs!

Capt Ringler literally ran to my office with the news, but by the time she got there, the Freedom Bird had already departed for the States with the Staggs on board. The culprit had escaped--for the time being. We'll have a Report of Survey and an Article 15[15] prepared and ready for young Airman Staggs when he returns.

♦♦♦♦♦♦♦♦♦♦♦

Even though SrA Staggs is gone, the mischief he performed before he left is still having an impact. Since Capt Ringler's pick-up has been in the Motor Pool for repairs since Wednesday, I've been lending mine to the Flights to pick up lunch time box bennies (they use the Maintenance truck on swings and mids). Friday, they were coming back from the chow hall with the grub when they were broadsided by a dependant wife. Fortunately, the guys in the truck did all the right things--didn't move the vehicles; called the Security Police to investigate; reported the accident to the Motor Pool and the 03rd's Vehicle Control Officer; and broke the news to me. The unit came up clean, but I was faced with a "no wheels" situation until my truck was fixed (probably about three weeks).

I went to see 1Lt Alan Johnson, the Vehicle Control Officer in LG, and told him my problem. He agreed the Ops Supe did, in fact, need a vehicle, especially with the I.G. Team in town and knowing they will conduct an exercise where I'll have to respond quickly. He got his list of vehicles out and said he'd call me when he found a truck for me.

---

[15] Used to administer "non-judicial punishment", which means punishment administered without the accused having benefit of the judicial process. A Commander's authority to levy punishment under Article 15 is derived from the Uniform Code of Military Justice. For further information on the Article 15, consult the "Glossary of Terms".

I returned to my office to wait, but when he didn't call in 30 minutes, I went back to see the Lieutenant. He was in Capt Jacoby's (his boss) office and didn't know I was standing right outside the door. Lt Johnson was saying, "Captain, the Chief *has* to have one of the LG trucks. We don't need to look at this thing as what's good for LG; we need to look at it as what's good for the unit overall."

A lot of LG people are notorious for their attitude of "put LG first and to hell with everyone else." Bruce Lewis was that way and Capt Jacoby is carrying on the tradition. But Lt Johnson seems different. With his "for the good of the unit" appeal when he didn't know I was within ear shot, he earned a lot of respect from me.

Before Capt Jacoby could tell the Lieutenant no, I went into the office and took them both off the hook. I said LG probably needed all their trucks as badly as I needed mine and they shouldn't have to give one up just so I could have wheels. But I did know a place that had a truck and could afford to give it up for just a little while until mine was fixed--the Orderly Room.

I reasoned that Capt O'Rourk has a car and, if he has to get to the Orderly Room in a hurry, he can use that. First Sergeant Duckworth lives in the dormitory right across the street from the Orderly Room and can walk there in less than a minute. On the other hand, I'm a 15-20 minute walk from my place of duty and need wheels for rapid response. Jacoby and Johnson agreed that the best plan was for me to take Orderly Room truck 'till the Motor Pool was finished with mine. I got the pleasure of personally breaking the news to O'Rourk. Thought he was going to cough up a fur ball when I told him, but he grudgingly gave up the keys and now I have wheels.

Sunday, June 20th

What a week! I now have a great appreciation for what the I.G. Team looks like from the receiving end. They really wrung us out. But it's over now. Yesterday was the last inspection day. They'll be here until next Friday, but they'll be putting the report and outbrief together and won't be doing any inspecting.

The thing I feared the most about the whole inspection was the recall/exercise because I didn't have a feel for how it would go. During the dozens of practices we had to get ready, it ran hot and cold; one time we'd do great, the next time we'd fall flat on our asses. Needless to say, I was a bit apprehensive.

Based on my experience with the I.G. Team, I knew the optimum time (for them) for the exercise was Wednesday night. They must have been running a little ahead of the inspection schedule, 'cause they kicked that sucker off Wednesday morning at 3 a.m. It was a seven hour affair, lasting until almost ten o'clock. My response time was excellent. I got the pager call at 3:08 and had the Operations Sub-Control Center (SCC) up and running at 3:28.

The exercise went amazingly well. There were a few "glitches" in the Ops Division, but nothing serious. Hell, exercises never go perfect. When the exercise was over, the inspector in the SCC said B.O. O'Banion and Brian Decker (my two assistants) and I had done well. I guess all those practices paid off. They were a pain in the ass, but they paid off. The only *major* problem we had was with the Emergency Destruction Team.[16]

Everything went pretty smooth until the Team got the classified material to the destruction site. While everybody was milling around getting the material into 50-gallon drums and setting the incendiary devices, one of the team members decided he just

---

[16] If an ESC unit ever comes under attack, there would be *A LOT* of classified material that must be destroyed lest it fall into enemy hands. This monumental task falls to a group called the Emergency Destruction Team. For more information on EDTs, see the Glossary of Terms.

couldn't wait another minute for a cigarette. So he lit one up not more than two feet from three hundred pounds of explosives!

Milt Joskey (the I.G. Safety Inspector) went nuts-oid! And rightfully so! That one stupid act caused us to get a Deficiency Finding[17], but I don't think it caused us to go "MARGINAL" in the exercise area of the inspection. The Safety area might take it in the shorts, but I think we'll still pull a "SATISFACTORY" on the exercise. I sure hope so. Col Meade promised before the inspection began that, if the exercise went well, SKIVVY NINE would be excused from the base-wide quarterly exercise in July. God knows we need a break.

The idiot that caused everyone to scurry for cover when he lit up next to the explosives was--ready for this??--A1C Billy Nagle! I've got to find the man who was foolish enough to assign Billy to the EDT and have a chunk of his ass. On the bright side, Billy only has six weeks left 'till he leaves Osan for Goodfellow AFB, Texas. I just hope I can get through them without killing the boy.

♦♦♦♦♦♦♦♦♦♦♦

The in-brief went extremely well on the first morning of the inspection. Surprisingly, the I.G. Team is still using the in-brief I wrote and the slides I made when I was on the team. Our portion of the brief just knocked their sox off. Maj Weber wrote the text (with a little help from his Ops Supe) and delivered it. The I.G. Team was visibly impressed. It was a good way to start off an inspection.

About half the team are guys that were on it when I was and their method of inspection hasn't changed. They conduct business in a professional manner and, even when they find something wrong, they're not nasty about it. Not so with the newer guys.

---

[17] A fancy I.G. term that, when simply translated, means "you fucked up".

For the most part, they're a bunch of flaming assholes and the Director of Inspections (DI) is the worst of all. Lt Col Don Brogan took Gentle Ben Hassinger's place and is as bad as Gentle Ben was good.

One of the functions of the DI is to backbrief the Commander every morning on how the inspection is going. Col Meade told me after the first day that the backbrief from Brogan was more like a brow beating session. Brogan treats Meade like a real scum bag. I feel sorry for the Colonel. This is his first experience as a Commander, he has no self confidence, and he's scared to death we're going to go UNSAT on the inspection. Brogan doesn't help his feelings at all with the way he conducts the backbriefs.

Wednesday morning during their daily session, Brogan dropped the big bomb. He told Col Meade that the unit's people failed to measure up to ESC standards in the area of courtesy, dress, and appearance. For Col Meade, this news was an absolute slap in the face. He was crushed. He's a real stickler on dress and appearance and the news that his people failed in that area was almost more than he could handle. He had made himself a very unpopular man with the troops when he first got here because he demanded they look sharp in uniform, but apparently, his efforts weren't good enough for the IG Team. When he asked for a specific example of someone that didn't meet standards, Col Brogan said the First Sergeant had been seen on several occasions with his hands in his pockets. That was the only specific example he could cite.

As soon as the session was over, Col Meade called in all the Division Chiefs and went on the rampage. He gave them their marching orders to go back to their Divisions and whip the troops into shape *now*.

Maj Weber came back to our office, called a meeting of the Branch Chiefs, and passed along the Colonel's concerns. When he said the specific example of poor courtesy, dress, and appearance was the First Shirt, I exploded. "Major, that is BULL SHIT! Despite all our disagreements, he's one of the sharpest guys I've ever seen. You can cut your finger on the creases in his uniform; you can shave yourself in the toes of his boots; you can see skin on the sides of his head; his body is hard as a rock. A guy that looks like that putting his hands in his pockets does not a dirt bag make!" There.

The Major agreed and told the Branch Chiefs not to over-react. He didn't think we had a problem (especially in Operations) with how our people looked or acted. They agreed. The Major gave them instructions not to pass on the Director of Inspection's concerns to our people.

When our meeting was over, I went to see Col Meade personally to reassure him that he was not in command of a unit full of slugs. We've got room for improvement just like any other unit, but we are not a disaster area, either. My talk with the Colonel calmed him down a bit and he asked me what I thought we should do. I told him I needed to have a talk with Chief Herb Heffner (the Team's AFR 35-10 guru) to see just how bad the "problem" really was. Then, I needed to talk to Col Brogan to refute his accusations and hopefully pour water on the fire.

That afternoon, I got together with Herb over a beer in my room and we had a very frank discussion. I told him that, either his Colonel was overstating the problem or my Colonel was over-reacting to it and that, between us, we had to come up with a fix.

He said, yes, the First Sergeant had been seen with his hands in his pockets, but that didn't make him a bad guy (35-10 wise). He said Brogan had some concerns that we wore so many different combinations of fatigue uniforms and some of our Maintenance troops' boots weren't shiny and their shirttails weren't tucked in all the way all the time. Additionally, some supervisors had been noted addressing subordinates by their first names, and many unit people didn't stand up when an inspector approached their work place.

After my talk with Herb, it was obvious where the problem lay. SKIVVY NINE did not have a problem; the Director of Inspections had a problem.

I backbriefed Col Meade on my conversation with Herb and he couldn't believe the pettiness of the whole situation. He wanted to get his Division Chiefs back together to recall his marching orders, but I advised him against it. That would make him look like he was vacillating and unsure of himself. He took my advise for once and OK'ed a meeting between Brogan and me.

The next morning (Thursday), Lt Col Brogan attended our weekly Commander's Staff Meeting. When it was over, I asked for an audience sometime later that day. He said he had the time right then, so I invited him to my office. When I told him what I wanted to discuss, he immediately launched into the old theory that the best defense is a good offense.

He said although the Group's dress and appearance was absolutely in the toilet, our "courtesies" were even worse. He used me as an example. He said that during the Staff Meeting, I had slouched in my chair, was not erect and attentive, and generally showed poor posture throughout the meeting--definitely not the kind of attitude I should display in the formal setting of a staff meeting and *especially* in the presence of an O-6! At one point, I even turned my chair sideways to the table and crossed my legs! Lordy! Lordy! Lordy!

And then at another point in the staff meeting, I had the unmitigated gall to call SSgt LaMora by his first name during a discussion about a supply problem. I apologized to the Colonel profusely for my outrageous behavior and assured him that my actions were unconscious and were in no way intended as a personal affront to Col Meade's O-6ness. I also told him that I hadn't realized that I was such a skuzz ball, thanked him for pointing it out to me, and promised to work hard to improve my image.

With my apologies for my wicked ways out of the way, we then moved on to other issues. First, there was the matter of our dirt bag First Shirt. I told the Colonel that he was sharper than any three members of the I.G. Team put together and, before he threw stones for hands in pockets, he might want to clean up the Team's act in that area. I had observed Ted Doyle, Capt Thornton, and two new members of the Team with their hands in their pockets that very morning.

As far as the number of different fatigue uniform combinations was concerned, every uniform was authorized by AFR 35-10 or Commander's policy letter. I also said that, although the I.G. Team wears the same uniform while they're on the road (blue trousers, short sleeve shirt, no tie, no ribbons), I know from personal experience from when I was on the team that, when they're back at the headquarters, they wear any number of different uniform combinations--all of which are authorized by either AFR 35-10 or I.G. policy letter.

And then we moved on to the slobs in LG who had muddy boots and shirt tails that weren't tucked in. Unlike most ESC units, we have working maintenance men in SKIVVY NINE. I reminded the Colonel that, at most ESC units, maintenance people perform their duties inside on electronic gear at spotless work benches and don't even get their fingernails dirty.

Our maintenance people crawl around inside the belly of aircraft, wallow in the muck, mud, and slush of Hill 170 where there are major antenna upgrades in progress, and maintain generator engines every day. I would be concerned if they *didn't* get dirty. I also pointed out that it's a little tough to keep your shirt tail completely tucked in when you're dangling from the top of a 100 foot tower trying to get an antenna to work that's vital to mission accomplishment. I was on a roll and feeling good.

The fact that some supervisors called their subordinates by their first names was no accident. "Believe it or not, Colonel, we do that on purpose."

I told him I had made a conscious effort to learn the first names of everyone in Ops and, despite his concerns over the practice, I would continue to use first names. I believe this practice fosters esprit and camaraderie among the troops if the leadership takes the time and effort to know their first names. I also reminded the Colonel that it is a time-honored military tradition for seniors to call subordinates by their first names. It's even done on the I.G. Team. On the other hand, subordinates calling supervisors by their first name was a no-no and, if he saw instances of that, I would take appropriate action. Otherwise, I couldn't get real excited about first name usage at the 6903rd.

As for the problem of unit members not standing when talking to I.G. Team members, I got a little pointed with the Colonel on that one. I told him that in the 6903rd, we stand for people in deference to their rank, not their position. I assured him that, should an officer member of the I.G. Team approach an enlisted member of the unit, the enlisted person will stand while talking to the officer. However, I would be damned before I would stand up for some not shit Master Sergeant just because he happened to be a member of the I.G. Team and I wouldn't have my people do it either.

At the end of the discussion, Col Brogan seemed completely oblivious to what had just transpired. He didn't rebut anything I had said, but said all the items I had discussed were problems and would be reflected as such in the final report. I said fine--I was sure Major General Mather (the ESC Commander) would find the I.G.'s observations interesting, especially since he had called us one of the sharpest units he had seen during his visit a couple of months ago. Brogan said, "Perhaps he will," and left.

I backbriefed Col Meade on my talk with Lt Col Brogan and included every gory detail. He was completely satisfied and seemed serene in the knowledge that no matter what the assholes put in the report, we're right, they're wrong, and we'll continue to step out smartly without changing anything.

Meanwhile, back in the Orderly Room, Capt O'Rourk was showing his ass again. The inspection was not going well for him and the whiffle balls who work for him. They are going to suck up five deficiency findings and, according to Herb Heffner, have a good possibility of being rated UNSAT. There *is* justice in this world after all!

One of the areas where they are in big do-do is the Weight Management Program (WMP). They've got it so barfed up it's unbelievable. When Herb identified the problem Monday, Captain O decided he needed to show him the program had teeth and decided to sacrifice a unit member in an attempt to cover his ass. The unfortunate object of his wrath was A1C Janette Hoover. The screwed up mish-mash of events in Janette's "fat girl case" goes something like this:

> **February 9th**: The unit holds a no-notice weight check. Janette is re-measured, shrinks a half inch, and goes four pounds over her maximum weight. She is placed on the WMP and instructed to weigh in on the 16th of each month until she goes under the max. In order to make satisfactory progress in the program, she must lose three pounds per month.
>
> **March 16th**: A1C Hoover weighs in with a three pound weight loss. Satisfactory progress.

April 16th: A1C Hoover weighs in with no loss (or gain) in weight. Unsatisfactory progress. At this point, Captain O'Rourk should have taken some sort of disciplinary action. He didn't.

May 11th: Janette weighs in five days early because she's going on mid-tour leave back to the States starting the 13th. She had lost three pounds (satisfactory progress) and comes in two pounds under her maximum weight. She heaves a huge sigh of relief because she's off the WMP and goes on leave.

June 15th (the first day of the inspection): A1C Hoover is summoned to Capt O'Rourk's office and given a Letter of Reprimand for failure to make satisfactory progress on April 16th. She acknowledges receipt of the letter by signing at the bottom, but has the presence of mind to date her signature June 15th.

The letter stated she is *still* on the WMP (even though she's five pounds under her max at the present time) and ordered her into a mandatory exercise program to be conducted during off duty time and diet counseling at the hospital twice a week. Additionally, she would be given a sub-standard Airman Performance Report (APR) when her next one came due, and she would not be allowed to meet the Senior Airman Below-the-Zone board (which meant she couldn't be promoted early) when it meets on June 23rd. Needless to say, the girl was a bit stupefied and upset.

June 16th: A1C Hoover shows up in front of my desk with her tale of woe. I literally could not believe my ears; I knew O'Rourk was an idiot, but this was ridiculous. Before I reacted, I needed to do some homework to make sure I (and A1C Hoover) was in the right. I dug into AFR 35-11 (the WMP regulation) and AFR 39-62 (the APR regulation) and talked to Herb Heffner. Herb's reaction was: "The bottom line is the Captain is both legally and morally wrong."

June 17th: I get back with SMSgt Duckworth to see if he can get the Caption to back off. The First Sergeant was blindsided by the situation; O'Rourk had not consulted him before he laid the LOR on Hoover. He said that, in his opinion, the Captain was wrong on this one (strange words from Duckworth) and he would talk to him.

June 18th (morning): I got back with the First Sergeant and, like a good soldier, he's reversed himself and is now backing his boss, O'Rourk. According to him, what the Captain did was "by-the-book right", so why was I making waves. At that point, I requested and received an audience with the Captain. I expressed my concerns to him; his reaction was, "The bitch is fat and she deserves anything she gets." Oh well.....

June 18th (afternoon): In to see Col Meade on the Hoover situation. He was utterly amazed that the Captain had displayed such bad judgement. I apologized to the Colonel for having to elevate the problems of an Airman First Class to his level. I'd been able to show the Captain the errors of his ways at times in the past, but he refused to budge on this one and I needed help.

June 18th (late afternoon): On the way back to my dorm, I noticed the Colonel's car parked outside the Orderly Room. At about six o'clock, Col Meade knocked on my door with some good news. The LOR on Hoover had been withdrawn; the next APR won't be derogatory; she will meet the BTZ Board next Tuesday. I asked the Colonel how the Captain took the decision and he said, "Not good, but who cares." I think he's finally coming around. I invited him for a beer. He declined. Maybe not.

♦♦♦♦♦♦♦♦♦♦

And as if my week wasn't complete, there was a near-mutiny on Able Flight. When Capt Ringler came to work Monday morning, half of Able Flight was waiting at her desk demanding the ouster of 2Lt Brian Walk, the Flight Commander. Without boring the reader with a lot of details, take my word for it, Lt Walk is a bona fide flake. And to make matters worse, he's a eccentric nerd (wears his uniform shoes with civilian clothing; has 14 pens in his shirt pocket; always wears long sleeve shirts no matter how hot it is and corduroy trousers).

Able Flight has been in a state of turmoil every since I've been here, but Capt Ringler has continually worked with Lt Walk to keep the lid from blowing off. But their Sunday night/Monday morning mid shift was the last straw.

After six weeks of no mids off and limited leaves while getting ready for the I.G. visit, Maj Weber put out the word (verbally) that supervisors should slack off--the I.G. is here, we've done all we can do, so start giving the troops hits and letting them go on leave.

The word got out to everybody but 2Lt Brian Walk. He told Able Flight that, until he saw something in writing from Maj Weber, the no hits/limited leave policy would remain in effect on his flight. That was the straw and Able Flight, led by the Surveillance and Warning Center (S&WC) Supervisor, was demanding relief from Capt Ringler.

The Captain was on the verge of tears when she came to see the Major and me. We talked about the situation for a long time, weighing our options, and trying to decide what to do. The best course of action would be to fire 2Lt Walk, put him off in some corner where he could do minimal damage, and replace him with another Intel Officer. Unfortunately, we didn't have another Intel Officer to replace him with.

So the next-best-thing was to send him to another flight and replace him with that Flight's commander. We chose Baker Flight because they're the strongest and can absorb the Lieutenant's incompetence and still function. Additionally, Baker Flight's commander, 2Lt Mary Jarvine, is a sharp kid--she's kinda new, but has already shown that she has the stuff to glue Able Flight back together. The switch was made swiftly with surgical precision. Lt Walk reported for duty on swing shift with Baker Flight that night and Lt Jarvine reported for work with Able on mids.

I told the Captain and Major that, in addition to the Flight Commander move, we had some fence mending to do. First, someone had to get with Baker Flight and explain why we were doing this to them.

Second, someone had to talk to Able Flight and let them know, in no uncertain terms, that they had not run the Flight Commander off. It had to be made perfectly clear that, just because they didn't like a Flight Commander, they couldn't get rid of him/her by raising a little hell. They had to understand that moving Lt Walk had been a management decision, not a response to their protest.

Lastly, someone had to talk to the Able Flight S&WC Supe. He's a Master Sergeant named Greg Guthier and about the most abrasive individual I've ever seen. He makes a habit of eating young Flight Commanders alive, and undoubtedly contributed to Lt Walk's failure. He had to be told if Lt Jarvine failed, he would be held personally accountable. She's a very sharp troop, not at all like Walk, and he had better make sure she succeeded.

The Major, the Captain, and I divvied up the assignments between us. The Major took the unsavory task of talking to Baker Flight. We were saddling them with a known loser and they had to understand that our actions were absolutely necessary. We knew that if they understood the whys, they would be good soldiers and make the best of a bad situation. The Major's mission was a success.

Capt Ringler didn't fare as well. She took the task of talking to Able Flight and, according to later reports, she came across like Attila the Hun. Not only did she convince them that they had not run the Lieutenant off, she convinced them that the Lieutenant's failure was their fault. She did a lot of ranting and raving and Able Flight was generally left with a bad taste in their collective mouths.

I came in early the next morning to catch Greg Guthier when he got off his mid shift. I read him the riot act about his new Lieutenant and how she had *better* succeed. When I was finished, he told me about the Captain's performance the night before and said he had actually expected me to fire him when he came to my office. She had said everyone's APR would suffer because of the Walk incident. Greg said they were all punchy because of the Captain's threats and something needed to be done. So I went in for the next mid shift to reassure Able Flight that their next APR would be based on merit, not on what happened to Lt Walk. I also challenged them to make Lt Jarvine a success and warned them of the consequences if they don't.

I thought everything was fixed and all the tracks covered, but Thursday morning, Lt Jarvine went to Capt Ringler and said she just couldn't live another minute with MSgt Guthier. The boy was riding rough-shod over her and she wanted to go back to Baker Flight. Well, I had told Greg what the consequences were; he had to be fired and replaced with another S&WC Supe.

Maj Weber and I spent almost all day trying to figure out how it could be done smoothly. Once again, without boring the reader with detail, MSgt Greg Guthier now works in Exploitation Management and MSgt Tim Gabrovsek is the new S&WC Supe on Able Flight. It looks as though everything is fixed and all the tracks are covered. I sure as hell hope so. Only time will tell.

And all this was happening with the I.G. Team breathing down my neck! But I'm 10 feet tall and bullet proof--I can do anything!

Wednesday, June 25th

First, a follow-up on A1C Jeanette Hoover, the young lady on the "Chunky Chicken" program who O'Rourk tried to dick away for not making satisfactory progress. Justice was served and she got to meet the Senior Airman Below-the-Zone Board. She was promoted to Senior Airman early in a cake walk; of the 14 people to meet the board, her's was the top score with 142 points. The low score was 81 and the guy who finished second to Hoover scored a 108. That gives an idea of just how sharp this young lady is, and O'Rourk wanted to blow her out of the water.

And speaking of Capt O'Rourk.....he's still up to his old tricks. I was sitting in my office yesterday afternoon when A1C Ellen Andrews came in crying like a waterfall because her assignment to the 6990th ESS in Okinawa had been cancelled. The reason for her dismay was her husband was stationed at the 90th and the assignment cancellation meant that they would be separated for God-knows-how-long. They got married at Goodfellow, applied for a joint spouse assignment, was turned down, and have been separated for eight months of their nine month marriage. And now, the assignment that would reunite her with her beloved had been canceled--get this--because of failure to progress on the Weight Management Program.

Ellen's story goes something like this. She entered in the WMP in February as the result of the same weigh-in that nailed Hoover. She had lost three pounds at the March weigh-in, but only lost two in April. At that point, the regs say that a letter goes in to the Personnel Office identifying the person as a non-progressor and they can not receive an overseas assignment. If they already have an overseas assignment, it's automatically canceled.

Now a thinking man would look at the situation as a whole. Here we have a young lady with a spotless record, progressing nicely in her training, with a *first time failure* on the WMP. Capt O'Rourk could have laid a Letter of Counseling on her and then nail her to the wall for a second or third time offense. But nobody ever accused the Captain of being a thinking man. Without even telling A1C Andrews the consequences of her evil ways, he sent the letter to the Personnel Office knowing it would cancel her assignment to Okinawa.

In May, Ellen lost four pounds and, this month, she lost five to go under her limit and come off the program. She thought everything was cool until the assignment cancellation paperwork hit her. O'Rourk had once again applied the letter of the law instead of the intent and spirit of the law. I reassured A1C Andrews that I would do everything I could to get her assignment reinstated and sent her on her way.

I went to see SMSgt Duckworth and he allowed as how the Captain may have overreacted on this one. But O'Rourk stood firm; "The bitch is fat. She didn't meet the standard. She deserves anything she gets." Oh well. Off to see Col Meade again (Gawd! do I ever *hate* to do that!) Once again, the Colonel stuffed it up Capt O'Rourk's ass and today a message went back to the Assignments people at the Headquarters requesting a reinstatement of A1C Andrews' assignment to Okinawa.

I told Maj Weber this afternoon that it used to be fun breaking it off in the Captain's ass. But he makes it so easy by being so stupid that it isn't even fun anymore.

Chapter Five

THEY'RE GONE

Sunday, June 28th

The I.G. outbrief was Friday morning and it went about as I had expected. The Unit came up with an overall MARGINAL rating. Duckworth, O'Rourk and their flunkies went down the tubes with an UNSAT; LG took some bad hits and went MARGINAL; Budget was non-existent and went UNSAT; Readiness went UNSAT based on the poor showing of the Emergency Destruction Team (Billy Nagle's revenge) and Chemical Warfare Gear management; the Comm Center went MARGINAL; Safety took a MARGINAL based on the Billy Nagle incident alone; and on, and on, and on.

Operations on the other hand came out smelling like a rose. We have 10 branches and all did well except the Computer Support Branch; SSgt Jake Conrad and his crew came up with a MARGINAL. The rating could have just as easily gone "weak SAT", but the computer inspector is a bit of a flaming asshole and took the hard line (even people on the I.G. Team can't stand this guy. They call him the "Baby Gorilla".) Five of the other branches were rated EXCELLENT (with Capt Ringler and her crew coming as close to an OUTSTANDING as you can get) and four were rated SAT.

Deciding on an overall rating for Operations with five EXCELLENTS, four SATISFACTORIES, and a MARGINAL had to be a tough job for the I.G. Team. We had a couple of situations like this when I was on the team, and I know how gut wrenching it can be. It could have gone either way--a *very* healthy SAT or a middle-of-the-road EXCELLENT. Once again, the hard liners, led by Brogan, won out and came up with a strong SAT. But I don't feel bad about it. We still done good!

It became obvious in the middle of last week that the unit, as a whole, was going to go TANGO UNIFORM[18]. The Director of Inspections was backbriefing nothing but bad news to Col Meade. The Colonel was passing the bad news on to Maj Weber and me. I told the Major if the unit went MARGINAL or UNSAT, the I.G. outbrief would really put our people in the dumps. What Col Meade said to them immediately afterward was absolutely crucial. If he said the right words, he could lift their spirits, send them out of the theater with a modicum of self respect, and point them in the right direction to put the unit back on track. If he said the wrong words, he could crush them even further into the ground and make unit morale lower than it already is.

The Major knows, as does everyone in SKIVVY NINE, that Col Meade has the knack for saying just the wrong thing at exactly the wrong time, so he went to the Colonel and told him what I had said about the Colonel's words and unit morale. Col Meade agreed that the right words had to be said, but didn't know what they were. So he sent word back with Maj Weber that I should write him a speech and he would deliver it right after the outbrief.

It took me all morning Thursday, but I finally came up with one typewritten page filled with what I thought were the right words. The talk was simple and, I estimated, would take no longer than two minutes to deliver.

> *"OK Guys, we came up a little short. But we're not going to waste our time crying over spilled milk.*

[18] Phonetics for the letters "T" and "U" as in ALPHA (A), BRAVO (B), CHARLIE (C), etc. TU is simply short for "tits up", which is a metaphor for something dead, lying on its back, mammaries pointed toward the sky. Confusing? It could only happen in GI jargon. TANGO UNIFORM = "It's dead. No need to bother with it anymore."

We're going to spend our time productively, press on to the future, and fix the things that need fixing.

"For the Divisions, Branches, and people who did well, I offer my sincerest thanks and appreciation for a job well done. But I also offer you this challenge: the folks who didn't do so well need your help getting their programs back on track. It's up to you to pitch in with your time, your people, and your ideas. I know you'll do it for the good of the mission, the good of the unit, and the good of the Air Force.

"We've all been under a lot of pressure for the past couple of months. First there was the hard work and long hours getting ready for the I.G. Team's visit. Then there were two weeks of intense scrutiny while we lived under the I.G.'s magnifying glass. Well, the ordeal is over and it's time to unwind.

"Even as I speak, there are dogs and burgers on the grill and beer and sodas on ice at the SKIVVY NINE Lounge. As soon as you're dismissed, I want every man and woman in this theater to go straight to the Lounge and let your hair down. Celebrate if you did well--cry in your beer if you didn't. But above all, relax and relieve those tensions.

"Use the weekend to get plenty of rest and relaxation because, come Monday morning, SKIVVY NINE is going to step out smartly and fix the things that need fixing. We'll do it quickly and we'll do it right. And while we're doing that tough job, we'll do it with our heads up and our shoulders back. When the I.G. Team comes back in six months or so, they're going to see the evidence of

> *our work and they're going to see a different unit. I know you can do it--you're good soldiers; you're professionals; you're SKIVVY NINE! Dismissed!*

When I gave the manuscript to Col Meade, I told him these were *suggested* words. I advised him that to read the talk to the troops would be disaster. He should take the main ideas and put them into his own words, sprinkle in a few "Meade-isms", then deliver the talk off the cuff. I had given him the words, I had given him the advise, I had given him my support, but when he stood up after the outbrief Friday afternoon, I didn't have any idea what to expect.

Maj Weber and I were on pins and needles wondering if he was going to blow the unit out of the water. After the I.G. Team delivered the bad news and left the theater, the Colonel went to the microphone and spoke.

"*OK Guys, we came up a little short. But we're not going to waste our time.....*" He had *memorized* the damn speech--word for word. When a speaker memorizes, it usually comes off stilted and artificial. But not Meade. His performance was spectacular. The audience didn't have a clue he was speaking from a prepared text and the talk came off like a dream.

When Col Meade started, everyone was slumped down in their seats, but as he spoke, I could sense them coming up. When he got to the last sentence, I could almost hear the backbones straightening: "*You're good soldiers*"-- CLICK!; "*You're professionals*"--CLICK! *"You're SKIVVY NINE!"*--CLICK, CLICK, CLICK!! And then they were on their feet with a standing ovation.

When the cheering died down, the Colonel deviated from the prepared text for the first time. Instead of saying "*Dismissed!*" like I had written in the speech, he said, "Last one to the Lounge is a rotten egg!!" And that brought the house down.

SKIVVY NINE!

While the audience was milling around heading for the exits, Maj Reardon jumped onto the stage, grabbed the microphone and yelled, "Wait a minute! Wait a minute, everybody. Before we leave, I think we should show the I.G. Team our appreciation by giving them the SKIVVY NINE yell. Are you with me?" Another cheer.

"OK, here we go. One--two--three. SKIVVY NINE! SKIVVY NINE! SKIVVY NINE! YOOOoooooooo! If you ain't SKIVVY NINE, you ain't SHIT!" And another cheer.

The wind down party at the Lounge went well. The atmosphere wasn't what it would have been were we rated EXCELLENT, but it wasn't a wake either. People were in a party mood and spirits were upbeat. The next six months aren't going to be fun, but it's not going to be as bad as it could have been.

♦♦♦♦♦♦♦♦♦♦

Well, I'm afoot again. Got a call from the Motor Pool saying the dent in the side of my truck was fixed, but during the inspection they always give when a vehicle comes in for body work, they discovered the cam shaft was bent. You guessed it; there's not a spare cam shaft on all of Osan Air Base so they had to order it through supply channels. Woe is me!

O'Rourk and the First Shirt whined enough for me to have to give their truck back. They reasoned that, with the inspection over, the chances for a recall are almost nil and they need wheels more than I do to conduct day-to-day business. That's bullshit, but the Vehicle Control Officer bought it and his opinion is the one that matters. They got the truck back and I'm hoofing it for the foreseeable future.

Wednesday, July 1st

It's been a pretty busy three days since my last entry. The big story was everybody's favorite dirt-bag, SrA Billy Nagle. Monday morning at 3:00 a.m., SMSgt Duckworth got a call to come down to the Security Police Office and pick the boy up. Billy was scheduled to leave for Goodfellow Air Force Base, Texas in a couple of weeks and Sunday night his newest honey (fiancée') told him she wasn't going to marry him and go to the States. His reaction to that sad news was to go out and get drunker than a one-pedal bicycle, return to his honey's apartment, and beat the living shit out of her. In retaliation, she looked up a razor blade and whittled on Billy's bod for awhile, mostly his arms and hands (he was probably trying to fend her off.).

All this happened in "Blow Job Alley" (where Billy's honey is employed) so when the Security Police got to the scene, they charged him for being in an off-limits establishment in addition to assault and battery and drunk and disorderly. Fortunately, they didn't charge him for dulling the girl's razor blade with his hands and arms.

The First Sergeant called me early Monday morning and asked what I wanted to do with Billy. As many tussles as I've had with Duckworth over disciplinary matters, he actually expected me to go to bat for Nagle. I told the Shirt he could hang the ass-hole out to dry, as far as I was concerned. I'll fight for the good ones, but the Billy Nagles of this unit can go to hell in a hand basket. Yesterday, the Shirt started the paperwork to boot old Billy out of the Air Force. I think both he and the Air Force will be happier.

♦♦♦♦♦♦♦♦♦

SrA Walker Staggs is back from leave and his ass is mine. He and his lovely bride arrived on Monday's Freedom Bird. It was easy enough to find out from the Orderly Room when they would be back, so when they came out of the passenger terminal after having gone through Customs, Capt Ringler and I were waiting just outside to meet them.

When Staggs saw us, he somehow sensed all was not well. But in a typical display of bravado, Walker turned to Kathy and said, "What a class outfit! SKIVVY NINE takes such good care of their low ranking people that they've sent a Chief and a Captain to welcome us back and give us a lift so we won't have to spend our meager earnings on a taxi." Kathy released a nervous giggle while the Captain and I walked toward them.

"Senior Airman Walker Staggs," Capt Ringler said as seriously as she could, "I am officially charging you with wrongful destruction of Government property." Then she fished out the small piece of paper from her BDU pocket that she had prepared earlier and continued. "You have the right to remain silent and any voluntary statements you may offer can and will be used against you in court-martial proceedings. You have the right to an attorney and, if you can not afford one….."

As Capt Ringler continued to drone on with the military version of the "Miranda blurb", Staggs' face went white and Kathy continued her senseless nervous giggling. I think they both finally realized just what deep shit he was in.

When Capt Ringler finished reading from the scrap of paper, she returned it to her pocket and began to ad-lib. "Kathy, you're free to go wherever you please. Airman Staggs, you will accompany Chief Beal and me to the Orderly Room."

"What Government property you talkin' about, Captain. I ain't done nothin'," Staggs stammered. I was already at his side. "That's bullshit, Walker. You trashed a truck. You know it, I know it, the Captain knows it. Now it's payback time. Lets go."

I led SrA Walker Staggs to the eight-passenger van we had waiting in the parking lot. Kathy decided to "stand by her man" and followed close behind with Capt Ringler. SSgt Jim LaMora was waiting behind the wheel and, as soon as we loaded the Staggs and their luggage, he fired up the engine and headed for the Orderly Room.

Capt O'Rourk and SMSgt Duckworth were waiting at the Orderly Room. I told Kathy to wait outside and escorted Walker into the Captain's office. He and Duckworth stood behind O'Rourk's desk where they had arranged three documents on the front where Walker Staggs would have easy access to them.

Capt O'Rourk could hardly hide his elation. He was about to nail a SKIVVY NINEr to the wall and he was loving every minute of it. As much as I wanted to see Staggs get his just deserts, having O'Rourk deliver the justice left a bad taste in my mouth. But after all, he is the Orderly Room Commander and this is part of his job.

O'Rourk took charge of the proceedings. "Senior Airman Walker Staggs, you have been charged with willful destruction of Government property. An extensive investigation has been conducted and there is irrefutable evidence that you are guilty of the offense". Staggs stood in front of the desk at parade rest, staring down at the documents, and shifting his weight nervously from one foot to the other.

O'Rourk continued. "The documents you see in front of you are an Article 15, a Request for General Court Martial, and a Report of Survey. I'll explain each to you to ensure you understand the gravity of your situation."

The Captain explained that SrA Staggs had some options. He could sign the Article 15 which outlined the particulars of the offense and the punishment that would be levied. Signing the document was an admission of guilt and Staggs would not have benefit of a trial.

If he truly believed he was innocent, he could opt not to sign the Article 15, but sign the Request for General Court Martial instead. In that case, the Government believed they had sufficient evidence to proceed with a trial where, if convicted, the punishment would probably be much more severe than the Article 15.

The third document, a Report of Survey, listed the damage that had been done to the truck and the amount of money required to fix it. The information in the Report of Survey would come into play only after Staggs either signed the Article 15 or was convicted by a Court Martial. In either case, Staggs pays.

O'Rourk finished his dissertation and paused to let Staggs absorb the information just given him. Walker leaned forward over the desk top and spent the next several minutes scanning the documents in silence. When he straightened up, he glanced in my direction and said, "I need to talk to Kathy."

I looked at O'Rourk who gave me an almost imperceptible nod. "OK, Walker," I said. "You've got five minutes to talk it over and then we want a decision."

He didn't need the entire five minutes. He was guilty as sin and he knew it. When he returned from the hallway, he walked straight to the desk, looked the Captain squarely in the eye, and said defiantly, "Got a pen?"

The Captain produced the writing instrument and Senior Airman Walker Staggs signed the Article 15. He is now liable for the $650 it took to return the truck to its original condition, confined to quarters in the dorm for one month (where the lovely bride can't get at his body), a demotion to Airman First Class (suspended), and eighty hours of additional duty washing vehicles at the Motor Pool during off-duty time.

Justice served--case closed.

♦♦♦♦♦♦♦♦♦

Lt Johnson, the Vehicle Control Officer, called me Monday afternoon to say the Motor Pool had found a cam shaft and the truck was ready to go. Halleluja!! I've got wheels under my ass again and it feels great.

♦♦♦♦♦♦♦♦♦

Late Tuesday morning, I had a meeting with the First Shirt and CMSgt Bob Estep (Bruce Lewis' replacement in LG) to talk about divvying up all the Senior Enlisted Advisor stuff I've been handling myself since I've been here. My original idea was to divide it up equally between the three of us but, I must admit, I let myself get steamrollered into dumping the responsibilities off onto the Senior NCO Council (SENCO). Both Duckworth and Estep thought it was a good idea, so I went along with them.

They proposed having various "committees" on the SENCO handle programs like the Airman/NCO/SNCO of the Quarter selections; the Recognition Breakfast; the Hail and Farewell parties; and the annual Dining Out. I don't think our Senior NCOs are ready to work hard to make these programs work and, if they're not, they'll fall through the cracks. I also believe Duckworth and Estep want to dump this stuff onto the SENCO because they're too damned lazy to do the jobs themselves. I don't know--it may work. But in any case, I've agreed to do it, so we'll see what happens.

Chapter Six

THE AFTERMATH

Sunday, July 5th

SHOCKER!! Col Meade has been fired! Every since the results of the I.G. inspection were released, the thought has been rumbling around in my head that he might be. Even though I had given it some thought, the announcement was still quite a jolt. And the *way* he broke the news was a show stopper.

Thursday mornings at 10:30, Col Meade holds his weekly Commander's Staff Meeting. All the Division Chiefs, Bob Estep, and I are the only attendees. It's usually pretty boring stuff (unless I have to square off with the Orderly Room hooligans) and last Thursday was no exception. Col Meade was almost 10 minutes late for the meeting. We didn't know it at the time, but the reason for his tardiness was he was getting the bad news by phone from Col Hoyt McMasters, the Commander of Pacific Electronic Security Division in Hawaii.

When he finally did arrive, Col Meade conducted the staff meeting as usual. He lets the Division Chiefs, Estep, and me make our inputs and he waits until everyone's finished to make any announcements he might have. This staff meeting was no exception. He nonchalantly went through everything on his list and the last item was, "I've been relieved of duty as your Commander. Col McMasters informs me that General Mather, the I.G., the ESC Chief of Staff, the Director of Personnel, and the Command Operations Officer agree unanimously that I must go."

Col Meade went on to say the new commander's name wasn't releasable yet, but he was coming out of the Headquarters and would be assigned on a one-year, unaccompanied, remote tour. The transition would take place quickly. Col Mead should be gone by next Wednesday and the new commander should arrive by next Friday. If it *has* to be done, that's the way it should be done--quick, clean, surgical.

I really do feel sorry for the guy. He should have never been assigned here as the commander in the first place. He spent his entire career in a B-52 cockpit, and then when he made Lieutenant Colonel, they gave him some kind of not shit job on the staff at Headquarters, Strategic Air Command.

When he made Colonel, they couldn't seem to find a place for him at SAC, so he was assigned to the ESC Liaison Office at Tactical Air Command (his *first* and *only* contact with ESC) to do another staff-type job. During all those years, he had almost no contact with enlisted people--an absolute must for ESC commanders who have to deal almost exclusively with enlisted people.

When he got the job here, there was a real rumble in the Headquarters. The question on everybody's lips was, "Who the hell *IS* this guy, anyway?" SKIVVY NINE has had a long list of seasoned commanders who had cut their teeth on smaller, easier to run units. Command of this unit was a real plumb given to the good guys as a reward for jobs well done at other units, and as a springboard to bigger and better things. At least four SKIVVY NINE commanders have gone on to make Brigadier General and higher.

Everyone knew that this was no place to "learn" to command, and couldn't figure out why the hell Col Meade was given the job in the first place. I hate to say it, but it's almost as though he was set up for failure. And fail he did.

During his year here, SKIVVY NINE went from being one of the shit hottest units in ESC to the pits. The results of the inspection showed that. Morale went from sky high to rock bottom. So although I personally feel sorry for Col Meade, the move to relieve him of duty was a good one and absolutely necessary. Majors Weber and Reardon, Bob Estep, and I can work 'till we're blue in the face to get the unit back on its feet and morale up, but unless we have the commander's support and understanding, we'll never get there.

And now, there's rampant speculation about who the new guy will be. Maj Reardon and I were talking it over yesterday and, given the information we had (0-6, coming out of the Headquarters on a one-year, unaccompanied remote tour), and the fact that they usually send a real hard-ass in to clean up a mess like this, the obvious choice is Gentle Ben Hassinger. He has all the prerequisites: successful Ops Officer in Berlin (tough unit); successful commander in the Philippines (another tough unit); Director if Inspections on the I.G. Team; currently in an artificial job that was created for him when he made Colonel and came off the I.G. Team; a kid in high school and a wife who don't want to move; and a house in San Antonio he can't sell. The perfect profile.

Gentle Ben would be my personal choice for purely selfish reasons. He thinks the sun rises and sets in my ass-hole and he *listens* to me when I give him advise. We got along great when we were on the I.G. Team together. He's a real creampuff on the inside, but he can be a rompin', stompin' hard-ass when he needs to be. He would definitely whip the unit back into shape, but no telling how many heads would roll in the process. As a matter of fact, maybe some heads *need* to roll.

Maj Reardon and I thought we had the replacement commander nailed down when SMSgt B.O. O'Banion (who had wandered up on the conversation in mid-stream) came up with another name we hadn't thought of--Col Jason Lucas. Col Lucas has almost the same exact background as Col Hassinger: successful commander in Okinawa; been at the headquarters for over five years and has the assignments people breathing down his neck to move on; a kid in high school and a wife that don't want to move; and a house in San Antonio that he can't sell. SKIVVY NINE is a tailor-made assignment for Col Lucas, too.

The big difference between Hassinger and Lucas is their modus operandi. Lucas isn't a hard-ass. He's a bona fide charmer who would get the unit back on its feet by making the troops love him enough to do anything he asks them to do. He would be just as effective as Hassinger and it would probably be less painful.

I'll be glad to see either one of them come in, but on the other hand, it may be neither of them. It could be some whiffle ball I never heard of. Lord knows the Headquarters is a bottomless pit of 0-6's looking for a meaningful job. They're probably fighting like crazy right now to become the next commander of the 6903rd Electronic Security Group.

Sunday, July 12th

One of our Tech Sergeants went a little astray last week and the incident resulted in yet another head-butting contest between Maj Weber/me and Capt O'Rourk/First Sergeant Duckworth. TSgt Dan Pinder (Morse Controller on Baker Flight), came to work his first day watch last Monday knee-walking drunk. The Flight Commander told him to go back to his dorm, go to bed and sleep it off, and report to work the next morning for disciplinary action. So far, so good.

Pinder left, but he failed to show up for work the next morning. The Flight Commander dispatched a search party, and they found him around 11:30 a.m. Tuesday morning passed out in a bar down town. Wednesday morning, the Flight Commander, working in concert with Duckworth, O'Rourk, and the Security Police, had Pinder's clearances pulled and ordered him to be evaluated for possible placement on the alcohol rehab program. I didn't have any problem with any of the actions taken against Pinder to this point, but Thursday morning the Orderly Room duo tried to really put the big time screws to Pinder.

Col Meade called a meeting of the "heavy hitters" to decide Pinder's fate. Majors Weber and Reardon, Capt Jacoby, MSgt Pat Aiken (Security Police), Bob Estep, and I pretty well agreed that perhaps an Article 15 with a suspended reduction in rank might be in order. But Capt O'Rourk and SMSgt Duckworth wanted Pinder charged with desertion and court martialed!

According to the "rules", folks with the kind of security clearances held by SKIVVY NINE people (Pinder included) get special treatment when they're "missing" for a period of time. If you're missing for less than 24 hours, you're considered Absent Without Leave (AWOL). Pretty serious stuff, but not devastating. But after 24 hours, AWOL turns into desertion. Now we're talking some serious shit! The dynamic duo contended that Pinder had been missing from 7:00 a.m. Monday morning until he was found at 11:30 a.m. Tuesday morning, a total of 28 1/2 hours.

Maj Weber and I argued that, since he had been excused from duty by the Flight Commander Monday morning, he wasn't missing until 7:00 a.m. the following morning when he didn't report for work as directed. When the First Sergeant accused us of "mother coddling these worthless dirt-bags", I had a million come-backs, all of which I would have been sorry for later. So I just withdrew from the conversation, didn't say anything else during the rest of the meeting, and drew doodles in my note pad. So there!

When the meeting was over, Col Meade dismissed everybody but asked me to stay behind. He said my non-verbals during the meeting were unacceptable. My input was needed to resolve controversial cases like Pinder's and, when I withdrew, he was denied my advise and council. He said he realized these situations were my most unfavorite things, but the least I could do was refrain from doodling in my note pad.

I apologized to the Colonel, and told him that when those two asinine bozos start making asses of themselves, it's best for me to clam up lest the meeting turn into a pissing contest or, worse yet, I get insubordinate with Capt O'Rourk. Col Meade said he appreciated my view of the Shirt and O'Rourk and that he sometimes has the same personality conflict with those two. He admitted that in similar situations, he too, had a tendency to withdraw and that's one of the things that probably got him fired. Then he said, "I don't want that to happen to you."

I just stared at him with what I'm sure was a blank look on my face. He thought about what he had said for a couple of seconds then kinda chuckled and said, "Chief, on second thought, I guess there's not a hellava lot anyone can do to hurt you, is there."

I said, "No, Sir." With that, the conversation was over. Oh by the way, cooler heads did prevail and TSgt Pinder won't be Court Martialed for desertion. He will receive an Article 15.

♦♦♦♦♦♦♦♦♦

Colonel Meade called a special meeting last Thursday to announce who his replacement will be. Col Jason Lucas will become the new commander effective 15 August. We all thought it would happen much quicker than that, but Col Lucas needs time to wrap up all the projects he was working at the Headquarters and also get his personal stuff in order. Col Meade leaves next week and, to fill the gap between his departure and Col Lucas' arrival, Col Bo Carlson (the Vice Commander of Pacific Electronic Security Division) is flying in from Hawaii. Don't know the guy that well, so I don't know what to expect.

Maj Reardon is a little miffed by this turn of events and, I think, rightfully so. He is, after all, the Deputy Commander and is to command when the commander isn't available. He thinks the folks back at Headquarters don't trust him to do the job and, naturally, that hurts his feelings. He doesn't really know where he stands with the powers that be.

♦♦♦♦♦♦♦♦♦♦

Had a straaaaange experience Wednesday afternoon. I took part in the change of command ceremony for the outgoing commander of the Korean unit we work with. Col Park, the outgoing commander, is being replaced by Col Choa. Col Park is being sent to a desk job deep in the bowels of DSA (Korean version of NSA). The Koreans recently had an I.G. inspection themselves and didn't do too well. Col Park was being fired, but at least the Koreans are sending their guy out with a little bit of class and dignity.

The ceremony was held in their chow hall and it was *very* hot--no air conditioning. There was a platoon of Korean soldiers standing at attention at one end of the room with their officers sitting in chairs along one wall. The American contingent sat along the opposite wall. The incoming/outgoing commanders entered accompanied by some Korean two-star general and Maj Reardon. Col Meade was too embarrassed to attend. The party took their seats facing the platoon.

When everyone was settled in, both commanders got up and gave a little speech in Korean followed by a speech in both Korean and English by the two-star. I was sitting there comfortably with my legs crossed and my arm propped on the back of my chair when I noticed everyone else was sitting at attention with the palms of their hands on their thighs. So I quickly followed suit and popped to. Then Maj Reardon gave Col Park a plaque from SKIVVY NINE, Col Park passed the Korean flag to Col Choa, and the ceremony was over.

From the chow hall, we fell out in front of the Headquarters building for a group picture (minus the Korean enlisted riff-raff).

After the picture, we went to the soccer field where they had set up three tables under open-sided tents. The tables were loaded with snacks and refreshments, but to a different degree by table. It was the strangest hodge-podge of food and drink I've ever seen.

Table one had cantaloupe, dried squid, water melon, hot green peppers, Ritz crackers, kimchi, apple sauce, cakes and pies, peanuts, ham slices, and (oh well, you get the picture). There were 10 or 12 place settings around the table and each setting had five full bottles of refreshments. There was a bottle of 7-Up, Fanta orange drink, Coca-Cola, mineral water, beer, and "Oscar" (rancid Korean champagne). Next to the cluster of bottles at each setting, there was a paper cup, a styrofoam cup, and a champagne glass.

Table two had the same strange mixture of snacks, just not as many of them. And the place settings only had two bottles--beer and Coke.

Table three was another story altogether. There were no place settings. There was a bunch of dried squid, a mound of kimchee, and green peppers with a couple of loaves of hard bread in the middle of the table. That meager repast was complimented by six huge bottles of Soju (rot-gut Korean whiskey).

Not wishing to commit a faux pas and embarrass the American contingent, I just kinda hung around the area of Table Two and watched where people of various rank and status were heading. The Korean enlisted troops went straight for Table Three, the mid-level officers (both Korean and American) sort of gravitated toward Table Two, and the General and his crew gaggled up around Table One.

Knowing the way Korean officers feel about enlisted swine, I assumed my place was at Table Three. I was headed that way (I saw SMSgt Kim (the Korean Ops Supe) there, so I thought I was on the right trail) when Maj Choa (the Korean Ops Officer) took me by the arm and guided me to Table One. He put me beside Maj Weber and said, "You stay".

I asked Maj Weber why I had been given this "honor". He mingles and socializes a lot with the Koreans, he knows how they think, so I thought he might have the answer. The Major said the one concession the Koreans would make where enlisted people were concerned was American Chief Master Sergeants. They see how Chiefs are treated by both lower ranking enlisteds and officers, so they figure they should treat them the same. But the concession stops right there; all other American enlisteds are scum bags, just like Korean enlisted scum bags.

The atmosphere at Table One was stiff and very formal. First, there was a toast to the General, then the Korean Colonels, and then to Maj Reardon (in his capacity as the acting 03rd Commander). There was a lot of small talk about the weather and golf handicaps and other such boring trivia. Meanwhile, at Table Two with the Lieutenants, Captains, and Majors, the atmosphere was relaxed and there was some shucking and jiving going on. Table Three was a madhouse! They were reaching and grabbing for squid and ripping the loaves of bread apart and snarfing wads of kimchee and drinking sohju out of the bottle. Toward the end of the affair, a wrestling match broke out at Table Three. Don't know why; maybe someone didn't get their fair share of squid.

On the General's cue, everyone at Table One shook hands all around and, just like that, the affair was over. On the way back to work, I told Maj Weber I had been very uncomfortable and didn't like doing stuff like that. He said he didn't either, but we both had to put up with it because it came with the territory. Ahhh--such are the joys of Ops Suping at SKIVVY NINE.

Sunday, July 19th

Tuesday morning, Col Meade came to see me with a very concerned expression on his face (hell, he *always* seems to have a concerned expression on his face). Every since he got canned, he's been in contact with a "mole" in the Headquarters getting daily updates on what's being said about/done to the 6903rd. He had talked with his underground contact that day and was told that more firings were in the offing. The I.G. had recommended that Capt Jacoby, Capt O'Rourk, MSgt Paul Aiken (the Top Cop), and (I absolutely could not believe it!!!) Maj Weber be relieved of duty as a result of the inspection. What he wanted me to do was call back to the Headquarters and talk to any contacts I may have to see if there was any validity to the story.

Wednesday morning, I went in to work at 5:00 a.m. so I would be sure to catch the people I needed to talk to before they left work (on their) Tuesday afternoon. I called three people I knew would:

1. Trust me enough to open up to me.
2. Know enough about what was going on to give me the information I needed.
3. Be honest enough to tell me the straight skinny, no matter how bad it might hurt.

I got the Command Post on the line and asked them to make phone patches for me to Col Marv Divany (Assistant Operations Officer), MSgt Teddy McCarthy (Operations Inspector on the I.G. Team), and Capt Hugh Bassett (Readiness Inspector on the I.G. Team). Between the three of them, I pieced together the real story.

It was true that the I.G. had recommended all four of the guys Meade's mole mentioned be relieved of duty. LG was rated MARGINAL, so they wanted Capt Jacoby booted. He won't be, because he's only been on the job for six months and hasn't had a chance to get LG in shape after a series of three notoriously bad

Officers in Charge and good old CMSgt Bruce Lewis. He'll be left on the job until the I.G. Team comes back for a reinspection. If LG gets a SAT, good on him. If they go TANGO UNIFORM, Capt Jacoby hits the bricks. Fair enough.

The Orderly Room was rated UNSAT and there were rampant stories about unfair, heavy-handed discipline, so the I.G. recommended Capt O'Rourk be fired. He won't be because he leaves in August and the problem will die of natural causes. However, he was scheduled to be the Orderly Room Commander at the 6924th Electronic Security Squadron in Hawaii and that won't happen. He'll be cut loose to the Air Force and given some not shit job where he can't do too much damage. Fair, but not fair enough.

None of the guys I talked to could give me much information on the status of our Top Cop, Pat Aiken. The Security Police shop had been rated a very strong SAT by the I.G. Team, but the I.G. recommended Pat be booted because of his unsightly personal appearance. What?!!? Granted, Pat ain't the prettiest guy in the world, but he's a good man and one hellava cop. He's big and mean looking, but his main problem (according to the I.G. Team) is he's hairy. You read right--*HAIRY*! Pat has so much hair on his chest and back that it protrudes out of his shirt collar and up onto his neck. And for the crime of having too much body hair, the I.G. wants to fire the guy. My contacts didn't know too much else, but I got the chance to get "the rest of the story" Wednesday afternoon.

Mr. Buck Evans (a retired Security Police Chief Master Sergeant) rolled in here for a one week visit Wednesday afternoon. He's a Civilian Employee in the Security Police Directorate at the Headquarters and is out here to oversee the security aspects of some new equipment we're installing. Soon as I saw him, I told him we needed to get together for a little chit chat. We met in the SKIVVY NINE Lounge for a beer Wednesday afternoon after work. Between pulls on his Budweiser, Buck laid out the sordid story.

He said that when Capt Mike Broom (the SP Inspector) and Lt Col Brogan came to the SP Directorate to backbrief on the inspection, Col Wayne Moryer (the head cheese of all Security Policemen in ESC) was away on a TDY, so they gave the backbrief to Buck. There were glowing words all through the presentation on what good shape the 03rd's security programs were in. And then they hit him with the news that they wanted to fire Pat because of his unsightly personal appearance. Buck, quite naturally, went ballistic and unloaded on Brogan and Broom.

"Do you mean to tell me that in a Air Force where it's illegal to discriminate against someone because of race, color, creed, age, religious preference, or national origin, you want to *FIRE* Pat Aiken because he's *UGLY*?" The answer was a startling, "Yes!".

Lt Col Brogan told Buck that he found Pat's appearance (and this is an exact quote) "personally repulsive". Using his overwhelming command of the English language, Buck responded, "I find you 'personally repulsive' too, Colonel, because you're a spineless broke-dick. But I'm not trying to get you fired from the I.G. Team because of it." That pretty much killed the conversation and Brogan/Broom slinked back to their lair.

The next day, Col Moryer was back from his trip and Mr. Evans broke the news about Pat to him. He, like Buck, went crazy. The two of them went straight to the I.G.'s office where Col Moryer gave Bergman (the I.G.), Brogan, and Broom both barrels. It was less than an hour before the I.G. was scheduled to brief General Mather on the results of the inspection--the forum they would use to recommend Pat Aiken be fired--so Col Moryer had to get his licks in fast. "If you ask General Mather to fire Pat Aiken, I will find some way to break it off in your ass so deep you'll never recover. And I will find a way. Hell, I'm ugly myself (and he really is) but I'm an eloquent son-of-a-bitch, and if you two fire the best Cop in ESC, I'll make you all look like the idiotic ass-holes you are."

The "Killer B's" backed off, but not much. Their compromise position was, they wouldn't ask General Mather to fire Pat, but they would brief the new commander, Col Lucas, on the problem and let him make a decision on what to do when he takes over at the 03rd. Pat has requested a one year extension of tour and they said they would recommend to Lucas that it not be approved. Moryer and Evans weren't real happy with the situation, but that's where it stands as of now.

When Lucas comes in, Maj Reardon and I are going to lobby hard for Pat to stay and for the extension to be approved. He's really done a fine job for us and we want to keep him. Hopefully, Lucas will exercise a little common sense and do the right thing. Meanwhile, Pat is on leave to the States and doesn't even know anything about the whole sorry mess. When he gets back, I'll fill him in on what's been going on. I'm also going to tell him that, unless the hair sticking out of his shirt has some sort of religious significance or he just can't live without it, he needs to consider trimming it up a little.

The news that Maj Weber's head was on the chipping block really shook me up. My sources told me that the I.G. Team did make the recommendation to fire him, but Col Jim Newkirk (Command Operations Officer) came to his rescue. The I.G. conceded that Operations here was in great shape and also revealed the reason Ops wasn't rated EXCELLENT. It was because Maj Weber personally had so many overdue performance reports, awards, and decorations. And the supervisors in his Division had a track record almost as bad as his. They reasoned that, although he might know how to run Operations, his tardiness in the performance report, award, and decoration arena showed a lack of concern for his people.

Col Newkirk's response to that was there might be a problem in SKIVVY NINE Ops, but that was no reason to fire (and quoting), "the best damn Ops Officer I've got." The compromise was Maj

Weber has until August 15th to clean up his backlog. That's the day Col Lucas assumes command and if the Major doesn't have his act together, Lucas' first official act will be to boot Weber out the door. Fair enough.

The Major shouldn't have any trouble meeting the deadline. As soon as the I.G. left, I convinced him that wiping out his writing backlog should be his Job One. He took me to heart this time and has been jumping through his knickers trying to catch up. As of Friday afternoon, he only has one overdue APR to write and his next one doesn't come due until the middle of August. What I've got to do now is hold his feet to the fire and make sure he doesn't get behind again.

◆◆◆◆◆◆◆◆◆

Friday was a full day. Went in to work early to do paperwork because I knew I would be out of the office almost all day. Got everything caught up by around 8:30, just in time to attend my first ever Court Martial at 9:00.

One of our people, Sgt Fred McNair, was being tried for taking classified material out of the compound and storing it in his downtown apartment. He had also taken a tape recorder to work, made classified recordings, and had those stored in his apartment, too. McNair was caught back in the middle of April, about two weeks after I got here. It was the first big problem I faced, but I was hesitant to put it on paper at the time because the whole thing was so hush-hush. Now that he's been tried in open court, the whole incident is out in the open.

McNair was found out by accident when his girl friend turned him in to the First Sergeant for possession of drugs. They had a fight and he roughed her up a little, and turning him in was her way of getting even. His clearances were immediately suspended and his urine tested for drug content. The test came up negative.

SKIVVY NINE!

The drugs the girl gave the First Sergeant was a plastic bag of white crystals. McNair contended the crystals weren't drugs at all--he used the stuff inside his guitar because it soaks up humidity and keeps the instrument from warping. The story sounded good, and McNair was an excellent worker and had never been in trouble before. We were almost ready to reinstate his clearances, but the First Sergeant suggested we have the crystals analyzed by the lab at the 121st Evacuation Hospital in Seoul. Just in case. For once, SMSgt Duckworth did something right.

The test came back positive. The crystals turned out to be something the dope heads call "Korean Crack". You can buy the stuff in any Korean drug store without a prescription, which is just one of the reasons Korean drug stores are off limits to GI's. They'll sell you anything in the place without a prescription.

When the results came back positive, Duckworth called McNair in again to break the bad news and asked him if he had any other drugs in his house. McNair said no, still insisting the crystals were used for his guitar, and volunteered to have his house searched to prove he was innocent. The Shirt took him up on his offer and he, McNair, and MSgt Pat Aiken went to McNair's apartment to conduct the search. They didn't find any more drugs, but what they did find boggled the mind. SMSgt Duckworth didn't recognize what they had found, but Pat Aiken sure as hell did. He got Majors Weber and Reardon and me down there in one hellava big hurry.

When I saw what McNair had in his apartment, I got sick at my stomach. He had classified material scattered everywhere. He literally had *everything.* At that point, we knew we had a serious situation on our hands, but didn't know exactly what to do about it. But Pat Aiken did. He got the Office of Special Investigations involved and made damn sure everything was done right so McNair couldn't get off the hook on a technicality later on.

The next couple of weeks were hectic, what with all the investigations, interrogations, and questioning going on. As the real story unfolded, it turned out that McNair was having trouble with his upgrade training for job proficiency testing. He had taken the stuff home so he would have time to study for his tests. Fortunately, he wasn't a *real* bad guy, just a bona fide, died-in-the-wool, dumb shit. No one but his girl friend had seen the material and she didn't read English at all and had no idea what the significance of the stuff was. When the investigation was over, Col Meade decided to go for a General Court Martial and McNair has been in pre-trial confinement ever since.

The court martial itself was a strange experience. Like I said, I had never seen one before and didn't really know what to expect. The first twenty minutes were spent going over the charges and making sure McNair understood what he was accused of. He was charged with violation of Air Force Regulation 205-1 (which sez you can't take classified information out of the compound) and Article 92 of the Uniform Code of Military Justice (UCMJ) (which sez he was derelict in his duties when he carried the recorder inside the compound).

The judge also outlined the maximum punishment should McNair be convicted; Dishonorable Discharge; two-and-one-half years of confinement with hard labor; reduction in grade to E-1; forfeiture of all pay and allowances; and a $2,000 fine. Then the judge asked McNair how he would plea. He pled guilty as charged.

At that point, I expected the judge to bang his gavel, sentence the boy, and adjourn the court. It didn't happen that way. Instead, the judge spent the next hour going over each specific in the case asking McNair to confirm or deny if it were true.

Judge: "Did you actually take classified material out of the secure area?"

McNair: "Yes."

Judge: "Did you know it was a violation of standing regulations to do that?"

McNair: "Yes, I did."

Judge: "Did anyone force you to take the classified material out of your work area?"

McNair: "No, they did not."

And so it went for what seemed forever. What was happening was, even though McNair had admitted he was guilty, the Judge was forcing him to prove beyond a shadow of a doubt that he was, in fact, guilty. When McNair finally convinced the Judge that he was really guilty, the Judge accepted the plea and then the trial moved into the sentencing phase.

This was the only part of the trial where the prosecution and defense attorneys actually got to argue the case. The prosecution was trying to prove that what McNair did was super serious and he should be punished to the fullest extent of the UCMJ. The defense was trying to prove that, although McNair had screwed up, it wasn't all that serious and he should be let off with a slap on the wrist.

The prosecution called two witnesses; Maj Reardon and the OSI Agent who investigated the case. Both testified that if the materials had fallen into the wrong hands, the mission of the 6903rd would be seriously impaired. The defense cross-examined, but they both done good and held their ground. The defense didn't call any witnesses and the Judge told both sides to deliver their final arguments.

The prosecution laid it on hard, emphasizing the *potential* of what would have happened if the stuff had gotten to the bad guys.

At the end of his argument, the prosecutor requested McNair be given a bad conduct discharge, confinement for 18 months at hard labor, reduced to E-1, and fined $500.

The defense countered that McNair may not have been too smart to do what he had done, but he didn't do it with malice or an intent to harm anyone or anything. He only did it so he could do a better job at work. His record in the past had been spotless and (get this) he had been a Boy Scout and alter boy when he was a kid.

The defense recommended a sentence of an other than honorable conditions discharge, confinement for three months (with the three months McNair had spent in pre-trial confinement taking care of that part of the sentence), and reduction to E-3. Both sides agreed that McNair shouldn't be hit with forfeiture of all pay and allowances since he had married his girl friend two weeks earlier and she was pregnant. If all his money was taken away, that would be punishing not only him, but his family as well.

The Judge called a recess to mull over what he was going to do with the future of young Fred McNair. It only took ten minutes. The sentence was: dishonorable discharge; one year confinement with no hard labor (and McNair would be given credit for time served); and reduction to E-1. There would be no fine, and McNair would receive E-1 pay while he's in jail. That should be just about enough to keep his family alive.

I watched McNair's face through the entire sentencing. Here was a young 25-year-old man with a brand new family whose life was in a shambles and his face showed absolutely no expression. The sentencing was cold and emotionless and the whole scene made the hair on the back of my neck stand up. But I didn't feel sorry for Fred McNair. What he did was too serious and a stiff sentence was needed to send the message to anyone else that might be thinking about doing what he did. The whole thing was kind of a downer, but it was something I needed to see.

SKIVVY NINE!

♦♦♦♦♦♦♦♦♦♦

After the trial was over, I rushed back to work to pick up my script for a speaking gig at the NCO Preparatory Course graduation at the NCO Club. I got the script OK, but when I got to the parking lot to get my truck and drive back to my form, THE TRUCK WAS GONE.

I found out later that while I was at the court martial, SSgt Jim LaMora took it to make a supply run and he wasn't back yet. It was almost 1:30 and it would take me 15 minutes to walk back to the dorm, 15 minutes to change, and at least five minutes to get to the NCO Club. In other words, I was sure to be late for the 2:00 ceremony. Panic!

Fortunately, MSgt Joe Del Ricco (my head admin guy) pulled into the parking lot coming back from lunch. He gave me a ride to my dorm and I made it to the NCO Club with five minutes to spare.

After the downer morning and the scramble to get to the ceremony on time, it was pretty tough to get pumped up to deliver the talk. The audience was packed with SKIVVY NINErs so I felt like I had to make a good showing. I put on my best "game face" and delivered the talk with all the conviction I could. It must have worked; the audience loved it.

The graduation was over by 2:45, but I was so emotionally wrung out, I told Maj Weber I wasn't going back to work. I wouldn't have been worth a damn for anything anyway. What a day!!

Chapter Seven

AND LIFE GOES ON

Sunday, July 26th

Got a disturbing phone call from CMSgt Ray Smith (Ops Supe at the 6920th Electronic Security Group in Misawa, Japan) last Thursday. They've been notified that the I.G. Team is swooping in on them around September 15th and, according to Ray, their shit is pretty stringy in Operations. Lt Col Dale Kline (my old boss on the I.G. Team) is the Ops Officer up there and he had Ray call me and request I come up and help them out with a pre-inspection inspection. Lt Col Kline seems to believe I might be able to identify a lot of problems they can fix before the I.G. arrives.

I told Ray I really didn't want to go to Misawa. The place is a real bummer, it's soooo expensive, and I'm up to my ass in alley-gators right here at SKIVVY NINE. He told me that was all well and good, but he's "cashing in his blue chips". Over the past year, the 20th has sent help to get us through a shortage of Admin folks, sent us two inspectors for our own pre-I.G. inspection, and an impartial investigating officer to take a look at the Fred McNair case. The boy had me over a barrel, so I reluctantly agreed to help him out.

That afternoon in the SKIVVY NINE Lounge, Maj Weber and I were discussing CMSgt Smith's request. MSgt Dick LaChance, who is visiting from Pacific Electronic Security Division (PESD), overheard our conversation and parachuted into the middle of it. "If you send Chief Beal to Misawa, Col McMasters (PESD Commander) and Col Carlson (PESD Vice Commander) ain't gonna like it even a little bit."

According to LaChance, both McMasters and Carlson firmly believe my place is here, helping the unit get ready for the I.G. re-inspect. The Major's response to LaChance's warning was: the movements of SKIVVY NINE's Ops Supe was none of PESD's business. He had some pay-backs to do and, if he didn't make those pay-backs, he would have the reputation as the biggest ass-hole in the Pacific Theater.

LaChance said he saw where the Major was coming from, but he was merely trying to pass along the PESD philosophy on SKIVVY NINE's Ops Supe. Maj Weber thanked him for his observations and invited him out of the conversation.

Friday morning, Maj Weber called Lt Col Kline and said I would make the trip to Misawa. He also told the Colonel that, when they send the formal message requesting the assistance, a copy should be sent to PESD. Kline said we should be getting the message sometime next week. So it's still up in the air; when the message hits PESD, they may give us a nasty call to say I can't go. On the other hand, they may figure that one of their units needs help and will allow me to go. We'll see.

Wednesday, July 29th

Well, here I am in the hospital with another flare-up of my old problem with urinary tract infections. It's been five years, so I guess it was just about time.

Went to bed early Sunday night in anticipation of the quarterly Base Exercise that was to kick of around 4:30 a. m. Monday morning. (If you remember, Col Meade had promised to get the 03rd excused from this exercise if we did well on the I.G. exercise. Well, since he's a "lame duck" commander, he was unable to keep that promise. So we have to play.) I woke up around 1:00 a.m. with a terrible back ache and a fair-to-middling fever. Went to take a leak and, sure enough, it hurt like a sombitch and I thought, "Shit!

Here we go again." I've had so many of these things, I know the symptoms well.

Went back to bed but couldn't sleep. I lay there 'till around four o'clock, debating whether I should go to sick call right now or tough it out and report for the recall when it came. I decided to go for the recall and break loose for the 12:30 p.m. sick call.

Finally got up and did my morning routine, laid out my uniform, boots, and field gear, and sat down to wait for my beeper to go off. It never did. At 6:30, the base siren went off, indicating a recall for the exercise was underway. The folks who were supposed to call my pager never got the word that the recall had started. Got dressed quickly in full battle gear and went to the front of my dorm to wait for B.O. O'Banion to pick me up.

My truck is *still* in the motor pool for its quarterly inspection, so I had made arrangements the previous Friday for B.O. to swing by my place and pick me up when the recall kicked off. I waited until seven o'clock. No B.O. I was standing there in the parking lot cursing that no-good SOB for letting his old Chief down when it hit me. Since there had been no 6903rd recall, B.O. had gone to work at his usual time, 6:00 a.m. When the base siren when off at 6:30, he was already at work under eight feet of concrete and 10 feet of dirt. No way he could have heard that siren and probably didn't even know there was a recall in progress. Bat shit!

I decided I'd better try to hoof it on in to work, but about half way there, I knew I had made a mistake. Going up Hill 180 kicked my ass. I broke out in a cold sweat; my knees began to wobble; those last 200 feet were the toughest I've ever walked.

By the time I got to work, the exercise was well under way. B.O. apologized profusely, but I told him to forget it; and besides, if he had come to get me, there would have need no one in the Operations Sub-Control Center and the whole exercise would have fallen flat on its ass. As it was, he had filled in for me admirably, and the SCC was purring like a kitten.

I tried to throw myself into the exercise, but it didn't take long for me to realize my shit was stringy. Sick call is between seven and seven thirty but, by the time I decided I needed to be there, it was 8:45. I didn't care. I got all my battle gear back on and walked outside into a torrential downpour (the tail-end of Typhoon Vern).

I put my slicker on over my uniform in an attempt to stay dry and it worked nicely from the knees up. By the time I got to the hospital, my trousers (from the knees down), boots, and socks were completely soaked. From the knees up, the rest of my bod was soaked with sweat caused by the slicker holding in all that fever-generated body heat. In other words, I was wet all over. But at least the walk from work to the hospital was down hill. I don't think I could have done that uphill gig again.

When I got to the hospital, they did my vital signs. Everything looked good except the old temp--102.4 degrees. The Doc I saw decided to admit me on the spot; he didn't want to put me on bed rest in the dorm because, with a 102-plus fever, he said I needed to be monitored at all times. Reason two: He decided to give me the antibiotics intravenously instead of orally. Well that nailed it. I was admitted to the hospital at noon.

The antibiotic IV they're giving me is administered every six hours. To keep from sticking me four times a day, they stuck me once and inserted a catheter in my arm. When it's feeding time, they insert the needle into the catheter and pump in the medicine. No pain (literally), no strain.

I've been in here two days now and I'm feeling much better. My temp is down to normal, the back isn't killing me any more, and it doesn't hurt to pee. The Doc sez even though the symptoms are gone, the bug may still be lurking somewhere in my bod. So they'll keep pumping the medicine into me and checking my urine and blood twice a day. If all goes well, I should be outta here by Friday, the last day of the base exercise (damn the luck!).

Even though I'm not having to play in the exercise, it's still very much a part of my life. The patient lounge on the ward I'm on is being used as a triage area during the exercise. At all hours of the day and night, they're bringing in "the wounded".

This morning at 2:00 a.m., I finally asked the nurse on duty if she could do something about the noise. It wasn't the doctors, nurses, or "patients" causing all the problems; it was the stretcher bearers (all 18-20 year old one, two, and three stripers) shuckin' and jivin' and raising hell right outside my door who were keeping me awake. After I talked to the nurse, I went to bed and (I don't know what she did) the noise stopped. I went back to sleep and, thirty minutes later, the med tech woke me up to take my vital signs. I give up!

My time here hasn't been all wasted. I wrote a Meritorious Service Medal recommendation on Lt Gary Ashmont for Maj Weber the first night I was in. I've also had Joe Del Ricco bring in the unclassified items from my in-basket every morning. On his way home at night, be brings me all the stuff that came in during the day and picks up the items I worked and puts them in distribution the next morning. Neat system; it keeps the paperwork moving and not piling up on my desk. But most importantly, it gives me something to do and keeps me from going nuts-oid.

While I was eating supper tonight, Maj Weber popped in for a short visit. Before he left, A1C Janette Hoover (remember her?) came by. By bedtime, I had had an almost unbroken string of visitors. Really made me feel good, especially considering the visitors (except for the Major) were all lower ranking folks. I would almost expect the high rollers to visit, but so far, (except for Major Weber), none have.

Sunday, August 2nd

I'm still in the hospital and now it looks as though I'll be here much longer than I had initially expected. Instead of a 4-5 day stay, it'll probably be more like 10 days to two weeks. The medicine the Doc originally prescribed isn't working. I'm not getting any worse, but I'm not getting any better either. So he prescribed an entirely new brew and I had to start over from day one.

Another contributing factor to my longer stay is the fact the tests have to be run to determine the dosage of the new cure juice. The Osan Hospital doesn't have the equipment to do the tests, so the blood specimens have to be shipped to the 121st Evac Hospital in Seoul. Until the results of the tests get back, the Doc is giving me a "best guess" dosage. I asked him why, since he had started me on the medicine anyway, did he need a medico at the 121st to tell him how much to give me. He said if the dosage was too light, the infection would never clear up. If the dosage was too heavy, it could nuke my kidneys! Oh, I see.

♦♦♦♦♦♦♦♦♦♦

The exercise ended Friday afternoon, but the noise it generated caused me to have to go into my flaming ass-hole mode Wednesday night. It was 2:30 in the morning and the war was over for the night. It had been noisy, but now that it was over, and I was looking forward to some sleep. The exercise participants, instead of going home and to bed where they belonged, decided to hang around the triage area (aka patient lounge) and have a little party.

They were making big time racket and I'm sure none of the other patients were getting any rest, either. I heard the nurse go to the lounge three or four times and tell the dudes to hold it down. She was doing the best she could, but she is a mousy, tiny little First

Lieutenant and these guys were farting her right off. After her last visit, I'd had enough, so I went to the lounge myself. There were about 20 guys in the place smokin' and jokin' and just having one hellava good time.

I didn't go into the room--just stood in the doorway in my jammies and robe until they kinda stopped talking one-by-one and gave me the old "Who the hell are you?" look. When I had their undivided attention, I said, "Look, Guys. There are a lot of sick people in this place and they need their sleep and rest to get better. They can't get it with you guys down here raisin' hell. So you're either going to have to hold it down or go somewhere else to party. OK?"

No one said anything. They just stared at me with blank looks on their faces. I turned and started back to my room when I overheard (as I'm sure I was supposed to hear) one of them say, "Who does that Mother Fucker think he is?"

That got a big laugh. I lost my temper for just about that (snap!) long and started to go back to the lounge. Instead, I returned to my bedside table, got my ID card out of my wallet, and then went back. This time, I didn't stand in the doorway. I went straight into the room and shoved my ID into the first face I got to. In the coolest, most controlled voice I could muster (which was *very* cool and *very* controlled) I said, "This Mother Fucker is Timothy W. Beal, a Chief Master Sergeant in the United States Air Force."

While I'm talkin', I'm walkin', shoving the ID Card in front of every face in the room. "Watch my lips, Boys. This is a lawful order. Unless you have exercise related duties or other official business to conduct in this hospital, you will leave the premises within the next five minutes. If you do not leave, I will notify the Security Police and have you physically removed. And then I will have you prosecuted for failure to obey the lawful order of a Chief Master Sergeant."

I finished the words before I finished showing the ID Card to everyone, so I continued all the way around the room until I made sure everyone had seen it. When they had, I went back to the door and asked, "Does everyone understand who I am?"

They gave me the old "Duh!" look. I said it again. "Does everyone understand who I am?" There were some mumbled yes's, yeahs, and uh-huhs. Then I asked, "Does everyone understand the lawful order?" I didn't have to repeat that one; they all went into "auto-bob" and answered, "Yes".

"Good," I said. "Then you gentlemen have a nice evening. Good night." I went back to my room.

I laid down and hoped like hell they would leave. I didn't want to have to follow through. A couple of minutes later, I heard movement going down the hall with some mumbling and grumbling and some names being called, and it was quiet for the rest of the night.

♦♦♦♦♦♦♦♦♦♦♦

The steady stream of visitors continues and it sure makes me feel good that folks are concerned with my welfare. The "trench troops" continue to come by and even the "heavy hitters" have had their obligatory face time--Maj Reardon, Capt Jacoby, Bob Estep, Capt Smith, Capt Ringler--but still no First Sergeant or Capt O'Rourk. I know they hate my guts, but it's their JOB to visit unit people in the hospital or in jail. Hell, they visit Fred McNair every week! But I guess it's just as well. A visit would be a hypocritical gesture and they would know it and I would sure as hell know it.

I kept looking for Col Meade to come by, but he never seemed to make it. I thought the guy had more class than that. Then yesterday morning, he showed up at the foot of my bed. He said he had been out-processing and just hadn't had the time to get by. He was literally on his way to the airport in Seoul when I guess his conscience got the best of him. He asked Maj Reardon (his driver for the trip) to swing by the hospital so he could tell me 'bye. Maj Reardon waited in the car and Col Meade didn't stay long.

He told me I was a great Chief and we had just gotten started turning the 6903rd into one hellava unit. He said we worked well together and, had he not been fired, we would have done great things. Pretty emotional stuff, actually. He seemed uncomfortable through the whole thing, but I was glad to see he had the guts to do what was right.

He had been standing at the foot of my bed during his dump, but when it was time to go, he walked around to the side of my bed. He stuck out his hand and said, "It was fun while it lasted, Chief. When you get out of that bed, you kick some ass."

I accepted his hand and tried not to notice the tear welling at the corner of his eye. "Colonel, you're a good man. I just wish it hadn't come down the way it did. Maybe another time." We shook and he was gone.

Wednesday August 5th

Here I am *still* in the hospital. Me and my roomie are the two oldtimers on the ward now. We've watched them come and we've watched them go, and we just keep hangin' in there. Hopefully, I'll be out of here by Saturday. My roomie still doesn't know when he'll be released. Hell, they still haven't decided what's wrong with him! They've treated him for everything from strep throat to flu to stomach virus and back again. He still gets chills and fevers and feels like shit. So I guess the old saying's true: No matter how bad you've got it, there's always someone else in worse shape.

I feel like a million, but I've got to stay here so they can give me antibiotics four times a day. I put a proposition to the Doc this morning: turn me loose and I'll come back at feeding time. I told him I was a big boy and knew how to show up at the appointed place at the appointed time. He seemed to buy off on it, but said it had to be approved by the "Head Doc". The "Head Doc" said no. So here I am killing time between feedings.

Sunday, August 9th

I'M FREE!! I got sprung yesterday morning. The Doc told me Friday morning that as soon as I got my 3:00 a.m. shot of juice Saturday morning, I would be free to go. I told him I wasn't *that* desperate to escape and would probably wait 'till a more reasonable hour to check out.

When the nurse came to give me my 3:00 a.m. jolt, I told her to go ahead and take the catheter out of my hand because I was leaving come first light. She said no--the doctor had miscalculated the doses and I had two more to go, one at 11:00 a.m. and the last at 7:00 p.m. She said I couldn't leave until the last dose was given. I said BULLSHIT! One way or the other, I'm walking come morning.

She called the Doc around eight o'clock, told him he had miscounted the doses, and she had one pissed off Chief on her hands ready to go AWOL. The Doc came up with a compromise: I was released at nine o'clock, but the catheter stayed in and I reported back at eleven and seven for my medication. That was fair enough. At least, I was out and about and not confined to that depressing hell hole.

Tuesday, August 12th

Back to work bright and early Monday morning and, as usual, the joint was jumping. Maj Weber was spring loaded to go on leave, and as soon as I showed up, he was out the door and hasn't been seen since. Although that left me with a mighty load to carry, I don't begrudge him a little time off. He needs it. He's been here almost 18 months maintaining a horrific pace. Burn-out has started to set in, but maybe this week of leisure time will recharge his batteries. In the meantime, I'll hold down the fort, joust the windmills, and do the best I can.

One of the first problems to bite me in the ass was a Korean-American riff on Able Flight (seems like *everything* happens on Able Flight). As I've mentioned previously in this missive, we have a weird set-up here. We work side-by-side with the Koreans, doing the same jobs, but under a different set of rules with different (and distinctly separate) chains of command. I've been leery of this set-up all along, but have been amazed at how well the Koreans and Americans get along. Monday night, however, that spirit of cooperation broke down.

TSgt Pete Albro (the American Morse controller on Able Flight) and MSgt Soo (one of Albro's operators) have been having a running gun battle for the past several weeks. MSgt Soo felt TSgt Albro was out to get him and hadn't been treating him fairly. Turns out MSgt Soo has been compiling a list of grievances against Albro and Monday, after Able Flight's first mid shift, he turned the list in to Capt Kim, the Korean Chief of Operations Production. Kim, in turn, slipped the list to Maj Chae, the Korean Ops Officer.

Maj Chae fired off--how dare that American Tech Sergeant (E-6) treat one of my Master Sergeants (E-7) this way! His solution to the problem was to show up for Able Flight's second mid shift, go directly to TSgt Albro, and jump dead in his shit. The American Flight Commander, 2Lt Mary Jarvine, was beside herself--just flat didn't know what to do. She called Capt Ringler (the acting Ops Officer during the Major's absence) in to try and get a handle on the situation. She couldn't.

SKIVVY NINE!

If there's anything a Korean officer holds in more contempt than an enlisted person, it's a woman in the military (officer *or* enlisted). That being the case, Capt Ringler got nowhere with Maj Chea who was demanding Albro be relieved of duty on the spot. She tried to call Maj Weber in his quarters (even though he was on leave), but there was no answer. She couldn't raise him on his pager, either. God only knows where he was. So the next best thing was, you guessed it, the old gray-haired Chief.

My beeper went off shortly after midnight. "Chief Beal. This is Capt Ringler. Report to the S&W Center immediately." I threw on some clothes, charged out to the truck, and got there as fast as I could.

When I arrived, the scene was bedlam. Chae was screaming at Ringler; Ringler was screaming at Kim; Kim was dumping on Albro; Albro was giving it to Soo; and Lt Jarvine looked like she had one foot nailed to the floor, turning in circles. The Mission Supe, MSgt Lars Eberly, was standing on the sidelines observing the pitiful sight with a wry grin on his face and shaking his head.

Instead of jumping into the middle of the mess, I got Lars off to one side and asked him what the hell was going on. He gave me a quick run-down and then I stepped in to try and calm Maj Chae down. Fortunately, he understands the role of American "Cheeps" (Korean for "Chiefs"), so he didn't fart me off completely. I convinced him that this was not the place to settle our differences and perhaps the best place to do that would be in my office the next morning. He wasn't real hot on the idea, but he agreed to meet with Capt Ringler, Capt Kim, and me the first thing the next morning. In the meantime, MSgt Soo was given the night off to cool down and get away from TSgt Albro.

The next morning, I made damn sure SSgt Jim LaMora (who speaks Korean like a native) was available to act as interpreter. Maj

Chae speaks pretty good English, but I wanted to make sure he and I didn't have a misunderstanding because of some language foul-up.

When the meeting started, there was a few minutes of accusations and counter-accusations, but we finally got down to the bottom line. MSgt Soo resents being supervised by a Tech Sergeant. I empathized with the Korean contingent on this issue, but told them there was nothing I could do about it. People on both sides at pay grades a lot higher than ours had agreed to this arrangement during negotiations on the Memorandum of Agreement. That agreement states that Americans are in charge, regardless of rank.

As it turned out, our skirts weren't completely clean. Seems TSgt Albro has a genuine dislike for Koreans (*all* Koreans) and had probably been giving MSgt Soo (and all other Koreans on Able Flight) a hard time. MSgt Soo, on the other hand, thought he should be the Morse Controller since he outranked all other 207X1's on flight, and was looking for ways to ding Albro. So what we had here was two bad guys who both needed their clocks cleaned.

Maj Chae's starting position was we should fire Albro outright and turn the Morse Controller position over to Soo. I raised the Bullshit Flag. An American will be the Morse Controller even if we have to use an Airman Basic. We *will* adhere to the Memorandum of Agreement. We negotiated back and forth for almost half an hour and Jim LaMora was magnificent. Not only did he translate the words correctly, but he threw in the unspoken words and subtle nuances: "He's really pissed now, Chief," he'd whisper, "Better back off a little." Or "He's not sure of himself. I think you've got him." The bottom line allowed Maj Chae to save face (a biggie for him) and allowed me to get things back on an even keel at the same time.

I suggested that, since Albro and Soo were both horse's patoots, they should both be fired. Maj Chae allowed as how that was probably a pretty good idea, so with his concurrence, Albro went to Dawg Flight and MSgt Soo was farmed out to Airborne Operations. Problem solved, case closed--maybe.

After the Koreans left, I asked Capt Ringler, Lt Jarvine, and Jim to stay behind. They all seemed to think that the Albro-Soo affair was just a manifestation of an overall, bigger problem between SKIVVY NINErs and their Korean counterparts. If that's the case, that's something that needs to be worked between Majors Chae and Weber, or perhaps Col Lucas (when he arrives) and Col Chae (the Korean Commander). In any case, that's a bigger problem than I need to worry about.

♦♦♦♦♦♦♦♦♦♦♦

Yesterday afternoon, I got another shot out of left field with a call from an Airman three-stripe at the 6990th in Okinawa asking for help. His wife is a Korean national and had returned to the country to conduct some business and visit her family. She had come up here on MAC Space-A[19] and planned to return the same way. She's been trying to get a seat on an airplane headed for Okinawa for the past 25 days. During that time, she's gone from number 125 on the waiting list to number 330. To complicate matters, the girl is pregnant as a pumpkin and due to deliver during the first week in September. The Airman three-stripe was beside himself. He wants his wife in Okinawa when she has that baby, and I can't say I blame him.

My first move was to call CMSgt Sam Knight, the guy in charge at the air terminal. He gave me no relief at all. Regs are Regs. The lady would have to wait her turn to get on a plane. He didn't want to incite a riot by putting her on in front of other Space-

---

[19] "Free" travel on Military Airlift Command aircraft on a Space Available basis. For a full explanation of MAC Space-A, see the Glossary of Terms.

A travelers. No balls. (Well, I never said the "Chief's Mafia" *always* works the way it's supposed to.)

Having struck out with Knight, I called Chief Hal Oliver, the head cheese at the Hospital. Since the lady was getting ready to drop a baby just any day, I figured this could be considered a medical emergency and he might be able to help me (her). Sure enough, Hal was appalled by the situation. She had to get back to Okinawa ASAP! Just so happened there was a MEDIVAC (Medical Evacuation) Flight this morning and the hospital has final approval for who gets on it, not the folks at the air terminal. Happy ending: the girl was on that airplane, and is probably in Okinawa with her hubby even as I write. (But the "Chief's Mafia" *usually* works the way it's supposed to.)

Friday, August 14th

I guess my little disagreement with Maj Chae about the Albro/Soo affair didn't completely alienate me with the Koreans. Thursday morning, SMSgt Kim (the Korean Ops Supe) invited me to a banquet that night to honor the Sergeant Major of the Korean Army, who was visiting Osan. I graciously accepted the invite.

I thought the attendees would all be enlisted men (that's the way we do it) but, when I got to the banquet, it was obvious that I was wrong. All the Korean heavy hitters were there: Col Chae, Maj Chae, Capt Kim, and a whole bunch of other officers that I did not recognize. And to top it off, guess who was the only American in the place--me.

I'm a really punctual person. I arrived at the NCO Club Brass Room at precisely 6 p.m., the time SMSgt Kim told me to be there. When I walked in, everybody was already seated at a huge U-shaped table and Kim was standing up giving some sort of speech.

There was only one empty chair and it was at the head table between Maj and Col Chae.

I didn't want to interrupt Kim's speech, so I just kinda stood there inside the door with my face hanging out waiting for him to finish before taking my seat. But he didn't finish. Instead, he stopped right in the middle of his talk, came to where I stood, and escorted me to my seat. Of course, everybody in the place was looking at me like, "Where the hell *you* been?"

After I was seated, SMSgt Kim finished his remarks. Of course, my first order of business was to apologize to the Sergeant Major and Col Chae for being late. The Sergeant Major just grinned and nodded his head. He couldn't understand a word I was saying. Fortunately, Col Chae speaks a little English. All he had to say about the situation was, "You are berry punctual, Cheep."

The food wasn't nearly as weird as it was at their change of command ceremony. It was the standard banquet fare: soup, salad, rib eye steak, baked potato, green beans, red wine, and ice cream for desert. The dinner conversation was a little strained to say the least. First, what do you talk about with these guys and, second, even though the Colonel spoke some English, the language barrier was still there. But I managed to muddle through.

After dinner, they all seemed to loosen up a bit and there was a lot of talk back and forth and a lot of laughing. Although I didn't understand what was being said, it was relatively easy to pick up the gist of what was going on. They were swapping lies about their sexual prowess and then that degenerated into telling (are you ready for this) Polish jokes!

After about 20-30 minutes of this madness, it was speechafying time. First, Maj Chae got up and mumbled some words, and then Col Chae said some things, and then it was the Sergeant Major's turn. I have no idea what they were saying, but they all had one thing in common. When they were sitting and engaged in one-on-one conversation, all of them had been very outgoing, sometimes bordering on the boisterous. But when they stood to speak, they were extremely quiet and reserved. Sometimes, I had to strain just to hear the sound of their voice. I don't know if this is a Korean custom or if they were just scared shitless of public speaking. Anyway, after the Sergeant Major was finished with his piece, SMSgt Kim turned to me and said, "Cheep, you do." I was bumfuzzled.

What do you say to a bunch of people who don't understand what you're saying? I didn't know, so I faked it. First, I apologized for not being able to speak their language. "No, No," Col Chae said. "We understand enough."

Then I thanked them for the honor of being invited and told them what a pleasure it was to meet their top enlisted man, Sergeant Major (you guessed it) Kim. I don't know if he understood anything, but he recognized his name and that brought a grin and some head nodding.

Then I got into the ticklish area. I said although we had cultural differences (an oblique reference to the Albro/Soo fiasco), it was important that we overcome those differences and work together against the common enemy to the North. I reminded them they were some of the most loyal friends and allies the United States have (which is true) and that I hoped we could work in a spirit of cooperation. I have no idea how much of what I said was understood but, when I finished, there was a polite round of applause. And then everybody got up and left! Apparently, I was the keynote speaker and, when I was done, the event was done.

One of the key questions that remained unanswered was how much did I owe for the meal. Here was another area where I didn't know if I was going to piss somebody off or not. If I offered to pay, I may be insulting their hospitality. If I didn't pay, somebody was out the price of the meal and I'm forever known among the Koreans as the "cheap Cheep". I tracked SMSgt Kim down and offered to pay, but he very politely refused the money. Kim's a good guy. I'm sure he didn't tell the other Koreans that I had offered to pay. In any case, I think I made it through the situation unscathed and Korean-U.S. relations were not completely destroyed.

Chapter Eight

THERE'S A NEW SHERIFF IN TOWN.....

<u>Sunday, August 16th</u>

Friday was an uneventful day and I got a lot of paperwork done (for a change). Friday night, I went to Capt Ringler's going away party. I'm really sorry to see her leave. She's a good one. SKIVVY NINE's officer corps isn't exactly top notch, but she's an exception. Good, solid leader and she's tough as nails, but fair. She's going back to Brooks Air Force Base in San Antonio to be the 6906th Ops Officer (a real feather in her cap), so she's getting her just reward for a job well done.

Left the Captain's party early so I could get back to my quarters to get some shut-eye. Col Lucas was supposed to arrive Friday morning, but his airplane broke down in Anchorage and his arrival was delayed until 3:00 a.m. Saturday morning. Since I was a member of the greeting party, I figured I better get some sleep so I would be bright-eyed and bushy-tailed when I met "the man" (first impressions, you know).

Got to the terminal around 2:45 to join Col Carlson, Majors Weber and Carlson, and First Sergeant Duchworth. (Don't know how Bob Estep and Capt Jacoby got out of going.) Anyway, the plane didn't show until almost 4:00, and by that time, my ass was dragging. Did a little "skin and grin" with Col Lucas then headed on back to the dorm and crashed.

Went to the SKIVVY NINE Lounge Saturday night to catch Col Lucas' first appearance in front of a group of unit people. The place was pretty packed when he showed up around nine o'clock. Maj Reardon immediately went to the microphone and announced his presence to the assembled multitude.

Col Lucas took over the mike and made a little speech that knocked the crowd's sox off. He only spoke for a couple of minutes, but when he finished, everyone knew that here was a leader. He talked about the flag, killing Commies, and Mom's apple pie. A little corny, but effective. He got a standing ovation and more handshakes than he could handle. I think they sent the right guy to do this job. What a refreshing change from the wimpishness of Col Meade.

Next week is going to be a real barn burner. We start off Monday morning with a change of command ceremony at the base theater. Col Lucas will officially take over from Col Carlson. The rest of the week, I'll be getting ready for my trip to Misawa; getting orders cut, making travel arrangements, reminding the houseboy to water my plants, etc. I'll be preparing for my trip around any panic situations that may crop up (and there *will* be panic situations--there always are.) Anyhoo, hopefully, I'll get it all done and be on a plane out of here come Saturday morning.

Thursday, August 20th

Col Lucas assumed command Monday morning and my shirt ain't touched my ass since. He's really got me going. But it's not just me. The entire unit is on the move. Seems like people are more energized. After a hectic day Monday and Tuesday, I decided to keep a running log yesterday. Here's a day in the life of an Ops Supe.

> **6:00 a.m.** Chief's Group meeting: Same old stuff. All the Chiefs on base getting together to see what we can do to make life a little better for our enlisted people. As usual, not much got accomplished. And then the subject turned to a continuing problem with the Chief's Group; how do we get more visibility. In

other words, how can we do good deeds and make ourselves look good at the same time. I listened to this gibberish for a while and then couldn't take it anymore. I told the gang that good press was not what the Chief"s Group was all about. Helping the troops is what the Chief's Group is all about.

I told them what Chief Hal Oliver and I had done for the pregnant girl who was trying to get back to Okinawa before her baby was born. I asked them what they wanted us to do, take an ad in the base newspaper telling the world what great guys we are?

To me, visibility is the last thing we should be worrying about. If you help enough people, the word will get out. And who cares if we're visible, anyway. Helping the troops is what matters. My little tirade didn't make me many friends among my brother Chiefs. But so what. The Visibility Committee remained in-tact and they will continue to look for ways to make the Chief's Group look good.

7:30 a.m. SKIVVY NINE Senior NCO Council Meeting: Left the Chief's Group meeting early and scurried over to the NCO Club to make the SENCO meeting. The SENCO has been TANGO UNIFORM for almost two years and I'm trying to breathe new life into the organization.

The meeting went well and interest seems high. The main order of business was an upcoming meeting with Col Lucas and what we were planning for BGen Phil Richardson's (ESC Vice Commander) visit next week. This whole thing may fall flat on its face after I'm gone, but while I'm here, SENCO will be a going concern.

8:15 a.m. In to work and pick up the master copy of the TDY orders for my trip to Misawa.

8:30 a.m. Take the master copy to Finance to get the right numbers and signatures that will make sure I'm paid for the trip.

8:45 a.m. Stop by the Traffic Management Office to arrange transportation to Misawa.

9:00 a.m. Take the master copy of the orders to the Admin folks to have copies made. They say it'll take three days and I say, "BULLSHIT, I'll pick up the orders the next morning." They give me 99 reasons why it can't be done. I say, "BULLSHIT, I'll pick the orders up the next morning."

On my way out the door, I ran into SSgt Steve Morgan. Steve had dropped off a set of orders the first day of August and they weren't done *yet*! He was going TDY the next day and wanted to know if I could speed things up a little. Back to Admin to tell them they would have orders in Steve's hands within the hour. Ninety-nine reasons why it can't be done. Ninety-nine reasons why they hadn't done them before this. "BULLSHIT," I said. I looked up SMSgt Robert Tolbert (the Director of Admin) and got him into the act to get things moving. With a great deal of reluctance, they had Steve's orders to him that afternoon.

10:00 a.m. Stop by Pat Aiken's office to have him send my security clearance to Misawa. Almost forgot to have that done. That would have been a real disaster.

10:30 a.m. Go to Financial Management meeting with Maj Weber, but had to leave early to make it to my next appointment.

11:00 a.m. Rush like hell to the PME Center where I judge the finalists in the Leadership School speech contest. A Senior Airman from Suwan Air Base is the winner.

12:15 p.m. NCO Club for lunch.

1:00 p.m. Get back to my office just in time to parachute right into the middle of a dispute between DOA and DOS. DOA has four guys coming in from the states accompanied by 600 pounds of computer gear. They need a truck to pick these guys and the computer gear up at Kimpo Airport in Seoul.

DOS is the only shop with a six passenger pick-up--a vehicle tailor made for hauling the computer gear and the passengers. DOA wants the truck. DOS insists they have to have it because it's their emergency response vehicle in case of a recall.

Compromise: DOS gives DOA their truck to pick up the travelers and computer stuff and I turn my truck over to DOS so they'll have wheels in case of a recall. Problem solved, but I'm without wheels.

1:30 p.m. Ops Staff Meeting: Every Tuesday and Thursday, Maj Weber gets all the Branch Chiefs together to pass out words of wisdom. The meetings usually run about an hour and this one was no exception.

2:30 p.m. Back to my desk to do a little paperwork, but not for long. Panic phone call from Capt Curt McGranahan, the top ranking Ops guy on Hill 170. The Pacific Air Forces (PACAF) I.G. Team is here and they're doing a facilities inspection of the base. Although the 03rd isn't subordinate to them, we are a tenant unit on their base, so we have to play by their rules. They were not happy with the way Hill 170 looked and gave Col Lucas a call to express their dismay.

Col Lucas went to Hill 170 to take a look for himself, and sure enough, it was not a pretty sight. So he button-holed Capt McGranahan and told him he had 'till sundown to get the place shaped up. The Captain had a big problem; an 0-6 breathing down his neck to get a job done and not enough manpower to do it. After some frantic phone calls, I had 10 bodies on Hill 170 by 3:30 to help the Captain out and the place was clean as a whistle by "sundown".

3:00 p.m. Finally got time to really dive into my in-basket. I work it hard 'till around 4:00 p.m. when Maj Weber gets a phone call saying Col Lucas wants a complete run-down on what Operations is all about by five o'clock. So we scramble around like crazy getting a briefing together and we're ready to enter the lions den by five.

5:00 p.m. Maj Weber and I go in to brief Col Lucas on the health of Operations. We're in good shape. The Colonel is satisfied. The briefing takes an hour.

6:00 p.m. *Finally* got to the SKIVVY NINE Lounge for a cool one.

7:30 p.m. On my way back to my dorm for a balogna sandwich when I meet the First Sergeant headed for the Orderly Room. He's gotten a call from Col Lucas saying he's not satisfied with the way the grass looks around the Orderly Room. Better get it cut and edged before the PACAF I.G. Team sees it. SMSgt Duckworth was on his way over there to mow the grass himself. BULLSHIT! He may be an ass-hole, but he's a Senior Master Sergeant ass-hole, and Senior Master Sergeants don't mow grass. Three phone calls later, I've got three guys from the swing shift to push the mowers and do the edging. The Orderly Room is looking sharp by "sundown".

And that was the day that was.

Sunday, August 23rd

The SKIVVY NINE softball team played the 51st Supply Squadron for the championship of their league yesterday. I got to the field a little late, and by the time I grabbed a beer and a hotdog at the concession stand, it was a little tough finding a seat. The stands were packed, but I managed to find one and settled in to watch what I knew would be an excellent softball game.

I just got settled in when I heard someone calling me by my first name. I thought it must be either Bob Estep or Randy Shell (the other two Chiefs in the unit and the only people who call me "Wyman"), but it wasn't. It was Maj Dan Scott, BGen Richardson's aide and a personal friend of mine. He was standing about three rows down at the end of the bleachers motioning me to come over and join him.

I knew BGen Richardson had arrived that afternoon for a five day visit, but I didn't know that Dan was a member of his entourage. I worked my way over to where he was and sat down with him.

While we were shaking hands and exchanging pleasantries, I realized I was in the middle of the VIP section. There was the General, Col Lou Hopkins (ESC Director of Personnel), Col Lucas, and a collection of "strap hangers" who always accompany the heavy hitters. Dan introduced me all around while any possibility of watching the game slowly slipped away. They all (except Col Lucas) started firing questions at me.

"What's wrong with the unit; why did it go MARGINAL; how could they help us get back to our feet; did Maj Weber have his performance report backlog cleaned up yet; how was I feeling now that I was out of the hospital; should Osan be a two-year, accompanied tour for everyone; and on and on and on."

I was quick to point out that, although the unit was rated MARGINAL overall, there were some parts of it that were *very* healthy indeed, especially Operations. They acknowledged that, and cited it as one reason they wanted me to take the lead in getting the unit ready for the I.G. re-inspection planned for January. They suggested that with my prior I.G. experience, I should be able to help out quite a bit. I assured them I'd do all I could.

Through all the I.G. re-inspection banter, I kept trying to divert everyone's attention back to the action on the field. I was a little uncomfortable in the limelight and besides, I *really* wanted to watch that ballgame. It took a while, but I finally got them focused on the field.

Going into the top of the last inning, SKIVVY NINE was leading 7-6. 51st Supply scored one run and, with the bases loaded and one out, threatened to score a whole bunch more. The next Supply batter hit a line shot over shortstop, but Earl Whitsell went high and caught the ball in the very tip of the webbing of his glove. All the Supply runners had been off with the crack of the bat because it looked like a surefire hit. Whitsell came down throwing and whipped the ball across to Maj Reardon at first base to double the runner off. End of rally--end of inning.

In the bottom of the seventh, SKIVVY NINE had Boomer Marshall and Marsh Marshall (the team's two homerun threats) coming to bat followed by Whitsell, a notoriously poor hitter. Boomer and Marsh both popped up for outs, then Whitsell stepped in and punched one out of the park. SKIVVY NINE wins 8-7 and Earl Whitsell is an instant hero.

Said my good-byes to Dan Scott, the General and crew, and headed out for the NCO Club to grab some supper. On a snap decision, I changed my mind and decided to go off base for some Chinese grub. Went to my favorite restaurant, ordered their version of yaki soba (fried noodles), and was waiting for my order to come when who should walk in but BGen Richardson and party. Rats!

They had a private room in the back of the joint reserved and nothing would do but I had to join them for supper. Col Lucas didn't look too happy about the whole situation, but what was I to do? I didn't want to infringe on his turf, but I was trapped. So I ate with them.

Fortunately, Scott and I have quite a bit in common so we could carry on a semblance of a conversation instead of all the small talk and pitter-patter that everyone else was doing. I wasn't too miserable and when we finally finished, I said my good-byes again and tried to make an exit. BGen Richardson would have none of it; I just had to join the group for cocktails at the Officer's Club. Rats!

There was an up-side to this whole thing; I finally got to see the inside of the Taj Mahal (the name hung on the O-Club by enlisted folk). There's a strict rule about not allowing enlisteds in the O-Club and vise versa (no officers in the NCO Club), so I had never been in the place. It's very nice from the outside; from the inside it's an absolute palace!

I certainly wasn't dressed to be in a palace--shorts, pull-over T-shirt (with a picture of a mosquito and the words "National Bird of Texas" on the front), and sneakers. I had originally started out just to go to a softball game (and dressed appropriately) and now here I was in the middle of the Officer's Club. Everyone else was in shirts, slacks, and street shoes. But I guess when you're a member of the General's party, you can get away with being an underdressed enlisted swine. Well, at least, nobody said anything to me.

Fortunately, there was something to do besides engage in small talk. There was a live C&W band performing, so that took the pressure off to scramble around for something witty to say. I stayed long enough not to appear rude, said my good-byes (*again*), and got the hell out of there.

Went back to my room to pack for my trip to Misawa. I'm really not looking forward to that.

Sunday, August 10th

Like it or not, here I am in Misawa. And by the way, the old saying "Getting there is half the fun" is BULLSHIT.

Headed out for the air terminal last Sunday and got there about an hour before boarding time. Was having a sandwich in the Snack Bar when I was paged over the public address system and told to report the Customer Service Desk. I just knew I was about to be bumped off the flight by a higher priority passenger. Well, I wasn't bumped, but it was almost as bad; I had been tagged for courier duty.

I went with the Armed Forces Courier Service (AFCOS) agent to a warehouse just off the flight line where I signed a whole bunch of paperwork to receive over 500 pounds of classified material that was being shipped from Osan to Yokota. Fortunately, I had a Staff

Sergeant helper (I was the courier; he was the guard) so I didn't have to carry a weapon. He did.

The AFCOS agent, my guard, and I rode in a pick-up truck behind the forklift carrying the classified to the airplane. When the pallet went onto the back of the C-141, I signed some more paper and the AFCOS agent went away. The guard and I settled in amongst all the freight to wait for the other passengers to board. About the only bennie to pulling the duty was we had special seats located right next to the cargo with plenty of leg room.

When we landed at Yokota, all the other passengers piled off while the guard and I waited for another AFCOS agent to relieve us of your very special cargo. More paperwork, more signatures, turn over the gun to the agent, and we were out of there. Took well over an hour to claim baggage, clear customs, and get out of the terminal. The process is *very* painful at Yokota.

Grabbed a taxi to the billeting office. I had made reservations in advance and expected no problems. Foolish me. They had no record of a reservation for CMSgt T.W. Beal in their computer. Fortunately, I had a confirmation number and, while the billeting people were making out paperwork to send me to a Japanese hotel off base, I dug through my briefcase and found the number. When I produced it and raised a little hell, the billeting people miraculously found a cancellation and put me up for the night.

Up the next morning at 4:00 a.m. for a 5:30 show time for a 7:00 flight. Was checking my luggage whey they announced a two-hour delay for the flight to Misawa. Just what I needed--four hours of sitting around the Yokota terminal waiting for a flight. In my 26 years in the Air Force, I can't even count the times I've been through the Yokota Air Terminal. If I had all the time I've spent in that terminal knitted together, I'd get credit for another whole overseas tour.

SKIVVY NINE!

My flight finally took of at 9:45 and, an hour later, we touched down in Misawa. SMSgt Karl Rushmeyer met me at the plane and took me to billeting to get a room at the Sunshine Inn. I couldn't get a place on base (or even close to the base) because the PACAF I.G. Team was in town. When they were finished up with Osan, they had made their way to Misawa. There's almost 100 people on that team (compared to 25 on the ESC Team), so when they hit a base, they're like a heard of locusts. They snarff up *everything*! They had made my life miserable at Osan and now they're doing it at Misawa.

While Karl was taking me to the Sunshine Inn, I couldn't help but notice we were going a looooooong way out into the countryside. He finally pulled in at a real dump and said, "This is it." At that point, it was obvious I would have to get a rent-a-car. Fortunately, I had put the authorization into my orders just in case I needed one.

There are no commercial car rental agencies in Misawa. The only game in town is the Base Exchange Concessionaire and they had no cars for rent. The lady at the B.X. informed me there wasn't a car for rent in all of Northern Honshu. They were all tied up by (you guessed it) the PACAF I.G. Team! There you go.

Spent the rest of the day at the 20th setting up for the self-inspection. When I was finished, Karl drove me back to the Sunshine Inn, stopping along the way to pick up some grub at the Burger King. Even though it was a couple of hours until meal time, I knew I wouldn't have the wheels to go get something later, so I better get something while I had the chance.

Karl volunteered to pick me up every morning and deliver me every night, but I still felt stranded. The next morning, I went to see Lt Col Kline, told him my tale of woe, and asked for help.

Kline put me in touch with the Admin type who's up here from the 6990th in Okinawa to help out with the self-inspection. He couldn't get a renter, either, but the guy's he's helping loaned him his second car so he would have a way to get around. He's been good about giving me rides when I need them, but I really hate to impose and I still have that stranded feeling.

Other than the transportation and billeting problems, the trip hasn't been too bad. The self-inspection went well. I think the 20th will get by with at least a SAT when the I.G. pays their visit.

Chapter Nine

.....AND HE'S A BAD ASS

Sunday, September 6th

I'm back home in Osan and, once again, getting here was not half the fun. A lot of folks think you fly Mother MAC for free. Not true. You don't pay in dollars and cents; you pay with heartache, grief, and monumental pains in the ass.

When I made reservations for the flight back, I didn't think to ask what kind of aircraft I'd be riding or where it would be going. And you can bet your ass that the Traffic Management Office Agent didn't volunteer that information, either. I had come into Misawa on a direct C-141 flight out of Yokota and assumed that was the way I'd go back. How foolish of me.

I was standing in line at the passenger terminal waiting to check my bags and pick up my boarding pass when I heard the ticket agent tell the guy in front of me that the arrival time at Yokota would be 5:00 p.m. With a scheduled take-off time of 10:00, it didn't take me a long time to decide that this was not a direct flight. And I was right; it was a Misawa-Fukuoka-Yokota flight. Woe is me! Miserable flight riding in jump seats made more miserable by a one hour delay at Fukuoka putting us into Yokota at 6:00 p.m.

Had better luck with Yokota billeting this time. They had my reservation, didn't give me any lip, and I was in my quarters in minimum time with minimum hassle. They didn't have any Chief's quarters available, so they put me up in Colonel's quarters, which are almost as good.

Rolled out the next day, did my morning routine, and headed for the terminal. Got there two hours before take-off time and, while I was standing in line waiting to check my bags and get a boarding pass, I overheard two dependent wives (who were traveling Space A) discussing how lucky they were to get seats on the KC-10 tanker aircraft headed for Osan.

When I finally worked my way to the front of the line, I found that I wasn't booked on the KC-10, which would have been a direct one hour flight from Yokota to Osan. Instead, I was scheduled on a C-141 flying Yokota-Kunsan-Taegu-Osan, a trip that would take six hours, counting ground time.

I told the agent I wanted to switch from the C-141 to the KC-10, but he insisted there was no way. I was a manifested duty passenger on the 141 and to transfer me to the KC-10 as a Space-A passenger would be a monumental paperwork hassle. I contemplated bringing my "Chiefness" into play, but decided it wasn't worth it and took my ticket on the 141.

Sure enough, it was a miserable flight made more miserable by the fact they wouldn't let us off the plane while they loaded/unloaded cargo at Kunsan and Taegu. So I ended up spending six full hours on the airplane. What really galled me was when I stepped off the 141 at Osan, there sat the KC-10--and it had been sitting there for almost five hours. Ah yes; Mother MAC works in strange and mysterious ways.

Took a taxi to the dorm, dumped my bags in the room, and headed for the SKIVVY NINE Lounge to catch the Friday afternoon crowd. Everyone seemed genuinely happy to see me back. Backbriefed Maj Weber on my trip, then he filled me in on what's been going on since I've been gone.

There were lots of little things, but the biggie was the 6903rd now has a six day work week. Col Lucas has decided that, if the unit is to be ready for the I.G. re-inspect, we have to spend every Saturday doing nothing but I.G. prep. Hey, that sounds like a good idea; so good in fact that that's just what Maj Weber and I had the Ops Division do before the I.G. visited *the first time.* And it worked. We did well. The rest of the unit went flat on their asses.

Maj Weber said the six day work week wasn't setting too will with the Operations troops, but I can't say that I blame them. They worked their asses off preparing for the first inspection, did good, and now they're being penalized because the rest of the unit scrod up.

The Major said he tried to explain all this to Col Lucas, but he would hear none of it. "We're a unit and we're going to work as a unit. I'm not going to have everyone else in the 6903rd working six day weeks while Ops works a five day week. That would demoralize the rest of the troops." What about the Ops troops? What about their morale? The Major listened patiently to my tirade, then shrugged his shoulders and said he would see me at work bright and early the next morning.

Saturday morning and I'm out of bed at 5:30 a.m. so I can make work by 6:30. Even though SMSgt Ozzie Harpster was sitting in my desk while I was in Misawa, my in-basket was overflowing (what did Ozzie do, anyway?). Worked the in-basket hard and had it cleaned out by 10:30. Got a call from 1Lt Loretta Lane (Col Lucas' executive officer) saying the Colonel wanted to see me at one o'clock.

I wasn't in his office but a couple of minutes when the Colonel wanted to know what I thought about the six day work week. I told him.....adamantly. He seemed to respect my opinion, but wouldn't budge on his insistence that the Ops troops pull "their share of the load" (whatever that means). I explained to him that on re-inspections, the divisions that were rated SATISFACTORY or above wouldn't be re-inspected. Hell, the I.G. Team won't even bring an Ops Inspector with them. Never-the-less, the Colonel wants Ops working a six day week to build unit cohesiveness. Oh well, I've got one thing to say for the man; when he makes up his mind, he sticks to it, no matter how asinine the decision might be.

The other thing the Colonel wanted to talk to me about was making "GET READY FOR THE IG" posters. He wants to put up five posters a week (one each for major locations where people work/congregate) to remind people that the I.G.'s coming and challenging them to give 110 percent to get ready. He wants me to make these posters--five a week--in my off duty time. Each poster would take four to five hours, so we're talking about a major extra duty here.

I explained to Col Lucas what making five posters every week entailed and how much time was involved. I pointed out that I'm about as dedicated as the next guy, but I do need a little leisure time to keep body and soul together. He offered a compromise: I would do the posters in my room on Saturdays instead of coming in to the office to work. My Gawd! I can not believe the generosity of the man!

Well, I'm going to give it a shot next Saturday. If I can knock them out in one day, I'll continue to do them. If the work starts to bleed over into my Sunday or I find myself working on the posters on week nights, I'm going to direct the Colonel to the base graphics shop. I'm the Ops Supe, not an illustrator and he'll just have to understand that.

Wednesday, September 9th

Here it is 7:30 p.m., and I'm just now crawling in the door from work. Starting yesterday morning (my first day at work since I got back from Misawa, unless you count the full day I put in Saturday), I've started going to work at 5:00 a.m. Last night, I finished up at six o'clock and tonight at 6:30, but by the time I ate supper at the NCO Club, it was way past seven.

This Col Lucas guy is something else. He does everything with "blue slips". They're 3X5 inch blue index cards with handwritten notes handing out tasking and giving a deadline when the job is to be finished. Maj Weber dubbed them "blue snow". There are so many of them flying around, it's like snowflakes coming out of the sky. After today, I'll be calling them the blue blizzard. Every time I looked up, there was a blue slip hitting my desk.

"Do this; suspense 9:00 a.m., September 10th"

"Do that, suspense COB (close of business) today"

"This performance report is poorly done; have it rewritten and back to my Exec by noon".

The six day work weeks are going to be bad enough; the 12 and 13 hour days are going to be even worse. It's going to be an interesting "rest of the tour".

I worked half a day Monday, even though it was Labor Day. I had to keep ahead of the blue slips. Of course, Col Lucas had worked Sunday and generated many, many blue slips and I figured I'd better work them instead of letting them pile up on me. Didn't want to have to play catch-up come Tuesday morning.

Sunday, September 13th

And the grind continues! Was in to work by 5:00 a.m. Thursday morning and Maj Weber was already there and hard at it. A little later in the morning, a tiny episode took place that goes a long way toward illustrating the climate in this unit.

Maj Weber said he hadn't had a chance to eat breakfast that morning and was starving. I suggested we go out to the Roach Coach when it came to grab a couple of sausage and egg biscuits. By the time we got outside, the Roach Coach had already gone. The

Major turned and headed back toward the office. He took a couple of steps and then turned back around and said, "Maybe we can run down to the Burger King and get something to go." He took a couple of steps toward his car, then turned around *again* and said, "No; I just don't have the time."

I give you that little anecdote just to show how hectic things are lately. Col Lucas is piling on the work so deep and keeping the pressure on so hard that Maj Weber and the other Division Chiefs don't even have time to eat. (By the way; the Major didn't starve. I went to the Burger King and got the grub for him.)

Since the Colonel started his rampage, I thought it couldn't get any worse but, apparently, it can. Maj Weber attended a meeting of the Division Chiefs Thursday afternoon where Col Lucas told them, "You ain't seen nothin' yet. I know you and your people are working 12-14 hour days, six days a week, but I'm going to turn up the heat even higher."

That brought out quite a few eye rolls. Then toward the end of the meeting, it got even rougher when the Colonel told the Division Chiefs, "I'm going to run you into the ground and then I'm gonna kick you in the ass 'till you get up and run some more. And when you go down again and can't get up, I'm going to run you over." Wow! Talk about motivating your people!

So here it is Sunday and Maj Weber had to go in to work to conduct a walk-through briefing for Col Butch Albright (PESD Commander) who's visiting the unit for a couple of days. Without saying so officially, I guess Col Lucas has upped the ante from six days a week to seven.

♦♦♦♦♦♦♦♦♦

After winning their league championship a couple of weeks back, the SKIVVY NINE softball team played its first game in the

Base Championship Tournament Thursday night. I got the money from the Lounge to buy 100 hot dogs and buns and took them to the game. Maj Weber brought the charcoal and his little habachi grill and we set everything up on the tailgate of my truck right behind the SKIVVY NINE stands.

Several people came over while we were setting up and warned us that the Morale, Welfare, and Recreation (MWR)[20] people weren't going to like what we were doing. The Major and I agreed that, if MWR asked us to leave we would, but until they did, we would cook dogs for the troops. So we pressed on and gave away all but ten or twelve of the dogs and everyone loved it. We're going to do the same thing for tomorrow night's game and will continue to do it until either the tournament's over or MWR shuts us down.

♦♦♦♦♦♦♦♦♦

Friday was a long, long day. It started with a fire drill in the unit dorm at 4:30 a.m. All the biggies (Col Lucas, Maj Reardon, Capt Terry Oakley (O'Rourk's replacement), SMSgt Duckworth, Maj Weber, and of course, me) were there to witness the event.

MSgt Joe Del Ricco (along with everything else he does, he's the Unit Fire Marshall) set off the alarm and we all stood back and waited. Nothing happened. The dorm residents farted the alarm right off!! Col Lucas began to froth at the mouth (as he damn well should have). He (and the rest of us) began banging on doors to get people out. When the room occupants opened their door to find a

---

[20] The organization on each Air Force Base responsible for providing just what their name implies for the troops. They are the people who run the golf course, gym, bowling alley, rec. center, library, child care center, hobby shop and provide softball fields, tennis courts, kiddy play parks, racquet ball courts, picnic areas, riding stables, marinas, ski slopes, and skeet ranges. They administer the intramural sports program and pay the people who officiate the games. Sound like nice folks? They're actually bloodsucking slugs. To see why, turn to the Glossary of Terms.

Colonel, Major, or Chief standing there, you can bet your ass they scrambled to get out of that dorm.

When they were all outside, Col Lucas gaggled them up and delivered a major league ass chewing. A couple of folks got special attention. One of the guys and two or three of the girls were fully dressed and the Colonel chewed their asses up close and personal. When he had finished motivating them, he sent the occupants back to their rooms and we had another dormitory evacuation exercise. He had Del Ricco set the alarm off three more times, keeping time on how long it took to empty the place. The third time around, it took a minute and ten seconds and Col Lucas decided that was good enough for the time being. We all left.

On the way back to our vehicles, the Colonel indicated that it was obvious more practice was needed. So he instructed Del Ricco to do a fire drill every night next week, all between midnight and 2:00 a.m. Fortunately, he doesn't want me or the rest of the gang to witness them. Guess he figures he and Del Ricco can take care of everything. Thank God!

The rest of the day was spent reacting to blue slips, but I did manage to convince Maj Weber to take a 45-minute break so we could get some lunch.

♦♦♦♦♦♦♦♦♦

Friday afternoon, I got a whole stack of Airman Performance Reports (APRs) back from the Command Section that looked like someone had bled to death on them. Most of the "problems" were with the endorsements. I had some trouble with that since I personally approve as written, re-write, or write from scratch all endorsements that go to the Commander for his signature. I may not speak the Queen's English too well, but I write that sombitch good. But apparently the Executive Officer, 1Lt Loretta Lane, doesn't think so.

Since she's been here, *every* endorsement I've written or OK'd has come back for rewrite. The fact that I get my feelings hurt when this happens is a minor thing. The biggie is it places a tremendous burden on our Admin people (who are already undermanned and over worked) who have to retype the damn things just because the Lieutenant wants to demonstrate what a literary genius she is.

I had already talked to Lt Lane about the kickbacks a couple of times and she promised not to change things "unless I absolutely have to." Well, the stack of APR's I got Friday didn't have "have to" type changes. It was stuff like changing "outstanding" to "superb"; "fantastic job" to "great job"; and my personal favorite, "---" to "..." (or vice versa. Whichever way it's done, it's always changed to the other way.)

I set up an appointment for Maj Weber and me to go in and talk to Col Lucas about the situation. We had Lt Lane sit in on the meeting so she would hear first-hand what we had to say. I put the stack in front of Col Lucas and told him, as far as I was concerned, the changes were so much bullshit. He reviewed the stack and agreed.

Lt Lane was instructed that only typos, misspelled words, words missing, and things like that would be changed on APRs coming out of my office. We'll see what happens. If things get better, good. If not, I plan to take it right back to the Colonel.

Bickering over nit-picky pucky like that really gets to me. I have better things to do with my time.

♦♦♦♦♦♦♦♦♦♦

Up early yesterday morning to get started on the posters Col Lucas has tasked me to do. Worked from about eight o'clock straight through to around five-thirty, six o'clock. I finished three.

Got into uniform and took the posters to Col Lucas' office for his approval.

There are a couple of key things in that last sentence that gives the reader some idea of what the atmosphere is here. First, the fact that I put my uniform on to deliver the posters (even on a Saturday night after 6:00 p.m.). Lucas' Rule One: No one can enter the compound in civilian clothing. The second key fact is that I *knew* he would be at work after 6:00 p.m. on a Saturday evening (he's *always* there).

Anyway, the Colonel was pleased as punch with the posters, but I explained that I couldn't possibly turn out five a week. These had taken nine hours and to do two more would require me to work most of the next day (Sunday). He wasn't sympathetic. His only response was, "I would like to have two more posters on my desk Monday morning. You just do what you think's right, Chief." And so I will.

Sunday, September 19th

About half of SKIVVY NINE's people (Staff Sergeant and below) live in dormitories that are sub-standard at best. Everybody knew that they were scheduled to be torn down so new dorms could be built on the site. Only question was "when?".

Week before last, our people living in the dorms started hearing rumors from their neighbors in other squadrons that the dorms were scheduled for demolition beginning October 1st. They were telling our people that their First Sergeants and Commanders had told them they would have to move before then. Because of a shortage of dorm space, Staff Sergeants and Tech Sergeants would have to share a room. Staffs and Techs have had single rooms 'till now. Our people hadn't heard *anything* about such a move, and naturally, they were a bit concerned. This was their home that was being messed with, and some of them started trying to find out just what the hell was going on.

The rumor worked its way all the way up to Col Lucas by late on Friday afternoon. He started looking into the rumor early Monday morning of last week. What he found was not a pretty picture.

The base had been planning for the 1 October move for months. There had been many First Sergeant meetings to decide just how it would be done. During these meetings, Col Jim McDonald (the Base Commander) had insisted on unit integrity in the dorms: i.e. everybody in SKIVVY NINE would be housed together, everybody in the Security Police Squadron would be housed together, etc. It was a good idea with one major draw-back; it would mean doubling up Staffs and Techs.

Col McDonald's plan also called for moving SKIVVY NINE's Staffs and Techs who were living in Air Force Village[21] back on base and giving the Village to the smaller units. That way, they could have unit integrity, too. The bottom line: SKIVVY NINE's people were getting *SCREWED*!

And what was SMSgt Duckworth, our fine First Sergeant, doing while all this was going on? The minutes of the meetings showed that he had been at every one and, not once did the protest or go to bat for his people. That was bad enough, but even worse was the fact that he hadn't kept the Commander (or anyone else) informed about what was going on. And even worse than that, he hadn't kept the troops informed about what was going to happen to them. Both

[21] Enlisted housing on Osan Air Base has always been in short supply. Since there never seemed to be enough dorm space, the U.S. Government leased an entire apartment complex on the outskirts of Song Tan and turned it into an enlisted housing area. All the units are two bedroom places that are occupied by two people and totally furnished. Very nice.

the Commander and the dorm occupants had to learn about what was transpiring through the grapevine. Needless to say, SMSgt Duckworth's shit was a little weak with Col Lucas.

The First Sergeant is on leave right now, so there's no way he can explain his actions (if, in fact, there is an explanation). The fill-in First Sergeant, SMSgt Robert Tolbert, and Col Lucas jumped through their ass-holes all last week trying to get the situation turned around.

First, they got the move postponed until 1 November. That gave our people time to plan for the move, pick roomies, etc. They got the transportation people to agree to ship stuff back to the states for storage if two people with a lot of junk (stereos, TVs, furniture, etc.) had to move in together. Lastly (but the biggie), they got Col McDonald to back off on the unit integrity thing. That means Techs won't have to double up, and only half our Staff Sergeants will have to share a room.

Tolbert and Lucas really did a great job of straightening out SMSgt Duckworth's mess. But while they were doing it, unit people didn't know what was going on behind the scenes and the rumor mill continued to grind out horror stories. One rumor had E-4's and below (who are already two to a room) moving into tents so the Staffs and Techs wouldn't have to double up. You can imagine how that made them feel. Everybody was coming to me demanding answers and I just didn't have them. Needless to say, things were pretty tense. Almost everyone I talked to had the attitude of "Why are *you* doing *this* to *me*, Chief?" It was like they thought I was personally responsible for their woes.

Went to see Col Lucas and told him that he and Tolbert were doing a magnificent job, but they needed to find a way to get "the word" down into the trenches. This rumor mill is killing us! The Colonel agreed, so he and Tolbert scheduled meetings with all dorm residents to pass out information first hand. They put in some horrendous hours (talking to Flights on swings and mids as well as day watches), but they got the job done and by last Friday afternoon, everybody had the real story.

As a result of the dorm flap (and a lot of other skeletons Tolbert has unearthed since he's been filling in as First Shirt), SMSgt Duckworth has got a big surprise in store for him when he comes back from leave. He won't even have to unpack his bags. Col Lucas is going to fire his ass and have him on the next plane out.

In addition, the Colonel is going to do everything he can to get Duckworth's assignment to the 6950th in Chicksands, England cancelled. He doesn't want him to have the opportunity to screw up another unit like he's done this one. As you can tell from previous entries in this missive, I've *always* known Duckworth was an ass-hole; I just didn't know he was an incompetent ass-hole. I'm just glad it all came to light and he's going to get what he deserves.

♦♦♦♦♦♦♦♦♦

At the same time the dorm flap was coming down, Col McDonald made another decision that put SKIVVY NINErs on the warpath. He's decided that the SKIVVY NINE Lounge will have to be turned over to Morale, Welfare, and Recreation (MWR), The dorm thing was bad enough, but losing the Lounge on top of that was like driving a stake through the heart of the unit.

Col Lucas and Tolbert fought that move, too, but they didn't make a whole lot of headway. By PACAF regulations, private lounges on base are illegal. You know the old story--you can't compete with MWR or the Exchange System. The PACAF IG is coming again next month and Col McDonald wants to make sure they don't find any illegal lounges on Osan Air Base.

There are over 50 lounges on base ranging from the biggest (51st Transportation Squadron which clears over $5,000 per month) down to the small two and three barstool operations. The three biggest lounges (51st Trans, SKIVVY NINE, and Red Horse) are to be turned over to MWR and all the rest will be closed altogether. Small lounge patrons will be asked to take their business to the three that remain open.

Although it's a proven fact that the lounges are big morale factors and bring in a lot of revenue to the units, Col McDonald is sticking to his guns on this one. By the letter of the law, he's right, so there's not much anyone can do.

When MWR takes over our Lounge, it won't stay open long. A boycott is already planned; no SKIVVY NINEr will so much as go near the place. Since MWR is profit motivated, when the dollars don't come in, they'll dump it fast. The SKIVVY NINE Lounge has been around since 1958 and is a legend throughout ESC, but the legend is about to die.

♦♦♦♦♦♦♦♦♦

What with the dorm fiasco, the Lounge closing, and the big-time pressure Col Lucas is putting on the unit, needless to say, rubber bands were stretched just a little tight last week. That's why I'm glad the softball tourney is going on. The ball games are a good opportunity for the folks to blow off a little steam in a healthy way.

The tournament lasted all week and (naturally) SKIVVY NINE made it to the championship finals. SKIVVY NINE making it to the finals was no surprise--their opponent was. The Hospital Squadron seldom has a winning team in *anything*, much less make it all the way to the big time. So, needless to say, their folks were pretty excited about the whole thing.

There was a possibility that we would have to play three games. SKIVVY NINE only had to take one game to win the championship, but Hospital had to win two since they came through the loser's bracket. Of course, we were counting on winning in one, but Hospital came from behind with a dramatic bottom of the last inning home run to win, forcing a second game.

I don't think any of our fans were disappointed. They were having such a good time, I don't think they would have minded if all three games had to be played. There were at least 300 people there and the stands were rockin' and rollin'. The team got their stuff together in the second game and we won it and the championship going away.

After the post-game ceremony where there was some speechafying and trophy awarding, there was a mad dash to the Lounge for the victory celebration. The place was absolute bedlam. It was probably the last big party in the place and everybody knew it, so they were determined to make it the party to end all parties. And it was. More beer got on people than in people.

Later in the evening, when people started to come down from the high of winning, it turned in to a pretty somber occasion. Talk turned to the MWR take-over and a wake broke out to mourn the demise of our beloved Lounge. By eleven o'clock, the place was pretty much cleared out (Saturday was, after all, a duty day) except for the old time "Lounge Lizards" who were crying in their beer and swapping lies about the Lounge's good old days.

October 1st - 30th

Back in San Antonio for a three day TDY at the headquarters to discuss how we're going to consolidate SKIVVY NINE under one roof. Took leave for the remainder of the month to be with my wife and kid and away from SKIVVY NINE regaining my sanity and recharging my batteries.

Saturday, October 31st

I'm back. Here it is at four in the morning with a full day ahead of me. More on why I'm making this entry at 4:00 a.m. later.

The flight back went pretty well, everything considered. The San Antonio-St. Louis leg was relatively uneventful except for the Mexican dude sitting next to me. This kid was in his early 20's , had on a purple shirt with yellow pants (very baggy, but tightly tapered at the ankle held up by a whisper-thin black leather belt). The ensemble was highlighted by a pair of silver blue, pointy-toed, alley-gator skin shoes with high heels. A real fashion statement. His English was just good enough that I could understand him if I strained real hard.

Turns out this kid is headed for Fort Leonard Wood, Missouri for Army basic training. I don't think either he or the Army knew what they were in for. He had never been on an airplane before and he was nervous. Real nervous. I was traveling in uniform, so he wanted to know if I was in the Coast Guard (No, I'm in the Air Force); was I an officer (No, I'm an enlisted man); had I ever flown before (Yes, many times); and so it went. I guess talking kept his mind off the fact that he was flying.

Talking and going to the rest room. The boy must have gone to the john 15 times. Ordinarily, I wouldn't mind, but he had the window seat and I was on the aisle; every time he had to go, I either had to get up or let him crawl over me. When the meal came (something brown, something white, something green, something wet) he ate it like it was the most fantastic meal he had ever eaten. (Maybe it was.)

Although I wasn't in any mood to socialize, I was civil to the young fellow. Felt kinda sorry for him actually. When he got off the plane, he and eight or ten other young fellows were met my an

Army NCO who gaggled them up and (yelling and screaming all the way) led them off to God-only-knows-where.

Claimed my luggage and did a bag-drag to the MAC Passenger Counter. The Airman behind the counter was very helpful when I requested a seat in the VIP section on the upper deck of the 747. When I boarded the airplane, I got the shock of my life. The Airman hadn't done me any favors; there is no longer a VIP section on Flying Tigers[22] aircraft.

I climbed the spiral stairs to the upper deck and found the big, wide, plush, first class seats I saw in April were gone, replaced by tiny, little, cramped, standard seats just like the ones on the lower deck. I guess Mother MAC, in all her wisdom, decided they weren't cramming enough people into the airplane, so the good seats had to go.

When the first class seats were on the upper deck, there was room for 10 people. Very comfortable for the Chiefs, Colonels, and Generals who were authorized to ride up there. Under the current set-up, there is room for 32 people. They had someone in every seat and, sure enough, mine was in the middle. To top it all off, the entire upper deck was a no smoking area. I mentally cursed the Airman, Mother MAC, and Flying Tigers Airline as I buckled into seat 22-J. (With a number like that, I shudda known.)

As soon as the plane was airborne and the seatbelt light off, I headed for the lower deck to check out what it looked like down there. If there was *anything* open in the smoking section, I intended to take it even if it was a middle seat. I may be uncomfortable, but

---

[22] A company founded by veterans of the fighter squadron which won fame in China before the United States entered World War II. They tried to "make a go of it" in the civilian sector, but soon discovered that there was more profit and security to be had by leasing their planes to the U.S. Government and flying military people all over the world.

at least I could have a cigarette and watch a movie (no movie screen on the upper deck) while I was miserable.

What I found on the lower deck defied all reason. The front one-fourth of the aircraft was packed with every seat taken. The middle portion of the aircraft was totally empty. You could have had a square dance and played a basketball game at the same time in the place. I ventured to the back one-fourth of the plane and it looked just like the front fourth. Packed.

I beat feet back to the upper deck, grabbed my briefcase, and found a seat in the smoking section in the middle of the aircraft--on the aisle, thank you. My ass no sooner hit the seat than the flight attendant showed up and asked if I were assigned to that seat. I said no. She said I would have to return to my assigned seat. I asked why. She said there were bunches of people getting on the plane at Oakland and this seat would undoubtedly be assigned to one of them. I said fine, when we get to Oakland, I'll go back to my assigned seat. 'Till then, I'm not moving. She said the number of meals they had prepared corresponded with the number of people they had sitting in each section. If I stayed where I was, I wouldn't get a meal. I said fine. I wasn't hungry, and besides, Flying Tiger food was not edible.

She left. In less than five minutes, she was back with the head flight attendant. The head flight attendant (whom I firmly believe was in China with the original Flying Tigers) told me I would have to go back to my assigned seat. I asked why. I guess they didn't have a real good answer, so they went away mumbling, and I spread out for a nice, comfortable ride to Oakland. (They did serve me a meal, by the way. I ate the roll and drank the coffee and left everything else. When the flight attendant came to take my tray away, she asked why I hadn't eaten anything. I said I wasn't hungry and besides, Flying Tiger food wasn't edible.)

SKIVVY NINE!

Just before the plane touched down at Oakland, I went back to my upper deck seat. I knew from prior experience they always deboard the upper deck first and I had a good reason for wanting to be one of the first people off the plane. There wouldn't be much ground time in Oakland, and I needed to make a trip to the MAC Passenger Counter.

I asked the guy behind the counter if all the seats were taken for the remainder of the flight. He said there were only eight people getting on in Oakland and, according to his computer, 23 were getting off in Anchorage and only 12 were getting on. I asked if I could change seats. He said sure. He punched some buttons, looked at the screen, and asked, "How would you like to have a whole row of seats by yourself?" I said that would be nice and he gave me a new boarding pass.

The flight from Oakland to Anchorage was a pleasure. I hunted down a pillow and blanket, made a bed on the four middle seats, and slept like a baby for four hours. Since I was so refreshed and wide awake, I used the Anchorage-Yokota leg of the trip to write my Trip Report. Now all I have to do is type it before I go to work Monday morning and I'm finished with it.

During the layover at Yokota (there's *always* a layover at Yokota), I was having a cup of coffee in the snack bar when two SKIVVY NINErs, SSgt's Billy Dotson and Katy Keller, joined me at my table. They were on their way to Leadership School at Misawa, but since they had a chance to bend the old Chief's ear, they took it.

They started off with small talk ("How was leave; did you enjoy the time with your family; are you glad to be back; etc; etc; etc), but the conversation quickly turned to the real reason they wanted to talk to me. They were both overjoyed to be going away to Leadership School, not because they had a burning desire for more education, but because it would get them out of the unit for five weeks. Seems Col Lucas has tightened down the screws even tighter while I've been gone.

They had lots of complaints, but the biggie was the constant recalls/exercises that the unit has been enduring for the past three weeks. The most recent one kicked off at 11:30 p.m. last Thursday night. It lasted until 4:00 a.m., which gave everybody just enough time to go back to their dorm to shit, shower, and shave, and get ready to go to work Wednesday morning. They both said that morale was even lower than when I left and pleaded with me to do something. I said I'd try.

The flight from Yokota to Osan was uneventful and gave me just enough time to do one last relook/edit on my trip report before going final. At the Passenger Terminal, I sat through the "Welcome to Korea" and customs briefings, then went with everyone else to pick up my luggage.

My bags always seem to be the last on the belt, so I didn't get too excited when I waited, and waited, and waited and still no luggage. But when it got down to the point where there was only two or three passengers left and I still didn't have my bags, I started to wonder. Finally, I was the only one left and there was no more luggage and the conveyor belt stopped.

Bat shit! They've lost my stuff!

I buttonholed the first baggage handler I could find and told him my problem. He looked at the nametag on my uniform and said, "Oh, I wondered where you were, Chief Beal. Your luggage had VIP tags on it, so we put it in the VIP Lounge so you could pick it up and not have to go through the customs hassle."

Luckily, he had taken note of my name embroidered on the bags, so when I approached him, he remembered where my stuff was when he saw my nametag. The best I can figure, here's probably what happened:

The nice young Airman at the MAC Counter in St. Louis had decided to give me a break and put VIP tags on my luggage. That luxury is usually reserved or Colonels and Generals. The VIP luggage comes off the plane first so they don't have to wait around with the rest of the riff-raff. And sure enough, mine came off first, went directly to the VIP lounge, and sat there while I stood at the conveyer belt and waited for them. Here Mother MAC was trying to give me a little special treatment, and I didn't even know how to handle it. Oh well.

Once I located my luggage, it was a snap going through customs because there aren't any in the VIP lounge. I walked outside the terminal to look for a taxi and there was MSgt John Watts with a six-passenger pick-up to give me a ride to my dorm. That sure was nice of good old John to think to pick up his favorite Chief at the terminal. Fat chance!!

After the preliminary small talk, he lit in on me about the latest morale crusher the base commander has come up with. John, and the rest of the Master Sergeants living in Air Force Village, are being evicted from their apartments. They're either going to have to move back into the dorms and share a room with another Master Sergeant, or find a place to live on the economy. John was pissed (big news) and wanted to know if there was anything I could do to help. I said I didn't think so, but I'd try--Monday. I didn't say anything to John, but I do wish they would at least let me get back to work before they start hitting me with all this bullshit.

Got back to my quarters, unpacked, and got Mr. Yi (my houseboy) to press the stuff that needed pressing. By this time it was 3:00 p.m. and, even though I wasn't sleepy, I laid down to try for a nap. No luck. I laid there for thirty minutes with my eyes big as saucers and finally gave up.

Went to the Orderly Room to sign in and then down the hall to the SKIVVY NINE Lounge. With the PACAF IG out of town, Col McDonald had softened his position a little and had decided to allow the Lounge to remain out of MWR's clutches "on a temporary basis". The place was packed and everyone seemed genuinely happy to see me and (thankfully) no one hit me with a problem.

B.O. O'Banion and Maj Weber were both overjoyed I was back. B.O. fessed up that if he had to sit in my desk one more day, he would pull out what little hair he has left. I asked the Major to run me out to work so I could get my pick-up. I needed wheels under my ass. He said it was in the shop for its quarterly check-up. Now that really pissed me off. I knew the check-up was due in October and gave Jim LaMora specific instructions to make sure it got done while I was gone so I would have it when I got back. He finally put in the shop last Wednesday and it won't be ready until next Wednesday. Bummer!!

I broke for supper at the NCO Club around 5:30 p.m. and went back to the Lounge for a few more brewskies. About half way through my first beer, jet lag hit me like a ton of bricks. I could hardly hold my eyes open. I didn't want to do it and I knew the consequences, but I stumbled back to the room and crashed at 6:30. And bigger than Dixie, at three-thirty this morning: PING!, my eyes popped open and I'm wide awake. I laid there for a minute debating whether to try to go back to sleep. I got up and began writing this entry.

Wednesday, November 4th

Monday was my "get back in the groove day". When I got to work, I couldn't believe my in-basket. It was literally stacked a foot high with paperwork. I asked Maj Weber what the hell B.O. did while I was gone. He just kinda chuckled and said, "He's the only guy I've ever seen who hates paperwork more than I do." Good old B.O. It took me the better part of the day to clean out that basket.

Tuesday was a more-or-less humdrum day. About the only thing of note was getting my truck back from the motor pool. I started bugging Jim LaMora the minute I hit the door Monday to get it back (*after* I chewed his skinny little ass for getting it into the shop late). He kept telling me "any hour now", but by noon Tuesday, still no truck.

About three o'clock, I got word from my secret source that there was going to be a recall this morning. I called Jim in and told him I *had* to have that truck because there was a recall coming. Now understand, no one (least of all the Ops Supe) is supposed to know when a recall is going to take place, but I had to tell Jim about this one to get his ass in gear. He asked to borrow my phone and I said OK.

Jim called Lt Johnson, the Vehicle Control Officer and, while I looked on in horror and disbelief, said, "Chief Beal said there's going to be a recall tomorrow morning and he needs that truck *now*!"

When he hung up, I said, "God dammit, Jim! I'm not supposed to know there's going to be a recall. Now the Lieutenant knows that I know. Why did you tell him that?"

He gave me his best sheepish grin. "Well, gee, Chief. It got results. You can pick up your truck at three-thirty." Well, I guess I can't be too pissed when he puts it like that.

♦♦♦♦♦♦♦♦♦

The only thing my source refuses to tell me about the recalls is the exact time they will kick off. So I rolled out of the rack at three o'clock this morning figuring it would hit around four. That's always a good time to have a morning recall. Did my morning routine, got dressed, and waited for my pager to go off. It didn't.

Long about 4:45, I was mentally cursing my source when there was a knock on my door. It was a runner telling me the unit was in a recall condition as of 4:00 a.m. It had taken 45 minutes for me to get the word and I was pissed.

After the exercise was over, I set about finding out why the Flight Commander hadn't called me on my beeper as soon as the thing started up. When I showed up in the Surveillance and Warning Center breathing fire, Lt Jarvine showed me the new recall roster dated yesterday. She said the mids Flight Commander told her he wanted to call me on my beeper like he always did. But this new roster showed Flight Operations was supposed to notify me.

He did the right thing; he had a roster showing it wasn't his responsibility to notify me and he didn't. But when I hadn't showed up by 4:30, he figured Flight Operations had dropped the ball, so he sent the runner to fetch me on his own initiative. Good man. Now it was time to look up the whiffle ball who made the change to the roster and find out why. It had always worked the old way. Why change now?

Finally tracked down the culprit, MSgt "Z" Zalegowski, the Plans and Programs NCO. "Z" had a reason for doing what he did, but it wasn't a very good one. He told me he had made the change because, during the last recall, it had taken too long for people to respond. He reasoned that the Flight Commander just had too many people to contact and that created a bottleneck. So he unilaterally moved some random people (including me) from under the Flight Commander and put them under other offices for them to contact. Bad move!

I tried to talk some sense to "Z", but he held his ground, refusing to change the roster back. So I took it up with Maj Weber, who talked to Maj Reardon (Zalegowski's boss), who told "Z" to make the change. So now I'm on the Flight Commander's recall roster again, but it really doesn't make any difference. I don't have my pager any more, so my response time is shot to hell anyway.

Got a call from the Comm Group this morning telling me they wanted my beeper back. I went through a real goat rope back in May to get a beeper from the Comm Group because the 03rd couldn't supply one to me. I was to keep the Comm pager while the 03rd ordered a new one and, when the one on order came in, I was to turn the loaner back to the Comm Group. Nice arrangement.

The Comm Group says they don't mind me using their beeper, but the PACAF IG is coming back again and they have to have all their spares for inspection purposes. Mine was one of those spares. I took it back (reluctantly) and then checked with our supply guys to see how long it would be before the one they ordered for me arrived. The incompetent ass-holes never ordered the damn thing! No excuse--they just never got around to placing the order.

So now I'm without a means for the Flight Commander to get in touch with me if all hell breaks loose. So tomorrow morning, I'm going to call the beeper keepers at the Headquarters and beg them to send me one and let us do the paperwork that makes it legal later. I sure hope this works.

Chapter Ten

TIGHTENING UP THE SCREWS

Sunday, November 8th

I'm finally back into the swing of things, and everything is going pretty smoothly. All the "powers that be" (Majors Reardon and Webber, Capt Jacoby, etc.) are enjoying the relaxed atmosphere while Col Lucas is back in San Antonio for the Commander's Conference. But he'll be back Thursday and everyone can go back to jumping through their ass-holes again.

Col Lucas' threat to run his staff into the ground is finally paying dividends. While I was gone, Capt Jacoby (who the Colonel rides especially hard since LG got a MARGINAL on the inspection) went to the Hospital complaining of chest pains and heart palpitations, but the Hospital folks said his EKG was normal. He's still having pains, but won't go back for fear people might think he's "gold bricking".

A couple of days later, Maj Reardon was sitting at his desk when his left arm went semi-paralyzed and his vision became blurry. Col Lucas and Maj Weber rushed him to the Hospital where he stayed for three or four days for tests. The medicos aren't sure, but they think he may have had a mini-stroke. He's scheduled to go to the 121st Evac Hospital in Seoul next week for more extensive tests. Sure hope they don't find anything.

Then Thursday night, Chief Randy Smaley (the NCO in Charge of our Detachment over on Hill 170) went to the Hospital with what we thought was indigestion. He was sick at his stomach and his legs were a little weak. They examined him and turns out he was in the middle of having a massive heart attack! They called in a chopper and air-evacuated him to the 121st right then. He's still in intensive care, but it looks like he'll pull through. I guess the Colonel will turn this place into a sharp unit or kill everybody in it.

♦♦♦♦♦♦♦♦♦

Maj Weber is still under the gun on late Airman and Officer Performance Reports. He's finally gotten his act together on the ones he's personally responsible for, and those are on time. But now, the problem is we're so short on Administrative Staff that they can't keep up with the typing and other administrivia, so there's still a back-log.

At the Commander's Staff Meeting week before last (while I was on leave), Operations had one late APR on the "Late APR Slide". Maj Weber said Col Lucas looked him in the eye and said, "Kelly, if you have one more late APR on that slide the rest of the time I'm here, I'm going to have your ass." The very next week, operations had *seven* late APRs on the slide! Thank God Col Lucas wasn't here; he would have killed the Major on the spot.

After the staff meeting was over, Maj Weber said he wanted me to take charge of the APR situation and make damned sure there aren't nay more late ones. Up to this point, MSgt Joe Del Ricco has been trying to ride herd on the problem, but he obviously isn't getting the job done. It's not that he doesn't try and, God knows, he works hard enough (12-14 hours a day, seven days a week). It's just that he's not very imaginative and he tries to do everything himself.

Job one was to sit down with Joe and get the specifics on exactly where the problem areas lay. After about 30 minutes with him, I had identified four of them and spent the rest of the day working solutions and relaying them to Joe.

<u>PROBLEM 1:</u> Manpower (or lack there-of)

Del Rico is authorized five people in the Admin Section and he only has two, himself and one other guy. The supervisors out in the branches are getting the APRs written on time (most of the time), but they all have to go through Del Ricco for quality control and other processing. That's where the hang-up is.

Since his shop is grossly undermanned, APRs and OERs will sometimes lay in Del Ricco's in-basket for six or seven days before he gets around to them and, by the time he does, they're sometimes late.

When I told him that we absolutely *had* to eliminate that bottleneck, he said, "I'm already working a 70-hour week and can't stay caught up. And I've got other things to do besides APRs and OERs: filing, cutting orders, tracking leaves, (and a bunch of other admin-type stuff that I can't (and don't want to) remember). If I lay everything else aside to do nothing but APRs and OERs, then my other programs will go in the toilet." He was right, but something (anything) had to be done.

<u>SOLUTION:</u> Redistribution of work.

I did a little checking around to see what kind of hours Admin people in other Ops Branches were keeping. Turns out the ones in DOF are humping their asses off, but the ones in DOO, DOA, DOT, and DOV are coming to work at 7:00 a.m. and leaving at 4:00 p.m. Not exactly an equitable situation when Joe Del Ricco is working 12-14 hour days. But I had a fix.

As of Thursday afternoon, the Admin guy in DOO is also Joe Del Ricco's file clerk; the one in DOA is responsible for cutting orders; the one in DOT handles leaves; and the one in DOV (the most underemployed of all) works a "split shift": four hours in DOV before lunch and four hour in DOE after lunch.

PROBLEM 2: Sloppy book keeping in the Orderly Room.

They are responsible for keeping up with which APRs are late and preparing the slide that's shown in the weekly Commander's Staff Meeting. I asked Joe if he ever double checked the accuracy of the slide and he said he didn't. So we checked the status of the late APRs that had been on that morning's staff meeting slide. For various and sundry reasons, only two of the late APRs on the slide were legitimate.

SOLUTION: Get with Capt Terry Oakley (O'Rourk's replacement) and show him what I had discovered.

Oakley was amazed and appalled. He promised to crack the whip in the Orderly Room and make sure the slide is correct from now on. Just to be on the safe side, he'll also coordinate with Del Ricco to make sure late APRs on the slide are *really* late. I told the Captain I was counting on him big time; my Major's ass was on the line.

PROBLEM 3: The biggie!

The APR/OER Section in the Personnel Office is responsible for notifying supervisors when one is due. Joe said that many times, notifications aren't received until four or five days before the report is due. No way the report can be written, run the gauntlet of endorsing officials (with the inevitable kick-backs), and make it to the Orderly Room on time. I asked Joe to show me some examples.

He showed me one he received from the Personnel Office that very morning (November 5th). It had a suspense date to the Orderly Room for November 9th with the 7th and 8th being a weekend. No way this APR is ever going to make it to the Orderly Room on time.

APR/OER notifications are made using computer "rips". Each rip has a date/time it was printed on the upper left-hand corner of the page. This particular rip had been printed on October 2nd! I asked Joe where the hell the rip had been between October 2nd and November 5th. He just shrugged his shoulders.

Off to the Personnel Office with Del Ricco in tow. I showed the rip to the APR/OER Section NCOIC and demanded an explanation. She didn't have one except her section was grossly undermanned and overworked and couldn't stay caught up. Not good enough. *EVERYBODY* is undermanned and overworked.

My next stop was CMSgt Webb Rawlings, the head beagle of the Personnel Office. I told him my situation and asked for help. Webb talked with the APR/OER Section NCOIC and they agreed that, in the future, if we get a rip that gives us less than 10 days to get the report to the Orderly Room, all Joe has to do is pick up the phone and call. The APR/OER Section will give us a 15 day extension on the suspense. That's fair.

PROBLEM 4: An easy-to-do. Some supervisors just are not getting the APRs written on time.

SOLUTION: Beal becomes a raging hard-ass.

> From now on, if an APR hasn't been turned in by the day *before* it's due to Del Ricco, he is to notify me. Then I'll go to the supervisor and give him/her a lawful order not to leave the duty section that night until the report is finished. If they fart me off, it's a letter of reprimand; if they fart me off again, it's Article 15 time. Harsh, but that's how serious the situation is.

I don't know if my fixes for the problems will work, but I sure hope they do. If they don't, it's Maj Weber's ass. Col Lucas wouldn't hesitate a second in ruining his career. The Major's too good an officer and has too much potential to let administrivia do him in.

After I spent most of my morning with Joe Del Ricco fixing problems he should have fixed long ago, Maj Weber came to me that afternoon with an interesting proposition. He had somehow found out that it was Del Ricco's birthday. He suggested that he and I give Joe a surprise party that afternoon in the SKIVVY NINE Lounge as a form of recognition and appreciation for all the hard work and overtime he had put in. Reluctantly, I agreed. After all, he may not have been too efficient, but he had been busting his ass. As usual, I was up to my ass in stuff, so the Major took care of the arrangements. He left it up to me to get Joe to the Lounge.

I used the "topic of the day" (late APR/OERs) to get Joe to the Lounge. I told him Capt Oakley wanted to see us so we could explain what we're doing to fix our lateness problem. I called ahead and gave the Orderly Room folks a heads up on what was coming down. When Joe and I showed up, they told us the Captain was down the hall in the Lounge getting a Coke.

The surprise was a success. Joe was taken totally off guard. But the big surprise came when I asked the Major how much it was going to set me back for my half of the tab. I had expected beer and pretzels; the Major had gotten a three layer cake and champagne! My part of the bill came to $18.00. Oh well, it was a nice gesture and I'm sure Joe appreciated it.

Wednesday, November 11th

Happy Veteran's Day, for whatever that's worth. Col Lucas got back from the Commander's Conference at 5:30 p.m. last night and called a staff meeting for 9:00 a.m. this morning. Naturally, I had to be there. So much of the holiday off. The meeting lasted almost three hours and, by the time it was over, everybody in the room had enough taskers to keep them busy for the rest of their tours. When I got out of the meeting, I figured what-the-hay, I've already worked half a day, so I might as well finish it out. So I worked 'till almost five o'clock then hung it up for the day.

For the first time since I've known him, Maj Weber's confidence is shaken--no--I think he's just plain scared. We have our normal weekly Commander's Staff Meeting tomorrow morning and there's going to be two reports on the late APR slide. Woe is me! But there's no way we can get them to the Orderly Room in time to keep them off.

These two reports came due while Col Lucas was at the Commander's Conference and he was the last endorsing official on both. But the Colonel is sly; he knew some reports would come due while he was gone so he pre-signed a bunch of blank APR forms before he left. Any reports coming in for his signature would be printed on the pre-signed forms and not have to lay around waiting for him to sign them--and be late. It was a good plan, but it failed to take one thing into account: fumble fingered administrators.

Our APRs are done on a computer and, when all the data is in, the Admin folks insert a form and print it out. But it's a very tricky operation. The form has to be lined up just right and you can't allow it to slip. Our Adminers haven't quite mastered the task and it sometimes takes them three or four tries to get it right. The bottom line is, by the time these two APRs came in for Col Lucas' signature, all the pre-signed forms had been used up. So they're laying in his in-basket waiting for his signature. And they're late.

Almost anyone could plainly see that it's not Maj Weber's fault that the APRs are late--anyone but Col Lucas. He gave the Major some simple marching orders: "No late APRs. No excuses!" So the Major and I are going into the Staff Meeting not knowing whether the Colonel will look upon this situation as a reason or an excuse. If it's the latter, God only knows what he'll do to the Major.

♦♦♦♦♦♦♦♦♦♦

Spent a good part of yesterday afternoon helping put tomorrow morning's Recognition Breakfast[23] together. Planning the monthly event was one of the things Kevin Novak took over from Teddy Tressler when our Senior Enlisted slot got chopped and Terry retired. Kevin did it for one month, passed it off to me (along with all the other SEA duties) when I came here, then left.

After three months of just barely keeping my head above water trying to stay up with the Ops Supe job and the SEA job, I passed the responsibility for planning the breakfast (and some other SEA functions) off to the Senior NCO Council. The Council formed committees to administer the various programs. For example, there's a Professional Performer Committee, a Dining Out Committee, and Airman/NCO/Senior NCO of the Quarter Committee, Recognition Breakfast Committee, etc, etc, etc. But you know how committees are; the chairman ends up doing all the

[23] Once a month at SKIVVY NINE, a ceremony is held at the NCO Club to recognize all the people who have done something special over the past month. The Commander passes out medals, letters of recognition and accomplishment, announces promotions, and anything else to recognize our people for a job well done.

work and that's certainly how the Senior NCO Council Committees have been since they were founded. And that's where the problem came in with the Recognition Breakfast Committee.

When the committees were former, I took the chairmanship of that one because no one else would volunteer for it. Unfortunately, I haven't been in on the planning of a breakfast since the committee took over. I went into the hospital the last part of July, right when the planning for the August breakfast should have been done. That one was the first one Col Lucas attended and, although I wasn't there, I heard it wasn't very good. When the September breakfast was planned (or not planned), I was in Misawa helping out with their pre-inspection. It was even worse than the one in August, and Col Lucas was plainly unimpressed. I missed my third breakfast in a row in October because I was on leave in the States. From what I've heard, it was an absolute debacle and Col Lucas came unglued. It was time for "Orderly Room to the Rescue".

Although he had already been fired and knew he would be leaving in just a few days, SMSgt Duckworth (our fine First Sergeant) volunteered the Orderly Room to plan and run all future Recognition Breakfasts. Capt Oakley allowed as how it was about time and now the Recognition Breakfasts would be done right for a change!

Long before the next breakfast came around, Duckworth went away, leaving the problem with Oakley (Duckworth's replacement hadn't arrived yet). Suddenly in the last week of October, Oakley realized that there's another breakfast coming up and it's time to start planning for it. He frantically looked around the Orderly Room for someone to do the job, but all his people were up to their asses doing their normal day-to-day jobs while trying to get ready for the IG revisit at the same time.

Capt Oakley called MSgt DAL Lawler (who was acting committee chairman while I was on leave) and tried to "beg off",

Maybe he had been a bit hasty in taking on the Recognition Breakfast, and now he was looking for help. DAL didn't buy it. "Tough shit," sez DAL. "You wanted it--you've got it." Good on him.

About this time, two Air Force Reservists (Admin types) I had begged, borrowed, and stole for during my trip to the Headquarters arrived at SKIVVY NINE. They put one to work in the Orderly Room and guess what her first job was? You got it; plan and run the November Recognition Breakfast. Hell, this girl had never even seen one of the damn things, had no training what-so-ever, and didn't have a clue about where to start.

Meanwhile, I got back off leave and learned of the coup 'de tat Duckworth had pulled off. Fine by me; not having to do the breakfast every month was a big load off my shoulders. Oakley called me and asked for help and I gave him the same treatment DAL did. Finally, last Friday, SSgt Millie Best (the unfortunate reservist), called me. She was frantic. The breakfast was scheduled to take place in six days and she hadn't even started working on it. She didn't know *where* to start.

My first inclination was to blow her off and let her sink, taking the Orderly Room down with her. But I couldn't do it. If it had been anybody else in the Orderly Room, I would have farted them off in good conscience. But she had done the unit a favor in coming over here and now the unit was shitting on her. That's a hellava payback for a favor, so I agreed to help her out.

But I made it plain right up front that I wouldn't physically do any of the work. My role would be that of advisor and that's what I've been doing. First, I made up a checklist of things that had to be done. She's been going down the list doing those things and when she runs across a snag, she calls and I tell her what she needs to do next.

By yesterday afternoon, she had almost everything done and all that was left was to write the script and reserve the ballroom in the NCO Club. I told her who to see at the Club and left her to do it. But she needed some help on the script, so I spent a couple of hours in the Orderly Room helping her put it together. The last bit of help that I'm giving her is a biggie: I agreed to be the Master of Ceremonies. The breakfast will be a quality affair, SSgt Millie Best will look good, and (this is the part that really rags my ass) the Orderly Room will come out smelling like a rose.

But there's a kicker. SSgt Best will only be here for 90 days. She'll do the November, December, and January breakfasts and, when she leaves, someone in the Orderly Room will have to do the one in February. I hope whoever that is is watching SSgt Best and taking good notes because when they come around looking for help from me, it ain't gonna be there.

♦♦♦♦♦♦♦♦♦♦

Came up against a real tough one yesterday morning. We got a brand new (came in on the same plane I did when I returned from leave) Communications Security (COMSEC)/Red Force Operator (AFSC 209XX)[24] that has turned out to be a real problem child. She definitely got off on the wrong foot. From the time she stepped off the plane (literally), she's been butting heads with MSgt John Watts and Capt Curt McGranahan.

As I mentioned earlier, John met me at the terminal and gave me a ride back to the dorm. But there were a couple of other people who needed rides and Sgt Jenny Burnell (the new 209) was one of

---

[24] These operators monitor telephone lines to make sure military people don't pass classified information using insecure means. Violations are reported to the base commander. The other half of the job entails playing the Red Force role during exercises where they jam "good guys" communications links and confuse them using bogus communications.

them. She had come over on the Freedom Bird in civilian clothes (beats hell out of me how she pulled that off) and John told her she would have to change into a uniform before he took her to the Orderly Room to sign in. She couldn't understand the reason for that (personally, I couldn't either), but after all, John was her new boss and, if he sez do it, you do it. But she persisted in arguing and finally, it came down to "You E-4 Sergeant--Me E-7 Sergeant. DO IT!" And that's how she started off.

After she in-processed, she showed up for work and things didn't get any better. First, she said she should have never been assigned to Osan, that the Personnel Office at her last base in Germany had screwed up (but she didn't say how).

Then she told John she didn't want to do the job he had her scheduled to do. It was a job normally reserved for people fresh out of technical school. She had four years of experience under her belt and she didn't want to start off at the bottom of the ladder. She wanted to start at the top. When John and Capt Mac gave her the tough shit routine, she went to Maj Weber with her story, which pissed the Major off because she jumped the chain of command.

Next, when Capt Mac told her she would be receiving an Air Force Achievement Medal at the next Recognition Breakfast, she refused to go and accept the medal. She said for the kind of work she had done in Germany, she deserved the Meritorious Service Medal or (at the very least) the Air Force Commendation Medal.

Then she threw them a curve ball; she said she would be leaving Korea in six or eight weeks (but didn't say why) and could see no reason why she should be entered into training. She followed that up by going to see Capt Oakley and asking him for a job in the Orderly Room. *That* was the straw!

John and Capt Mac came to see Maj Weber and told him they were going to write a Letter of Reprimand on the girl for a bad attitude. The Major supported their decision but, before they did it, he wanted me to talk to the young lady in an attempt to turn her around. After I talked to her, she would have a week to get her act together. If she didn't, they would slap her with the letter.

I called Sgt Burnell yesterday morning and arranged a 9:00 a.m. meeting on neutral turf--the SKIVVY NINE Lounge. I didn't want to talk to her in my office (too formal) and I didn't want to talk to here where she worked (no privacy). The Lounge is always empty at nine in the morning, so it was the perfect place.

I started off by telling her that she had gotten off on the wrong foot, but there was still time to get her act together. She countered with, "How dare they question my attitude!!" I reminded her that, as right as she may be, the military isn't a democracy (hell, it ain't even always fair) and if she insisted on butting heads with a Master Sergeant and Captain, all she could do was lose.

We went down the list of things she had done to piss off John, Capt McGranahan, and Maj Weber. She agreed that perhaps she had been a little bitchy. But when we got to the issue of not going into training because she would be leaving in six to eight weeks, she hit me with the *real* problem. She was two months pregnant. It's a little known fact (although *she* knew it) that if an active duty female becomes pregnant, her tour in Korea is curtailed and she's shipped back to the States to have the baby. And that's where this whole thing got started way back in Germany.

Jenny got pregnant about a month after she got the assignment to Korea. She went to the assignments people and informed them of her condition. She wanted to be extended in Germany until after the baby was born or have her assignment changed to the States. "Not possible," sez the assignments people and she was sent to Korea even though she was pregnant. She knew she would never pull the one year tour.

When she got to Osan, one of her first stops was the OB-GYN Clinic where they confirmed she was preggy and started paperwork to get her out of here. I asked her why she hadn't laid this news on John and Capt Mac right up front. That would have explained a lot of her actions. In this day and age of sexual freedom and single parenthood, she was too ashamed to tell them she was pregnant out of wedlock.

At this point in the conversation, things went to hell in a hand basket. Her emotional rubber band was stretched just about as tight as it could go and, once the truth came out, she decided to dump. She started squalling and told me that the guy who knocked her up doesn't even know she's in a family way. She loves the dude and wants to get married, but is afraid to tell him what's going on for fear of what his reaction might be. He might "do the right thing by her" or he might tell her to take a hike. That's a problem, but it can't compare with the fact that her parents don't know her condition either. They are staunch, hard shell, Southern Baptists and she just knows that when they find out, they're going to disown her. Sticky.

I reminded her that I wasn't a professional guidance counselor and suggested that she might want to seek help from one. She poo-pooed that idea out-of-hand and asked what I thought she should do. Hell, I didn't know what she should do but, since she insisted, I took a stab at it. So far as I could tell, two things had to be done.

First, she had to let her boyfriend and parents know what was going on. Second, she needed to get out of the 6903rd and out of Korea as soon as possible. She wasn't doing herself, the unit, or anyone else any good here. She needed to be in the States. I couldn't help her with the first one; she'd have to take care of that herself. But I told her I would do everything I could to get her a stateside assignment as soon as possible.

I wrapped up the interview by telling her that, until I could get her on a plane, she should keep her nose clean and not make any waves with MSgt Watts and Capt McGranahan. I said I realized that she was a little "ragged around the edges", but she's still a Sergeant in the U.S. Air Force and she damned well needed to conduct herself like one. She needed to do what she was told to do and she agreed that was probably the best plan.

From the lounge, I went to Manning Control at the Personnel Office to see what kind of progress they were making on getting Jenny out of here. They had the paperwork from the Hospital, but said they couldn't do anything until Sgt Burnell got Lt Gen Reynolds (7th Air Force Commander) to sign a letter authorizing her tour to be curtailed. This revelation simply amazed me. I told the personnel guy she wasn't *requesting* a curtailment; she was being *kicked out* of the country because she was pregnant.

We kicked that one around for awhile and, finally, he agreed that since she was an ESC asset and didn't belong to PACAF, he would accept a message from the personnel people at ESC Headquarters as authorization to curtail her tour. I haven't had a chance to call the Headquarters yet, but I'm pretty sure they'll buy off.

Just to make sure all the bases were covered, I called CMSgt Gene Miles (7th Air Force Senior Enlisted Advisor) and explained the situation to him. He said that if ESC don't provide the message to make things happen, he will grease the skids into Gen Reynolds' office. He'd make sure any necessary paperwork got out of his office within a couple of days instead of the normal two-three weeks. Hopefully, Sgt Burnell will be gone (one way or the other) by the end of November, first of December.

Got together with MSgt Watts, Capt McGranahan, and Maj Weber yesterday afternoon and laid out the revelations I had uncovered. Needless to say, they were a little taken aback, but agreed that getting Sgt Burnell out of the country ASAP was the best for all concerned. In the meantime, John and Capt Mac agreed they need to be a little more sensitive to Sgt Burnell's bitchiness.

I think what happened here was an unfortunate situation where both sides were right. Sgt Burnell had a personal problem that contributed to her bad start in the unit, and John Watts and Capt Mac had an understandable reaction of "Who the hell does this bitch think she is?" But I think we've got a handle on things and everything will work out.

Sunday, November 15th

First, the Airman Performance Report situation: GRIM! In my last entry, I made mention of two reports on the Late APR Slide that were going to show up at the Commander's Staff Meeting. I didn't know what Col Lucas' reaction would be, but now I do. When the Late APR Slide came up on the screen, Col Lucas very quietly (but loud enough for everyone in the room to hear) said, "Kelly, I want to see you in my office after this meeting is over."

The 30 minutes it took to finish the meeting was the longest half hour in Maj Weber's (and my) life. The Major followed the Colonel to his office where a Letter of Reprimand lay on the Colonel's desk with a pen beside it. Maj Weber didn't say anything--just picked up the pen and signed the bottom of the letter to acknowledge receipt.

Col Lucas told him that this was the desk drawer variety Letter of Reprimand. That means the Colonel will hold onto it instead of sending it to the Orderly Room where it would automatically trigger the establishment of an Unfavorable Information File on Maj Weber. That would be disaster! The next late APR will generate another LOR and both it and this one will go to the Orderly Room and into a UIF. If there are no more late APRs between now and the time the IG Team arrives (mid January), the Colonel will tear up the letter.

I waited for the Major back in our office while all this was going on. When he came in, his face was the color of chalk. He said, "Chief, we have *got* to do something about APRs. I can't stand up under this kind of pressure." After a lot of discussion and soul searching, we came up with a solution that neither of us likes, but we've got to do if he is to survive.

We've got to bring SSgt Ruby ("The Viper") Irons back to Ops Admin and make her the Ayatollah of APRs. Ruby has a personality like lye soap and absolutely detests me and the Major. But she's a damned efficient administrator that's organized and will kick ass and take names to make sure APRs get turned in on time.

Ruby used to work in Ops Admin, but I had to reassign her to Ops Production (DOF) back in May because of some personal problems she had that I won't go into here. DOF generates by far the most APRs of any branch in Operations, but since "The Viper" took over, there hasn't been one late APR coming out of that branch. So we've decided that, if she can keep our biggest branch caught up, she can do it for the whole damned division.

Ruby's not going to like the move. She was happy to get out of Ops Admin and loves working in DOF. Capt Jean Henke (Chief of Ops Production) isn't going to like the move. She'll be losing the best Admin person in the unit. Joe Del Ricco won't like it either. He'll feel like he's being fired (and in a sense, he is) from being the division APR Monitor. And Lord knows, Maj Weber and I won't like the move for reasons I've already mentioned. But it's got to be done, and done now. I've arranged a meeting of all concerned on Monday morning at 8:00 a.m. to break the news to them. If this don't fix the problem, I don't know what will.

♦♦♦♦♦♦♦♦♦♦

SKIVVY NINE!

As predicted in my last entry, the Recognition Breakfast went smoothly, not without some minor glitches, but still smoothly. For her first time to plan one, SSgt Best done good, but she did let a couple of items fall through the cracks. It took a little scrambling in the few hectic minutes before the program and a lot of tap dancing on my part during the ceremony, but everybody seemed to be satisfied with the outcome, especially Col Lucas, and that's what counts.

Capt Oakley was so satisfied that he said he looks forward to me working with SSgt Best on the next one. "Nay, nay, my good Captain," sez I. "This is *your* program and, since I've walked Sergeant Best through planning one of these things, I'm sure she can do the next one on her own. And as far as MC-ing the thing is concerned, that's something that needs to be rotated among our Senior NCOs. Builds character. So far as I'm concerned, I'm out of the Recognition Breakfast business." Thank God!

One of the people we honored during the ceremony was TSgt Tom Ritchey for being promoted this month. What we didn't know at the time was Tom hadn't *really* been promoted. He's still a Staff Sergeant.

Tom's line number[25] came up in October, so he sewed on his stripe the first of November. But as of the day of the Recognition Breakfast (12 November), he still hadn't received his promotion orders. He needed the orders to update a lot of his personnel stuff, but the biggie was to take a copy to Finance so he could start getting Tech Sergeant pay. After the breakfast, he went to the Personnel

---

[25] When an Air Force member is promoted, they are placed on a Promotion Roster which ranks each person by time-in-grade. The person who has been in grade the longest has Line Number 1 and is promoted first. And so it goes until you reach the person with the least time-in-grade who is promoted last, sometimes as much as a year later.

Office one more time to try and get things straightened out. That's when he found out the real truth--he hadn't been promoted after all.

The whole sordid mess started back in February when the Orderly Room had that infamous weigh-in that nailed Jeanette Hoover and Ellen Andrews as fat girls. That same weigh-in caught Tom Ritchey who had been 20 pounds over weight at the time. Tom had just been promoted to Tech in January, and was waiting for his line number to come up. Capt O'Rourk put him on the Weight Management Program (WM P), but told him the action wouldn't affect his promotion. He would still get the stripe--he just couldn't sew it on while he was on the program.

Tom was required to lose five pounds per month and he did well in March and April, losing seven and eight pounds respectively. Then in May, he slipped up and only lost four. Capt O'Rourk called him in, counseled him, and placed him on the Control Roster.[26] The Captain had lots of options he could have chosen, but he chose this one--the strongest possible. O'Rourk told Tom once again that his promotion wasn't in jeopardy, that the Control Roster action was taken "just so we can keep a closer eye on your progress." That was a lie.

What Tom didn't know at the time was when your name goes on the Control Roster, it comes off the Promotion Roster--permanently. This all took place in the privacy of Capt O'Rourk's office, so the only people who knew about it was him and Tom Ritchey. Tom's supervisor wasn't even notified. Shame on O'Rourk.

Time marches on. Tom continues to lose more than five pounds per month until he comes off the program in July. But he didn't stop

---

[26] Promotion Rosters are good; Control Rosters are not. A person is placed on the Control Roster for doing bad things. While on this Roster, bad guys are monitored very closely. If they screw up again, they are nailed. Being on the Control Roster is like walking on egg shells.

there. He continued to diet and exercise until he lost almost 50 pounds! He never told anyone about the Control Roster action and just waited around for his line number to come up. Finally, the message came in saying, "Promote line numbers 5,399 through 6,294" and Tom sewed on the Tech stripes (his number was 6,154).

When the Personnel Office broke the news to Tom last Thursday that he was still a Staff Sergeant, he thought there must have been some kind of monstrous administrative SNAFU. He came back to work and told MSgt DAL Lawler (his supervisor) what had happened and DAL brought the story to me. We did a little checking around in the Reg that covers Control Rosters and, sure enough, there it was in black and white; if someone is awaiting promotion and is placed on the Control Roster, their name is "red lined" on the Promotion Roster. I got sick at my stomach.

Before the day was out, I had briefed everybody in the unit who could possibly help turn this hideous miscarriage of justice around: Majors Weber and Reardon, Col Lucas, and Capt Oakley. They all agreed that it would be a tough, up-hill battle, but we had to make every effort to get Tom Ritchey's promotion back.

Wednesday, November 18

Boy, it sure feels lousy out. I've got a major league case of the galloping Korean crud and it just won't go away. And the weather doesn't help matters either--dark, overcast, windy, misty rain, bitterly cold. Actually, it's only about 32 degrees, but it cuts right through to the bone.

Went to the NCO Club for brunch last Sunday and bumped into our new First Sergeant, SMSgt Jimbo Gambill. He invited me to his table and we talked about SKIVVY NINE and its problems and how we could work together to solve them. We also talked at great length about the old Orderly Room crew (O'Rourk, Duckworth, et al) and how screwed up they were. I told him some of the horror stories and he agreed that the situation had not been good in the past. But he promised not to let it get that way again. He'll work closely with Bob Estep and me on all people problems and consult us before taking any disciplinary action. He said he wouldn't mother coddle anyone, but he wouldn't slam dunk everyone that slips up a little either. Fair enough.

Before I realized it, we had been talking for two hours. I told Jimbo I had Christmas shopping to do and he asked if he could tag along for the company and to learn the ropes in the big city. He hasn't been here long enough to make a trip down town. I said sure.

We spent the afternoon rambling through back alleys and shops. I showed him where to get eel skin catalogues, the best place to by sneakers, polo shirts, and luggage, and what was a good buy and what wasn't. Every now and then, we'd take a break in a Country & Western Lounge, listen to some sweet sounds, rest up, and warm up. (Jimbo is a black guy, but he really likes C&W). Then back out on the streets for some more heavy duty shopping. I finally ran out of money around six o'clock, so we called it a day. He may be pulling the wool over my eyes, but so far, Jimbo seems like a pretty good guy, a very nice contrast to the old First Shirt. I sure hope he doesn't bust my bubble.

One of the things that surfaced during our bullshit sessions was the straight skinny on the Tom Ritchey (the guy who thought he was promoted but wasn't) fiasco. Turns out that when Tom was placed on the Control Roster, it was his second time on the Weight Management Program. The first time (last fall), he failed to progress three months in a row.

First time: Verbal counseling with a Memo for Record.

Second time: Letter of Counseling.

Third time: Letter of Reprimand with a statement that if he busted the program again, he would be placed on the Control Roster.

He got his act together, lost the required weight, was taken off the program, and placed on one year probation. When he was weighed in February, he was put back on the program and should have been placed on the Control Roster then. For whatever reason, he wasn't. When he was busted again, O'Rourk nailed him. Fair enough. So this reduction in grade will stand. Sad, but at least he wasn't screwed over the way I thought he was.

Tuesday morning was the third one of the month which meant time for the Chief's Group Breakfast followed by the monthly SKIVVY NINE Senior NCO Council meeting. What a way to start the day! Col Jim Michaud, the 51st Tac Fighter Wing Commander, has started attending all the Chief's Group Breakfasts to keep us up to speed on what's going on around the base.

The hottest topics this meeting, of course, were what's happening with the dorm situation and the fate of the hooch bars (i.e. SKIVVY NINE Lounge). The dorm thing is still up in the air, but the bottom line seems to be doubling up won't be as extensive as we had originally thought. It looks like Techs and Masters will escape, but the Staffs will just have to suck it in. Col Michaud said the plan for managing the hooch bars was still to put them under MWR and AAFES except for one--the SKIVVY NINE Lounge. That revelation caught everyone (including me) by complete surprise.

All the other Chiefs went immediately on the attack demanding to know how the 6903rd had escaped the wrath of MWR and AAFES while *their* hooch bars will still be gobbled up. Col Michaud said ours was the only one whose skirts were semi-clean; we had a charter, we kept immaculate books, we funneled *all* our profits into worthy projects, and we could stand scrutiny of any auditor who might want to inspect us. Seems Col Lucas, Maj

Reardon, and CTC1 (Sea Sergeant) Gerry Wise (the Lounge manager) pled our case one last time while I was on leave and Michaud bought it. So while the lounge is closed up tighter than Dick's hatband while the PACAF IG Team is here (no use waving a red flag at a bull), when they leave, the Lounge will re-open, unchanged, in all its former glory.

From the Chief's Group Breakfast, I went to the SKIVVY NINE SENCO meeting. It was already underway when I arrived and Col Lucas was ranting and raving about the lack of ticket sales for Saturday night's Dining Out[27]. He was expecting to have 300 people attend the function, but as of yesterday morning, only 126 tickets had been sold. The Colonel allowed as how it was a disgrace that there was so little support for this gala affair and said it was up to us, the Senior NCOs, to convince the average two and three striper to buy tickets. I wasn't real surprised that tickets weren't exactly going like hot cakes. Tickets are $14 per person. That's a little steep for an E-3 or E-4. Anyway, Col Lucas challenged each Senior NCO to sell five tickets between then and close of business Thursday (the last day for ticket sales). Everyone marched up to MSgt Earl Romano (chief potentate for ticket sales) and got their five tickets.

That afternoon and today, I button-holed every two and three striper that came within six feet of me and didn't sell one ticket. I figured everyone else was having the same kind of luck, but when I talked to Earl this afternoon, the guest count was up to almost 250. I don't know what the rest of those dudes are doing to sell tickets, but then again, I probably don't want to know. Gawd only knows what this will do to morale. It'll either sink lower (if that's possible) because these kids were forced to go to the event, or it will go sky high because they had a good time (Dinings Out really are fun). We'll see.

---

[27] A "black tie" affair that pokes fun at black tie affairs. See the Glossary of Terms for more details.

Sunday, November 22nd

The performance report problem is looking a little rosier. We haven't had a late one since the Major got his Letter of Reprimand. But it hasn't been completely painless. I have to watch the whole thing like a hawk. I had Joe Del Ricco build a display that shows the exact status of where we are on APRs. I've given marching orders to the Branch Chiefs that every time they walk through Ops Admin area (and each of them does at least two or three times a day) they are to check the wall display to see if they have an APR coming due in the next day or so. But even with this seeming fool-proof system, there are still screw-ups.

Around lunch time every day, I have Del Ricco report to me with any APRs that are due to him the next day. In most cases, he's already received them but, occasionally, there's a supervisor who still hasn't made good on the suspense. When that happens, I go to the duty section and look up the guy or gal and ask what the status of the report is. Sometimes, there's a rough draft, sometimes it's partially finished, and on a couple of occasions, they haven't even started writing the damn thing yet. No matter what stage of development the APR is in, my orders to the supervisor is the same: they don't leave work that day until it's finished. And the Branch Chief stays with them to make sure it gets done. Not a very popular policy, but if that's what it takes, that's what it takes.

If the tardy APR happens to be coming out of the day shop, the supervisor/Branch Chief get pretty pissed off. But if the offender is a shift worker, they *really* get pissed. To a shift worker, their off duty time is sacred and not to be tampered with (and I was the same way when I was a shift worker). That not withstanding, if there's an APR due from someone on Charlie Flight and Charlie Flight is on break, I have the Chief of Ops Production call that someone in to write the APR. You talk about rip shit! But they do it because I say do it.

On the positive side, the word is starting to get around; the Old Gray-Haired Chief is a pretty nice guy most of the time, but he's a real son-of-a-bitch when it comes to late APRs. As a result, I'm having to be a prick less and less because they're starting to realize I mean business and they're getting them in on time.

♦♦♦♦♦♦♦♦♦

I finally got around to having the Come to Jesus meeting concerning bringing SSgt Ruby "The Viper" Irons out of Ops Production and putting her in Ops Admin. It caused such a rippit that I decided to hold out just a little longer to see if Del Ricco can get a handle on things.

Maybe the picture I painted of him earlier was a little uglier than he really is. Joe's not a bad guy; he's just a little slow on the up-take. His section is grossly undermanned, he works hard, he means well, but he's just not bright enough (or creative enough) to address problems head-on and make them go away. Maybe now that I've pointed him in the right direction and gave him a kick in the ass to get him going, he might be OK. But believe me, I'll be looking over his shoulder every step of the way making sure everything is still on track.

♦♦♦♦♦♦♦♦♦

Friday afternoon, Maj Weber held the Ops Staff Meeting at one of the Chinese restaurants down town. He calls them "working lunches" and it's the third we've had since I've been here.

The theory is to get all the Branch Chiefs together in a relaxed atmosphere for some good food, a couple of brewskies, and some frank, open discussions about any problems we may be having. Believe it or not, the theory works and we usually get a lot accomplished. Everyone is in civilian clothes (no visible rank showing), in a social environment, with no time constraints, so things often get down and dirty. Friday was no exception.

The big topics were the Gestapo tactics employed by our Computer Resources Branch (DOY), the continuing rift between Ops Production (primarily 202s and 207s) and Flight Operations (exclusively 208s), and the projected severe shortage of 208s we're facing later this year. This is how it came down.

> DOY was the only Operations Branch rated MARGINAL during the IG inspection. One of their major problems was a lack of accountability for computer programs and equipment in the unit. In other words, they didn't know where their shit was.
>
> Another biggie was their inability to show the amount of time the computers are being used. The computers and programs are located all over the unit, but DOY has the overall responsibility of knowing where the stuff is and how often it's used. Since the inspection, DOY has been doing no-notice mini-inspections. If a piece of equipment has been moved or people aren't using the usage logs when they sit down at a terminal, the DOY people leap dead in the Branch Chief's shit.
>
> The Branch Chiefs feel like DOY are a bunch of bullies intent on making their lives miserable. DOY feels like they're under the gun to get ready for their re-inspection and the Branch Chiefs aren't cooperative and will cause them to go TANGO UNIFORM again. There was a lot of discussion on this one (yelling and screaming, actually), but the bottom line from the Major was this:
>
> DOY has got a job to do and we want it done! But they can do that job with a little finesse, tact, and diplomacy, not like a bull in a China shop. On the other hand, they're under a

lot of pressure to get ready and the Branch Chiefs will cooperate with them *in every possible way* to make sure their stuff is nice when the IG returns. Case closed.

The rift between Operations Production (DOF) and Flight Operations (DOR) wasn't that easy because it has several deep-rooted, long-standing, ingrained causes.

CAUSE 1: Linguists (208s) have always tended to feel intellectually superior to Analysts (202s) and Morse Operators (207s). Since DOR is exclusively 208s, they have an inherent disrespect for the "dummies" who work in DOF. On the other hand, the 202s and 207s look upon 208s as self-righteous, pompous, arrogant, prima-donnas, which is also misguided prejudice.

CAUSE 2: 202/7/8s are supposed to work as a team. But DOF is located in one building and DOR is in another and the only communication link between them is a secure telephone. To further compound the situation, DOF works a different shift schedule than DOR, so people in both Branches never work with the same guys on a day-to-day basis. As you may imagine, this set-up is not conducive to a spirit of teamwork.

CAUSE 3: In the overall scheme of things, the Surveillance and Warning Center Supervisor (a 202) is in charge of everything and everybody while he is on duty. This is awfully hard for a 208 to swallow--"How dare a lowly 202 tell *me* what to do."

Wednesday afternoon, all three of these conditions came together to create an intolerable situation. During a hot, fast-breaking activity, the S&W Supervisor called up the Ground Mission Supervisor (his counterpart in DOR) and directed him to do something. The GMS disagreed with the

S&W Supe's decision and refused to react. Since they were both Master Sergeants, neither would accept an order from the other. To break the impasse, they both called Maj Weber on the secure phone to plead their case like a pair of bickering siblings arguing over a toy. All this while a potential operational emergency was on-going and nothing was being done about it. Not good!

During the working lunch, Maj Weber and I allowed the DOF and DOR Branch Chiefs to yell and scream and flail their arms and beat their chests and vent their spleens. Then we put out the bottom line(s):

BOTTOM LINE 1: There's no way we can force 202/7/8s to love and respect one another. We can't legislate feelings. But we *can* demand all concerned to act like professional military men and women. If they don't, heads will roll.

BOTTOM LINE 2: The different shift schedule/ different building thing is being worked. In fact, that was my number one priority when I came here to be the Ops Supe: get DOF and DOR under one roof, working one schedule, to become one team.

That philosophy has met with a lot of resistance, both here (primarily in DOR) and at the headquarters, which is one of the reasons I visited there in October. But the consolidation *will* take place. It was supposed to occur in February of next year, but the move was rolled back to October because the equipment can't be installed until then. Until the consolidation happens, we'll do the best we can with a bad situation.

BOTTOM LINE 3: Maj Weber made it perfectly clear to all concerned that, no matter what else happens, the S&W Supe *must* be in charge. If he gives an order, it will be carried out, even of the GMS (or anyone else) disagrees. On the other hand, the S&W Supe will not have a dictatorial attitude and will treat everyone with respect. After the smoke clears, a complete investigation will be conducted and, if it turns out the S&W Supe was in error, he'll be dealt with. But in the heat of battle, he has to be in control and everyone else must react accordingly. Case closed.

Having laid down the law on that issue, we moved on to the projected shortage of 208s later this year. This problem didn't have a solution, at least not at our level. We've got to depend on the Personnel folks back at the Headquarters to get us the bodies we need to perform our mission. But even if that happens, the training time for the new people coming in is so extensive that we won't have enough trainers to do the job. So the reality is we're going to be undermanned for the foreseeable future and we've got to find a way to deal with our dilemma smartly.

It was a painful decision, but everyone agreed that the day shops will have to be the ones to suffer the impact of short manning, not DOR or DOF. I've got to give the day shop Branch Chiefs a lot of credit on this one. They acted like big boys, swallowed their medicine, and agreed to suck it up until times get better.

♦♦♦♦♦♦♦♦♦

After the working lunch, it was back to my quarters to do some calligraphy work on the place cards for the Dining Out. The final count of attendees was 269 and I had to do a place card for each person. It took an average of two minutes per card, which comes out to almost nine hours to get the job done. Around nine o'clock Friday night I finished the last one and called it a day.

♦♦♦♦♦♦♦♦♦

SKIVVY NINE!

Went to watch SKIVVY NINE's football team play for the base championship Saturday morning. Was there any doubt? We won 14-6. The team will now represent Osan Air Base in the Korea-wide Football Tournament. Hopefully, we'll do as well as we did in softball. By the way, the Football Championship put us over the top in points for the Commander's Trophy[28] for the fifth year in a row.

After the football game, I delivered the place cards to the NCO Club to be put on the tables for the Dining Out. I hadn't thought about a system to get the right cards to the right seat at the right table. To my surprise, it was a bitch--very time consuming. There were quite a few people in the club getting the place ready, so I commandeered some help. But even with the help, it took almost three hours to get all the place cards to the right place. We finished up just in time for me to get back to my dorm for a shower and get my mess dress on to make the Dining Out on time.

On the whole, the function was a success; lots of pomp and circumstances and symbolism. When it was all over, I did a little circulating through the crowd to get a feel for how the trench troops really felt about the program. To my amazement, the general consensus was that the whole affair was too formal and stuffed-shirt. There was also a lot of concern over being virtually forced to attend. Oh well, you do the best you can and let the chips fall where they may.

---

[28] Every Air Force base has a Commander's Trophy. It's usually huge and is awarded to the organization on base which has the best athletic teams over a given year. Points are awarded for first, second, third (and so forth) place finishes in league play. You amass the most points during the year, you get the trophy.

Chapter Eleven

AND THE BATTLE LINES ARE DRAWN

Sunday, November 29th

Burrrrrrrr!! The *real* Korean winter is finally here. Twelve degrees with a 20 mile-per-hour breeze to put the wind-chill factor somewhere down around 18-20 below zero. I repeat: Burrrrrrrr!!!

Lets start off this entry with the good news. The Base Commander declared the Friday after Thanksgiving a down day (no work). This news hit Col Lucas pretty hard because it presented a BIG problem for him.

He's been preaching ever since he arrived that the 6903rd *is* going to be a part of this base. We *are* going to play in their exercises; we *are* going to participate in their recognition programs; we *will* help them with their clean-up details; we *will* attend their social functions. We *are* going to do everything they do!

After all that, when Col McDonald gave the base Friday off, Col Lucas was placed in a very interesting predicament. He didn't want to give SKIVVY NINE a day off, but he had to live up to his commitment to do everything with the rest of the base. After a lot of soul searching, he decided he *had* to give us the day off. But he waited until three o'clock Wednesday afternoon to announce his decision.

♦♦♦♦♦♦♦♦♦

Wednesday was a real ball buster. It started at 3:00 a.m. with a runner beating on my door to announce that there was a general recall and I was to report to work. The recall kicked off at 2:30, but it took thirty minutes to get word to me because I don't have a beeper anymore. By the time I got dressed, picked up SMSgt Brian Decker (one of my helpers in the Operations Sub-control Center), and drove to work, it was 3:35, over an hour after the exercise kicked off. Not good.

Overall, the exercise went pretty well, but one of the shortcomings identified in the post-exercise debrief was the Ops Supe's late arrival. Col Lucas had an instant fix: he turned to Maj Reardon and instructed him to turn his beeper over to me. This did not set well with Maj Reardon; after all, he *is* the Deputy Commander. But the Commander decided it was more important for the Ops Supe to respond to an emergency than it was for the Deputy Commander. Ergo, I got the beeper.

After the exercise, the rest of the day was a real wall-pinger and mostly a blur. But the biggie was SSgt Clarance Butler's APR. It was late and Lt Lane sent me a note directing me to write a letter of justification outlining why it was late. The letter below is my response to her tasking.

I thought it was a pretty good little letter showing exactly why the report was late, but in the Command Section, they didn't see it that way. Two parts of the letter gave them some real heartburn: paragraph 2e, where I pointed out that they had held the APR for six days; and paragraph 4 where I suggested a one day turn-around. Lt Lane went absolutely bug fuck when she got my letter and immediately ran to Col Lucas demanding my head on a platter. She got it.

FM: 6903 ESG/DO *25 November*

SUBJ: Late APR, SSgt Clarance Butler

TO: 6903 ESG/CC

1. Try as hard as we may to ensure all Airman Performance Reports meet suspenses, sometimes our efforts are overcome by events--in other words, the APR is "snake bit". That is the case with this one; everything that could go wrong, did.

2. Following is a chronology of events for this troublesome report:

a.	*10 Nov:*	*APR arrives in DOE from DOF. Good job; suspense met.*
b.	*12 Nov:*	*Errors identified in report; returned to DOF for corrections.*
c.	*16 Nov:*	*APR sent back to DOE from DOF with corrections made.*
d.	*17 Nov:*	*Forwarded to Command Section for CC signature.*
e.	*20 Nov:*	*Suspense for DOE to have the APR to the Orderly Room comes and goes. The APR is now officially late.*
f.	*23 Nov:*	*Command Section finds minor errors, returns APR to DOE.*
g.	*23 Nov:*	*DOE passes the report on to DOF.*
h.	*24 Nov:*	*APR arrives back in DOE, but <u>one</u> typo is discovered. Back to DOF!*
i.	*25 Nov:*	*Once again, the APR comes back to DOE and, once again, <u>one</u> typo is found. Report returned to DOF for correction where it languishes even as this letter is being written.*

3. As you can see from the above, everyone who handles APRs must do so in a more timely manner. DOE held the report for two days before returning it to DOF for error correction the first time--too long. DOF waited four days before making the correction--way too long. And the Command Section held it for six days before returning it to DOE--waaaaaay to long. If every office that handled this report had done so on a "one day turn-around" basis, it would have made it to the Orderly Room by the 20 November suspense date despite the numerous corrections.

4. We in DO plan to shoot for a one day turn-around on all APRs received from other offices. We sincerely hope this goal can be adopted in the Command Section.

T. WYMAN BEAL, CMSgt, USAF
Operations Superintendent

At 5 p.m., Col Lucas called Maj Weber and said he wanted to see the Major and me in his office immediately. When we arrived, he closed the door and proceeded to chew my ass like a bulldog on an old shoe. I wanted desperately to fire back on him, bit I kept my Chief's Rule Number One firmly in mind: "When Chiefs and Colonels fight, Chiefs lose"[29]. So I bit my lip and took it.

He accused me of harassing Lt Lane and trying to start a pissing contest with her. He also said he took the letter as a "personal affront" (his very words) to himself. I said it wasn't intended to be. I was just trying to point out the reason the APR was late. He didn't buy that even a little bit. He said if I *ever* wrote another inflammatory letter to his Executive Officer, he would have my ass. I thought, "Holy shit! After what he's giving me now, what does he consider 'having my ass'?"

I left the Colonel's office in a daze. Boy, what a shock that was! I definitely *did not* expect that letter to get *that* kind of reaction!

[29] The philosophy I live by. That philosophy is a list of five rules I think one must follow to be a successful Chief Master Sergeant. Rule one is stated above; to see the full list, go to the Glossary of Terms.

But I guess it established in no uncertain terms where the Colonel and I stand. Now there's no mystery, and I guess that's a good thing.

Back in my office behind closed doors, I told Majors Reardon and Weber that for the next four months, I'll be a good little boy, but don't expect any flashes of brilliance from me. In front of the troops, I'll continue to be the model Chief, but behind the scenes, I'm just waiting out my time and counting the days. They both understand and empathize with my feelings.

After the ass chewing session, I dragged what was left of my buns back to my dorm and got into some civvies. Although the day had begun at 3:00 a.m., there were still a lot of things I had to do. First on the list was the grand re-opening of the SKIVVY NINE Lounge.

The PACAF IG Team finally got out of Dodge, so I guess things are pretty much back to normal, Lounge-wise. Everyone was in a real party mood; the Lounge had been closed for three weeks and the word was out that the unit was going to get to keep it and operate it just like always with no MWR or AAFES interference.

Around nine o'clock, we started cooking Thanksgiving dinner. Several of us had kicked in a couple of bucks each to buy the food and Danny Zeller and Boomer Marshall put together a crew of cooks and bottlewashers to prepare it. We had four turkeys, a ham, Earl Romano kicked in a duck (not a clue where he came up with a duck) and all the usual trimmings just kinda showed up. I'm no cook, but they needed all the hands they could get to chop celery, peel onions, and break bread for the stuffing. So I pitched in and did what I could.

Up Thanksgiving morning at 10:30. Maj Weber came by at around 11:30 so we could put in some face time with the troops, wish them a happy Thanksgiving, and make sure they were getting properly fed. We no sooner walked in the door of the S&W Center when all hell broke loose. It was just as well we went in when we did; we would have been called in anyway.

Without going into painful detail, suffice to say we were jumping through our knickers for the next hour or so. Ended up calling in Col Lucas, Col Short (6th Tactical Intelligence Group Commander) and Col Hibbert (7th Air Force Ops Officer). By the time the smoke cleared, it was after one o'clock and we still hadn't visited everyone we should. So we said 'bye to the guys and gals in the S&W Center (their Thanksgiving dinners were still in their styrofoam containers, cold as January) and walked around to see everyone else. We hung around until about two o'clock when the swing shift came in so we could say hiddy to them, too.

From Ops, it was back to my room to get out of my uniform and into civvies. Dropped by the Lounge to sample the food Boomer and crew had stayed up all night to prepare. For something that was thrown together by a bunch of know-nothing whiffle balls, it was delicious. Everything but Earl Romano's duck--I guess its an acquired taste. The place was pretty well packed with folks who didn't want to go to the dreary chow hall and didn't have anywhere else to go.

Went back to my room around 6:00 p.m. and laid down for a short nap. The reason for the nap was the impending arrival of Chief Master Sergeant Buford Thompson, the Ops Supe at the 6924th Electronic Security Squadron in Hawaii. He was due to arrive at 11:30 p.m. and I had to be there to meet him.

Buford sent me a message a couple of weeks ago asking if I minded if he came over for an orientation visit (which translates to "Christmas shopping" at this time of year). I sent him a message back to come on down and told him I would be his host. Soon as I answered Buford's message, I hot-footed it down to the billeting office to make reservations for a Chief's suite[30].

The guys in the billeting office almost laughed in my face. Not only were there no Chief suites, there's *nothing* to be had on base and contract quarters down town are almost all gone. The reason for the billeting crunch is there are over 400 people coming into Osan today for an Exercise TEAM SPIRIT[31] planning conference. I ended up getting him a place down town, but it was a real pain in the ass.

Tomorrow night, I have a repeat performance. A crew of three from the ESC Headquarters Reserve Affairs Office is coming over for a Staff Assistance Visit which, at this time of year, also translates to "Christmas shopping". They had the gall to ask me to meet them in Seoul and drive them down to Osan, but I told them to piss up a rope--nicely. So they'll ride a bus, or taxi, or whatever down here like everyday people. That may sound a little tough, but I'll be damned if I'm going to give the red carpet treatment to every Tom, Dick, and Harry coming over here to do their Christmas shopping. But I'll still go to the billeting office in the middle of the night and wait around for them to arrive and get them a place to stay. Woe is me.

And it's not just the 03rd that gets all these visitors this time of year. Every unit on base has the same problem. It's so bad people stationed here can hardly get to the Post Office for all the visitors standing in line to send those super inexpensive Christmas gifts back home. It's almost criminal.

---

[30] Special transient quarters set aside for visiting Chief Master Sergeants. See Glossary of terms for more details.

[31] A three week "mock war" held every year in March to test how well U.S. and Korean forces work together. A lot of planning goes into the exercise because literally thousands of U.S. troops are airlifted into Korea every year to participate.

Wednesday, December 2nd

Gawd is it ever cold! Today was *really* miserable. This morning when I went to work, it was nine degrees. By two o'clock, it had warmed all the way up to 22--the high for the day. The really disconcerting thing is the old timers who say the worst is yet to come. They keep saying, "Just you wait 'till January, Big Boy. That's when the real shit hits the fan." I can hardly wait.

This week has been absolute bedlam; visitors coming out the wazoo!! There are four Chiefs visiting the 6903rd this week. Between Bob Estep and me, there was no way we could host them all, so I farmed them out to other Senior NCOs. If the Chiefs get their feelings hurt because they're not being hosted by another Chief, tough shit. They're all over here on tennis shoe runs[32] anyway, so I'm not feeling too bad about not exactly busting my ass to make them feel at home.

Buford Thompson didn't even make any bones about it; he openly admitted he was on a shopping trip. He arrived at 11:30 p.m. (it was almost one o'clock before I got him bedded down), spent all day the next day shopping, had me give him a guided tour of Operations the morning of the second day, and took the rest of the day off to do more shopping. The next day of his visit, he didn't even make an attempt to contact me and left the next day to return to Hawaii. Now that's a hard working TDY.

The group from Reserve Affairs was even worse. They arrived Monday night about the same time Buford did the night before and, once again, it was well after midnight before I got them to their hotel. Naturally, I was at work the next morning at six o'clock, but the folks from the Headquarters took a sleep-in and didn't come in

---

[32] Since Nikes, Adidas, LA Gear, etc are some of the most popular items purchased by visitors, the term "tennis shoe run" is applied to any visit to Korea where shopping is the sole purpose.

'till noon. When they got there, I spent the remainder of the day giving them a tour of Operations. And while I was tour guiding, the blue slips from the Command Section just kept on coming. I worked until almost nine o'clock last night just to get them cleared up.

Today, the Reserve Affairs folks started around nine o'clock inspecting the way I was handling the Air Force Reservists assigned to SKIVVY NINE. They finished up around three o'clock this afternoon, which leaves the whole day free tomorrow to squeeze in a little shopping before they leave Friday. Add it all up and it comes to three people traveling from the States to Korea for a four day visit to look at one not-shit program. Sometimes, I really can't believe people actually have the cajonies to pull that kind of stunt.

Sunday, December 5th

The APR issue continues to be my number one priority and causes me the most heartache and grief. I've almost got the problem licked, but I'm not quite there yet.

Went to the Commander's Staff Meeting Thursday morning and, for the first time since I've been here, there were NO entries on the Operations portion of the Late APR Slide. Maintenance and Admin had one, but for Ops, it was a big zero. Bit it didn't come easy; I stayed at work with Joe Del Ricco Wednesday night until 6:30 wrapping up three APRs that were due that day. If we didn't get them turned in to the Orderly Room that night, they would show up on the slide Thursday morning.

I called Capt Oakley at 4:30 (normal end of the duty day) and told him the APRs were on the way. He said he would wait in the Orderly Room until I delivered them, no matter how long it took. That's the kind of cooperation I've been getting from the Orderly Room under the Oakley/Gambill administration.

Del Ricco got everything finished, called people in from off duty time to sign the reports, and I delivered them at almost 7 p.m. It was a lot of jumping through hoops, but well worth it to see a blank slide the next morning.

It's hard to believe that when I first got here, it took two slides to show the Operations Late APR List. Naturally, I felt pretty good about my involvement in shrinking that list down to zero, but all that came crashing down around noon Thursday.

I had been out all morning helping baby-sit a visitor and, when I got back to my office, Del Ricco was fit to be tied. He had received a stack of APR computer rips from the Orderly Room that morning (4 December) and almost half of them had deadlines for the finished APRs to be back to the Orderly Room by 8 or 9 December. It was another case of the rips being printed in the Personnel Office back in early November and the distribution system taking over a month to get them to us.

I had had a deal with the APR Section in the Personnel Office where they would give automatic 15-day extensions on rips like these. But the deal went sour when the Section Chief I struck the agreement with went away and a flaming ass-hole took her place. So I had to turn elsewhere for help. That elsewhere was the Orderly Room.

The short deadline thing happens all the time, but since Oakley/Gambill came on board, it's been a simple matter of calling the Orderly Room and getting a 5-6 day extension. That's the only way we've been able to keep our collective heads above water. But when Del Ricco called for an extension Thursday morning, the APR Monitor refused to give him one. She said she was turning him down on the orders of Capt Oakley. Considering how cooperative he had been, I couldn't believe he would do that. Maj Weber and I jumped in the truck and headed for the Orderly Room to find out what the hell was going on.

We walked into Capt Oakley's office breathing fire and he knew why we were there. We weren't even into his office good when he came from behind his desk holding a piece of paper in front of himself at arm's length like a shield. "My hands are tied, Fellas. There's nothing I can do."

The piece of paper was a note from Col Lucas to Capt Oakley saying he was not to give extensions on suspenses for Operations APRs. No other division was mentioned in the note--just Ops. Gawd, it's great to be loved! The Colonel's bottom line was, "No extensions--no excuses." I knew my letter to the Exec had pissed the Colonel off, but I couldn't believe the vindictive son-of-a-bitch would resort to this kind of below-the-belt cheap shot.

Capt Oakley was apologetic as hell, but he said he couldn't go against a written order from the Commander and give us the extensions we so desperately needed. I couldn't blame him; I would probably do the same thing.

Maj Weber and I headed straight to see Col Lucas. Fortunately for us, he was tied up with some visiting General and we couldn't get an audience with him until three o'clock that afternoon. If we had gotten in to see him right then, there's no telling what kind of asses we'd have made of ourselves. We were definitely two pissed off puppies.

The wait gave us time to cool down and decide exactly what we were going to say to the good Colonel. While we waited for our appointment with his imminence, I couldn't sit still. I don't know how many miles I put on my office floor and by the time we went to the Command Section, my stomach felt like it was tied in a knot. For once, I used a little common sense and told the Major do the talking. He wasn't quite as emotionally fired up as I was--or at least he didn't show it.

SKIVVY NINE!

Col Lucas let us cool our heels in his outer office before calling us in. Maj Weber and I knew exactly what he was doing; he was showing us who was the boss even before we went in.

When we finally did get in, the Major was calm, cool, and collected. But he didn't waste any time beating around the bush. He told Col Lucas right up front that if he made his "no extensions--no excuses" policy stick, he might as well fire both of us right now. There was no way we could meet 4-5 day deadlines on APRs and there was no reason to try when we knew we were doomed to failure. The Colonel was unmoved.

I finally broke my silence. I was very respectful and didn't raise my voice, but the Colonel knew I was giving him the no bullshit facts. I told him we had been doing the best job we possibly could do, and even with the good cooperation we had been getting from the Orderly Room, we were just squeezing by. If he didn't rescind his "no extensions-no excuses" policy, he was setting the Major and me up for failure. I continued that he may as well get a new Ops Supe now because this one wasn't going to get himself in such a tizzy that he ended up going back to the States the way CMSgt Randy Smally did--air evaced out with a heart attack.

I reasoned that since I was in a no win situation, why bother to try to win. The result would be the same either way. So, that being the case, I'd just sit back and let the chips fall where they may. If the APRs were on time, fine. If they were late, that'd be fine, too. I tried not to sound like I was giving him an ultimatum. I just wanted him to know I was fed up and it was time to either get me the hell out of here or give me the tools to do my job and stay the hell out of my fecal matter.

Col Lucas took a few seconds to mull over what Maj Weber and I had said. Finally, he said he knew we had been working hard to fix the APR problem, but he felt like getting the extensions made our program look like it was healthier than it actually was. He felt getting extensions was an artificial fix. Maj Weber said that may be true, but without those extensions, we were dead meat.

The Colonel was now in a very difficult position; he could either fire his Ops Officer and Ops Supe on the spot or go back on his policy and lose face. Finally, he made the only decision he could make. He picked up the telephone, called Capt Oakley, and told him to tear up the note. He allowed the Captain to give us extensions, but only on those APRs where we had been given less than a 10-day deadline. Maj Weber and I said that was fair enough; getting APRs rammed through the system was damned hard, but it *could* be done in 10 days. That's all we wanted--a chance to succeed.

When we left Col Lucas' office, I was emotionally drained. I had broken Chief Beal's Rule Number One: "When Chiefs and Colonels fight, Chiefs lose." Maybe I should amend the rule to read, "When Chiefs and Colonels fight, Chiefs lose--except when the Chief is in the right."

After all the turmoil on Thursday, Friday was really a laid back day. No crises, no jumping through my knickers, no career-ending stand-offs. For a change, I got out of work at a reasonable hour. There was an NCO Prep Course graduation at three o'clock, a Hail and Farewell party at four, and a celebration party for the Football Team for winning the Base Championship at five. Then there was a Bean Run for Kenneth Flaharty at seven. He's one of our best troops, so I made an appearance at that. All in all, a *much* better day than Thursday.

Wednesday, December 9th

Major Weber is in Hawaii this week to attend the Pacific Electronic Security Division Operations Officer Conference, so I've pretty much got it by myself. Capt Jean Henke (Chief of Ops Production) is "officially" in charge. She's a nice lady, but she's not up to speed on how to be an Ops Officer. But I don't mind. Her heart's in the right place, she's not an ass-hole, so I give her all the help I can. Together, we're muddling through.

For this place to suck as bad as it does on duty, off duty is great and getting better. Last Saturday night was a good example. I went to Boomer Marshall's place in Air Force Village to attend my first muster (meeting) of the 69th Carrier Task Group (CTG).

The 69th CTG is the brainchild of TSgt Danny Zeller, SSgt Steve Morgan, and Sgt Gary Bertram. They hatched the idea while in a drunken stupor watching "Top Gun" for the fifteenth time on the SKIVVY NINE Lounge's vide system.

Ever since the Lounge got its copy of "Top Gun", it's been on the monitors constantly. The Lounge has over 250 video tapes available for viewing, but "Top Gun" is the movie of choice. Some of the Lounge Lizards have seen it so many times they can recite lines simultaneously with the actors. And every time one of the more popular songs in the movie comes on ("Great Balls of Fire, "You've Lost that Loving Feeling", "Take My Breath Away", etc.) *everybody* sings along. It was in this atmosphere of Top Gun Mania that the 69th CTG was born.

The original concept of the CTG was simple. Danny elected himself commander, then appointed Steve as his Executive Officer (XO) and Gary the Master at Arms (MA). Having established their chain of command, the threesome headed for the 'ville to get "uniforms" and perform their first operational mission.

The uniform consisted of a black baseball cap with "TOP GUN" embroidered on the front in white letters embellished by red wings on each side of the letters. Each man's position within the group (Commander, XO, and MA) was placed on the right side of the cap and their aircraft callsign (Z-Man 69, Sky Hawk 69, and Bull Dog 69 respectively) on the other. The entire ensemble was topped off by placing "chicken shit" on the visor of each cap. All this was done on magic sewing machines by super-talented Korean tailors while the drunken trio waited.

From the tailor shop, they headed for the Stereo Club. The disk jockeys in most clubs take requests, so Danny worked his way to the DJ booth and requested "Danger Zone" (the theme music from "Top Gun"). The request seemed a little strange to the DJ (after all, "Danger Zone" isn't one of his most requested numbers), but he shrugged his shoulders, found the record, and queued it up to play.

Soon, the driving drum beat that begins "Danger Zone" was booming from the huge speakers on each side of the Stereo Club's stage. The scantily dressed dancers on stage exchanged quizzical, almost dumbfounded looks ("What the hell is the DJ doing playing this stupid song?"), shrugged their shoulders ("What the hell-I can dance to *anything*), and began their stilted gyrations. But they had an even bigger surprise coming.

Z-Man 69 was first. He came flashing in from the side of the stage, did a diving belly-flop on the floor, and skidded (not-so-gracefully) between one of the dancer's wide-spread feet. She was still trying to figure out what had happened when Sky Hawk 69 went streaking between her legs. She was in the process of regaining her composure when Bull Dog 69 began his run for the third carrier landing. Unfortunately, Bull Dog 69 was slightly off the glide path. His shoulder caught the luckless dancer's left shin and the impact sent her ass-end-over-tea-kettle off the stage. When she came off the floor, she was one pissed off Korean lady. The Stereo Club bouncers weren't all that happy, either.

The bouncers and all three dancers pounced upon the CTG and soon they were on the sidewalk outside the Stereo Club licking their wounds and trying to regain their pride. Everything had not gone as planned, so the members of the CTG wandered back toward the base to regroup and plan strategy for their next mission. Such was the ignominious beginnings of the 69th Carrier Task Group.

Over the next couple of weeks, the CTG enjoyed more success by adopting the "hit and run" strategy. When they entered a club, they maintained a low profile, didn't bother to request "Danger Zone", waited for exactly the right moment, and came up from the carrier landings on the run--toward the door. Their exhibitions always drew loud roars of approval from the American clientele and groans of exasperation from the Korean management.

And they began to expand their ranks with an active recruiting program. Danny Z "rooms" with SSgt Janette Lynn and Steve Morgan does the same with SSgt Angie Monet, so they were enlisted as "The Lady's Auxiliary of the 69th Carrier Task Group". The women balked at the idea of wearing baseball caps, but they had to have "uniforms", so they had the Korean tailors make flight attendant-type headgear with the TOP GUN logo on them. Janette and Angie were close friends with A1C Rene' Chamberlain and has talked her into becoming the third member of the Lady's Auxiliary.

Meanwhile, additional members of the male persuasion were being brought into the ranks. Sgt Waco Williams (second banana in the Security Police Office), MSgt Jim Watts (remember him from the Jenny Burnell incident?), and MSgt Boomer Marshall (the unit's bona fide softball superhero and unabashed lady's man) became members of the CTG.

And at the same time, the Group began to gain some degree of legitimacy. It didn't take the Korean club owners long to realize their patrons loved the antics of the CTG and it didn't take the CTG long to figure out which clubs they would be welcomed/tolerated in and which ones where they would not. So they avoided the hostile clubs and did their carrier landings in the ones that were hospitable. And they became near legend.

CMSgt T. Wyman Beal

Last Wednesday, I was making my rounds when I stopped by Danny Zeller's desk to shoot the bull for a few minutes. I mentioned I had heard of his hearty band and he went on for a few minutes about how much fun the Group has together. Then, surprisingly, he asked if I wanted to join.

At first, I was a little hesitant--after all, I *am* the senior enlisted member of the 6903rd Electronic Security Group. How would people react to the old gray haired Chief doing carrier landings with this bunch of crazies? But I gave it some more thought that afternoon and dropped by Danny's desk on my way out the door and gave him a "thumbs up". What the hell--I'm entitled to a little fun, too.

So Danny called a muster (read party) of the 69th CTG for Saturday night at Boomer's place to induct its newest member--me. I stopped by Mike's Tailor Shop on my way to Boomer's and had my b-ball cap made. I chose "Senior Enlisted Advisor (SEA)" for my position in the Group and "El Jefe' 69" (Spanish for "The Chief") for my callsign and had them embroidered on the cap. Then I jumped a taxi for Air Force Village.

When I got to Boomer's, the joint was jumping. His stereo was spewing forth the soundtrack (naturally) from "Top Gun", the place was packed with people (mostly guests of members and CTG "wanna be's"), and Boomer was holding court at the barbecue grill on his patio even though the temperature was well below freezing. The smell told me we were having my favorite Mexican food, fajitas.

When Boomer announced that chow was ready, everyone lined up to dump some fajita meat on a tortilla, scoop pinto beans and rice onto their plates, and grab another beer. Good stuff!

After we ate, everybody gaggled up in the living room for my induction. The ceremony was simple. The centerpiece for the whole affair (besides me) was a little device called the snorkel[33]. Boomer brought the snorkel back from his mid-tour leave in the States about a month ago and, since then, it has become an icon of the 69th CTG.

With the crowd gathered in the living room, the CTG Commander called the newest member of the Group to the center of the floor. Danny Z said a few words welcoming me to this elite organization, then handed me the snorkel. I took it, shot it down, and handed the empty glass back to Danny. There was a polite round of applause, the stereo kicked in again, and that was it. I was a member of the 69th Carrier Task Group.

---

[33] A two ounce, hour glass shaped, shot glass used by pouring a "chaser" into the lower part of the contraption (one ounce) and the booze of choice (in the case of the CTG, Jim Beam) in the top half (one ounce). The design of the glass doesn't allow the liquids to mix, so the effect when you drink from the snorkel is a straight shot of Jim Beam followed immediately by the chaser. Repeated use of the snorkel will fuck you up in one hellava hurry.

Chapter Twelve

IT DON'T GET MUCH WORSE THAN THIS

Sunday, December 13th

The relationship between Col Lucas and me is very strained, but I'm trying to deal with it as best I can. I don't volunteer any information to him any more. If he asks for something, I give it to him. Nothing more; nothing less. I don't go see him unless he calls for me. I'm maintaining a professional appearing relationship with him, but suffice to say, we're not exactly buddy-buddy. Right now, I'm just trying to get through this thing one day at a time. Hellava situation when the relationship between the senior enlisted man and the senior officer in the unit degenerates to this.

But all is not bleak. IT'S CHRISTMAS PARTY TIME!! Every organization in the unit who's having a party has invited me. The grind started yesterday.

Flight Operations' Baker Flight (DORB) had their party starting at noon in the SKIVVY NINE Lounge. A lot of food; a lot of drink; a lot of people sitting around like knots on a log looking at one another. Booooooring!

About the only highlight was a video tape one of the guys on the flight made. DORB calls themselves "The Bastard Stepchildren of SKIVVY NINE" because so many of them seem to end up getting in trouble. They're not a bad bunch--it just seems they get more than their share of flake-o's. Remember Sgt Fred McNair and A1C Billy Nagle? Both were on Baker Flight. Their video tape centered around what a bunch of screw-ups they were and it was really well done. Pretty funny stuff, actually. But when the tape played, that was it. For all intents and purposes, the party was over. I stayed another 15-20 minutes and left.

Over the next 10 days, I have eleven more parties on my schedule with a couple of them taking place on the same day. I'm sure I'll enjoy some of them, but even if I didn't, I'd go to every one. I look at it as part of my job. If they think enough of me to invite me, then I feel obligated to go, even if it's just to put in an appearance for a few minutes and then leave. On the positive side, these things will keep me busy and I guess that's good.

Sunday, December 20th

The Christmas party grind is almost over. And that's just what it was--a grind. If I never see another piece of turkey or ham again, it'll be too soon.

Of all the functions I attended, the unit party last Monday night was the worst. It was a semi-formal affair (to suit Lt Lane) at the Hill 180 Club. I got to the party around 6:30 p.m., just in time for the cocktail hour. They weren't having a meal (thank God; no ham or turkey), just heavy hors 'd oeuvres. When they opened up the food tables, I had time to have one egg roll before Capt Jacoby called me over.

The Captain and I had been working on a special project since the previous Thursday. Capt Jacoby's maintenance guys had set up some electronic equipment for my Ops guys to use during the project. We talked about it late Thursday afternoon and he said he could have the equipment up and ready to go by the next morning if he had his people work all night. I told him that wouldn't be necessary. As long as the stuff was ready to go by sometime Monday morning so my guys could test everything, that would be fine.

As it turned out, the maintenance guys had to put in some horrendous hours anyway. They should have been done Friday, but they ran into some kind of technical problem and ended up working around the clock Saturday and Sunday to get everything ready to go. My folks went up to Hill 170 around one o'clock Monday afternoon, checked everything out, and were set to begin operations at 8:00 a.m. Tuesday morning. That start time was just about to get changed.

Col Lucas cornered Capt Jacoby at the party and asked what the status of the project was. The Captain told him the equipment was ready but, so far, the Ops people hadn't done anything with it. Lucas was furious! He told Jacoby he was scheduled to brief Lt Gen Reynolds (7th Air Force Commander) at seven o'clock the next morning and he was be damned if he was going in there and brief "the equipment is ready to go". He wanted operational results to brief to the General.

Lucas told Jacoby to tell me to have my people in place by 3:00 a.m. They were to give a full report to him at six o'clock so he could brief Reynolds at seven. Notice the Colonel told the Captain to tell me. He didn't come to me directly--guess that gives you an idea of where my stock is.

What all this meant was I had to leave the party and round up all the people involved in the project so I could give them the bad news. Kick-off time had been changed from 8:00 a.m. to 3:00 a.m. I went to my office, dug out the recall roster, and made phone calls to the ones who had phones. Four of them lived down town (no phones), so I dug out the maps and went off base to find them. All this took a little over two-and-a-half hours, but Col Lucas *would* have something to tell the General the next morning.

By the time I got back to the party, I was starving (hadn't had anything but an egg roll to eat since lunch), so I went to the hors 'd oeuvres table. It looked like it had been hit by a herd of vultures. There was absolutely nothing left to eat. Tickets to the party cost $12.00, so my meal turned out to be a twelve dollar egg roll. Believe me, it wasn't worth it.

On the brighter side, they had started holding a raffle just as I walked in the door and mine was the first name drawn. Since I came up first, I had my pick of all the prizes. There were some nice ones (the raffle prizes were what had driven the ticket prices so high), but I searched around under the Christmas tree until I found just the right prize. I picked a package of salami/cheese/crackers, took it to the bar, opened it, and snarffed it down on the spot. Raised a few eyebrows, but what the hell.

Got back to my room around ten o'clock and crashed hard. My beeper went off at 3:00 a.m. RECALL!!! Nice touch, eh. Have a recall the morning after the unit Christmas party. 'Tis the season to be jolly. After the last recall, Col Lucas announced that during the next one (this one) he was going to hold everybody in their duty sections (shift workers included, which really sucks) until every person in the unit was accounted for. It looked like it was going to be a long day for SKIVVY NINE.

We reached 90 percent present and accounted for within two hours of START-X. That's always been our goal, but since so many people live off base with no telephone, I didn't think we would ever make that goal. The best we've ever done until this recall was 65 percent at the two hour mark. In addition to so many people living off base, another contributing factor to the poor showing has been the whiffle balls living in the dorms either responding too slowly or (in some cases) farting the recall off all together. This time, I had a fix for that.

After Col Lucas announced he wouldn't end the next recall until everyone in the unit was present or accounted for, I picked out seven hard-ass Senior NCOs to be in the dorms when the next recall kicked off. Their job was to instill a sense of urgency in the dorm rats--in other words, kick ass, take names, and make sure *everyone* responded in a timely manner. They were with the Exercise

Evaluation Team when they went to the dorm and kept time on how long it took people to respond after the recall started.

If dorm residents weren't out of their rooms and on their way to work within 15 minutes after being notified, one of the seven "enforcers" went to the door, knocked again, and told them they had five more minutes. That seemed to work in most cases, but there were still the stubborn few. For those, the First Sergeant used his pass key and he or an enforcer went into rooms to forcibly get them on the stick. Also, those names were turned in to me so I could write Letters of Reprimand on each. There were 18 in all.

And then there were the rooms where there was no response. If a knock wasn't answered, it meant one of two things: either the room was empty, or someone was hiding out in it. Jimbo Gambill found five of these unfortunate souls when he used his pass key. All five will receive Articles 15 for failure to report to the appointed place of duty. That's pretty serious stuff. But maybe word will get around that recalls are pretty serious stuff, too, and that I mean business. I really and truly hate to be a hard-ass, but sometimes I guess it's called for. I think this was one of those times. We reached the 100 percent mark in just over three hours. Fantastic!

But during this drill, there was one unfortunate "Catch 22". When the runner knocked on Sgt Sarah Bruno's door, she answered it, put on her helmet, gas mask, canteen, and flack jacked and responded quickly. Just what she was supposed to do. Good troop doing a good job.

And then things went bad. Jimbo hadn't kept up with which rooms had responded and which had not, so he hit every one with the pass key. When he opened Sgt Bruno's door, there stood a nude dude with a bit of a startled expression on his face. When Jimbo chewed his ass and ordered him to respond to the recall, the young fella said he didn't have to. He wasn't a member of SKIVVY NINE--he was assigned to the Supply Squadron. Oops! Sgt Sarah Bruno was in big trouble with the First Sergeant. She was in violation of PACAF Reg what-ever and Jimbo wanted to hang her from the highest tree.

I talked to him later that morning about the incident and asked what he planned to do about it. He said normal punishment for this particular no-no was an Article 15. I said I thought that was a little stringent for Sgt Bruno's case. If she was a dirt bag with a long history of screw-ups, I would go along with giving her the slam dunk treatment. But she wasn't a dirt bag. On the contrary, she was a super troop. Always reported for duty on time; did quality work; never on the ration control list; had never passed a bad check; no weight control problems; in other words, squeaky clean until this incident. So I told Jimbo that instead of an Article 15, perhaps a verbal counseling would be more appropriate.

He backed off to a Letter of Reprimand and Control Roster. Then I pointed out that if we punished everyone in this unit who had ever had a member of the opposite sex in their room overnight, half the people in SKIVVY NINE would be on the Control Roster. Sgt Bruno had just been unfortunate enough to get caught, so maybe a Letter of Counseling would be just about right.

We dickered and bargained and argued for about 20 minutes before we reached our compromise: she would get a Letter of Reprimand but no Control Roster. I said fine, as long as it was the desk drawer variety, meaning it wouldn't go to the Personnel Office and become part of Sgt Bruno's records. Jimbo agreed, and that's the way it came down.

I would never have been able to work like that with SMSgt Duckworth, the previous First Shirt. He would have insisted on the Article 15, it would have ended up in a pissing contest, the commander would end up making the final decision, and we would both look like a couple of unprofessional ass-holes. But I can work with Jimbo--good man.

♦♦♦♦♦♦♦♦♦♦

I've got another people thing to work with Col Lucas next week and boy, do I ever dread it. The Colonel has been down on Joe Del Ricco and wants to burn him on his next APR. Joe has worked a lot of overtime getting the APR backlog cleaned up, but the colonel doesn't have any problem with that. Hell, he *likes* to see his people work overtime. His problem is Joe isn't making his people work overtime with him. Col Lucas views this as weak leadership; Joe should be making his people work the same hours he does.

Joe's APR comes due week-after-next and, even though Maj Weber is supposed to write it, I wrote it myself. (The Major is still a notorious procrastinator when it comes to writing.) When I got to the suggested endorsement for Col Lucas' signature, it went something like this:

> *Stalwart performer! MSgt Del Ricco has been a real workhorse in cleaning up our APR/OER backlog. Because of the backlog, he was forced to have his people work a 55-60 hour week but, at the same time, MSgt Del Ricco was working 70 hour weeks. That kind of leadership by example gets the job done every time. He deserves that seventh stripe now. Promote!*

When he sees that suggested endorsement, Col Lucas is not going to be a happy camper. It's taking the very thing he doesn't like about Del Ricco and putting it in a positive, even virtuous light. He'll probably have a large chunk of Maj Weber's ass (and mine, too), but I intend to go to the wall for Joe and the Major says he'll support me all the way. Joe Del Ricco isn't the flashiest, brightest, most charismatic guy I've ever seen but, dammit, he's a hard worker who's done the best he can with limited resources and he doesn't deserve to be burned. We'll see how it goes.

Sunday, December 27th

Wednesday morning at 4:00 a.m., we had another recall. These things are starting to be old hat now. I know the routine in my sleep. Strangely enough, this one wasn't called by Col Lucas. As a matter of fact, he (nor anyone else in the 6903rd) didn't even know it was coming. It was a complete surprise to the whole unit because the 51st Tac Fighter Wing Commander, Col Michaud, called it. But true to Col Lucas' credo of "We're going to do everything the base does", we responded and played the game to the hilt.

Once again, our response time was good, but not because I had Senior NCO's in the dorms to get everyone up and moving, but because of some incredibly good luck. Without knowing there was going to be a recall, Col Lucas decided to have another fire drill in the dorms Wednesday morning. The fire drill kicked off at 3:50, ten minutes before the recall, so the dorm residents were already up and milling around. It was a simple matter of putting on their fear gear and hi-tailing it in to work. We reached the 90 percent present or accounted for mark in an hour and thirty minutes. Col Lucas was "pleased as punch".

For a change, I my response time was good, too. The exercise kicked off at four and my beeper went off at 4:07. By the time I got dressed, rousted my rider (SMSgt Brian Decker) out of bed, scraped a ton of frost off my windshield, and drove to work, it was 4:27 when I arrived. Twenty-seven minutes from START-X and twenty minutes from notification. Not bad.

Since my response time was good, I wasn't behind the power curve when I walked into my office. I was able to pick up my check-list and start at the beginning of the exercise instead of half-way through it. Looks like we've *finally* worked out the kinks on who's supposed to notify me, when they're supposed to do it, and how (beeper, not runner) they're supposed to do it. Then Wednesday afternoon, a monkey wrench came flying into the works.

The Comm Group has recalled my beeper--AGAIN!! I thought we had everything worked out, but they're really being ass-holes about this thing. When SSgt John Kilmer (the base beeper keeper) called and said he wanted my beeper back, I really got hot. I played a little "My Daddy's bigger than your Daddy" with him--told him Col Lucas had personally arranged for me to have the beeper and was he *sure* he wanted to pull it back. He said that was all well and good, but *his* Colonel had ordered him to get the beeper back. So we had us a stand-off.

We arranged a meeting time so he could come to my parking lot to pick the damn thing up. I met him at the appointed place and time and, just as I was handing the beeper, batteries, and charger through the window if his truck, Col Lucas walked by. What an incredible stroke of luck! He wanted to know what the hell was going on and, when I told him, his face went red as a beet. He was furious! He said, "Come with me."

We left SSgt Kilmer sitting in the parking lot and went to Col Lucas' office. He called the Comm Group Commander (also a Colonel) and demanded an explanation. Of course I couldn't hear what the other guy was saying, but apparently, it was, "Chief Beal can not have one of our beepers"--in no uncertain terms.

Now it was time for Col Lucas to play "My Daddy is bigger than your Daddy". He said, "I hate to get General Heffner (7th Air Force Vice Commander) involved in this, but if I have to, I will." There was a long pause while Col Lucas listened to the Comm guy's response to the threat. I don't know exactly what it was, but it had to be something like, "Knock yourself out, Ace." Another stand-off.

Since it was late in the day, Col Lucas didn't want to call the General right then. He tried the next day, but since it was Christmas Eve, it was a down day for the rest of the base (but not SKIVVY NINE) and General Heffner wasn't in. So the Colonel sez he'll call first thing Monday morning and get this thing ironed out once and for all.

I simply can not believe a General Officer has to get involved in something as nit-picky as whether or not I have a pager. But he will. Lucas won't just roll over. He's adamant that I will have a pager; not because I'm such a nice guy and one of his favorite people, but because if the bad shit comes down, he wants his Ops Supe in to work in one hellava hurry to cover his ass. And that's fair. It's my job to cover his ass. That Monday morning call to General Heffner should be interesting. We'll see.

♦♦♦♦♦♦♦♦♦

Had another tiff with Jimbo Gambill Wednesday afternoon. I got a letter from him dated 22 December at 4:00 p.m. on the 23rd. The letter contained a list of people who were to report to his office on the morning of the 24th. The first person on the list was scheduled for 7:00 a.m. the next morning. When I looked him up in the Alpha Roster, I found he was on DAWG Flight, had gone on break at 2:00 p.m. (two hours before I got the letter), and wouldn't be back to work until the 26th swing shift. No way was I ever going to get in touch with him in time to make the appointment with the First Sergeant. The last paragraph of the letter stated anyone not showing up for the appointment would be issued a Letter of Reprimand. Say what?

I called Jimbo and asked what was so hot that he absolutely had to see these people on such short notice--and give them a Letter of Reprimand if they didn't show up. He said they hadn't paid their November dues at the NCO Club! What chicken shit! I told him if I put forth a super human effort and jumped through my ass-hole, I *might* be able to round up half of the list and have them in his office the next day. But for delinquent Club dues? Not likely. I said I'd contact the readily available ones, but the others would be no-shows. And there best, by God, be no Letters of Reprimand. He said, "OK." Coming to an understanding was that simple.

The big difference between Jimbo and Duckworth is, although both of them are unreasonable pricks (must be something they teach in First Sergeant School), I can reason and compromise with Jimbo. Jesus--I just wish I didn't have to!

♦♦♦♦♦♦♦♦♦♦

Christmas Eve was a normal duty day for SKIVVY NINE even though it was a down day for the rest of the base. So much for the "doing everything the base does" bullshit. Long about one o'clock, Col Lucas found a soft spot in his heart and gave everyone (except the poor SOBs working shifts, of course) the rest of the day off. Maj Weber and I finally got out of the office around 3:30 (we had stuff we *just had* to get done before we left), which was a refreshing change from the five-thirty or six-thirty routine.

Went to the Lounge to make sure the Christmas dinner preparations were well under way (ham and turkey again-yuk!). The action was pretty much a repeat of the Thanksgiving dinner preparations except we had more help. Word got around that we had a lot of fun that night, so when the call went out for volunteers, we had a great response.

The atmosphere in the Lounge was somehow a little "softer" that night. Instead of the customary movies on the TV monitors, images of the Jimmy Stewart classic, "It's a Wonderful Life" flickered silently on the screen. The rock and roll that usually blasted from the sound system was replaced by "Silent Night", "Noel", and "Silver Bells". And the crowd that is normally so rowdy and boisterous sang along with the carols while they worked at putting the next day's meal together. Even the 69th CTG had the spirit; our TOP GUN b-ball caps were decorated with sundry Christmas ornaments.

Took a bit of a sleep-in Christmas morning then met up with Maj Weber to make the rounds, pump up the troops, and wish them a Merry Christmas. I was surprised and pleased to find a lot of Day Whores working. They had come in to give a few shift workers a Christmas hit. I guess the Christmas spirit lives. Good on them.

Flight Operations got their grub from the Chow Hall. The food was excellent, but the Chow Hall ran out of plastic utensils and the guys didn't have anything to eat with. But good old GI ingenuity came through again. The Flight's Store sells instant ramen noodles and each package comes with a set of chop sticks. So they ripped off the chop sticks from the noodle packages and ate their meals with them. Now when the Flight's Store sells the noodles, there won't be any chop sticks to eat them with but they'll cross that bridge when they come to it.

After our walk-around in Operations, the Major and I headed for the Lounge where I had some turkey and ham. They put the food out in staggered shifts so everyone would have a shot at it, no matter what shift they were working. After the last group had eaten, I helped clean up the mess, then got involved in one hellava cut-throat Hearts game. Played until midnight, then headed back to my room for some shut-eye. Merry Christmas.

Chapter Thirteen

ROCK BOTTOM

Sunday, January 3rd

Here I am at the end of the worst week I've had since I've been here--possibly the worst week of my life. Monday started off pretty uneventfully. We had two APRs in the Command Section awaiting Col Lucas' signature. I sent Joe Del Ricco up to remind them that we had to have them back that day so we could meet our deadline to the Orderly Room. We do that all the time. Nothing unusual.

When Joe came back, his face was flaming red and he was so mad he could hardly talk. One of the admin people in the Command Section (more on her later) told Joe that those APRs had just been delivered that morning and she didn't know if she could get them out by the end of the day or not. She informed him (he's an E-7 and she's an E-4) she was tired of jumping through hoops to get signatures just because of our incompetence and she wasn't going to make any special efforts any more. So there!

When Joe finished his remarkable tale, I went to the Command Section and asked Lt Lane what the hell was going on. I told her I thought this was a team effort. We were supposed to be working together to get the APRs through the system on time, not putting up roadblocks. She agreed and said she would ask Sgt Loftus to try and get those pesky APRs back to us by the end of the day. She asked me to try to get them in sooner in the future, if possible. I said I'd try.

When I got back to my office, Captain Henke was there waiting for me. She was moving from her old dorm to a new one that afternoon and wanted to know if she could use my truck. Se said her moving crew would be at her place by 3:30 and I agreed to have the truck there immediately after Commander's Call[34] which should be over about that time.

Toward the end of Commander's Call, Col Lucas opened the floor to questions. Someone asked why shift workers can't get hot meals delivered to them from the Chow Hall. The same question had been asked over and over in the BITCH BOX[35] for weeks.

Even though this horse had been beaten to death many times over, the ass-hole in the audience insisted on raising the hot meal issue one more time. Col Lucas looked over to where I was siting and said, "Boy, are we lucky today! We just happen to have the expert on that very subject in our audience this afternoon. Chief Beal, would you like to explain to the audience why we can't get hot meals for the shift workers?"

I thought that was a pretty smart move on the Colonel's part. After all, I had been talking to the Chow Hall supervisor, the Services Squadron Commander, researching all the Air Force Regulations, and had written the answers for the Bitch Box. It made sense to have me answer the question.

While I was walking to the front of the theater, I was trying to organize my thoughts. Speaking in front of a large audience is tough enough, but with absolutely no preparation, it's double tough. But I'm an experienced speaker, right? No problem.

---

[34] Information from the Commander to the trench troops is normally passed through the chain of command. But if the Commander wishes to go directly to his people, he calls them together so he can talk to them all at the same time. Traditionally, that was done aperiodically, but in recent years, Commander's Call has become a recurring monthly affair.

[35] One of Col Lucas's favorite projects. See the Glossary of Terms for a detailed description of the BITCH BOX.

The first thing that came out of my mouth was a brain fart. "I thought we had beat the hot meal issue to death in the "Bitch Box Bulletin" and that horse was dead. Apparently, it's not. As you all know, the Colonel doesn't have time to answer all the complaints you guys drop in the Bitch Boxes. He farms them out to the experts to research and answer. Well, I'm the guy who's been handling the hot meal thing. All I can do is rehash and review all the answers I've written over the past few weeks, so here goes." And then I launched into the 99 different reasons hot meals for shift workers were not possible.

The words were no sooner out of my mouth when I realized what I had done. Maj Weber was sitting in the front row and when I said I had written the responses, he got a panicked look on his face. All I could think was "Oh Shit!". I had put my foot in my mouth, so I guess the Colonel had a right to be pissed off. He didn't say anything to me after Commander's Call, just gave me the icy stare routine as I left the theater. Just one more wedge in the schism between us.

From the theater, I went to Capt Henke's dorm to lend her my truck. When I got there, she was by herself. Her moving crew of fellow officers didn't show up. I couldn't bring myself to leave her stranded, so I offered to help. It took almost two hours and four truckloads to get her moved.

Most of the stuff was pretty easy, but four of the pieces really kicked my ass. There was a TV set that wasn't all that heavy, but it was so big I just couldn't get a good hold on it. Awkward. Then there were the two stereo speakers made of solid oak; and the real ass kicker was the microwave oven that *had* to weigh 85 or 90 pounds. I muscled all four pieces to and from the truck by myself and by the time I got that last item in her new dorm, I was one beat puppy.

SKIVVY NINE!

The next day (Tuesday), Joe Del Ricco took leave to go to Seoul and attend his nephew's wedding (he's married to a Korean lady). It was probably the biggest mistake of his life. I learned more about what has been going on in his office in that one day than I had ever known before. TSgt Anne Jensen (one of the Reservists I had brought in from San Antonio to help out in the Admin area) kept digging up skeletons in Ops Admin. Finally, I called Dave Dixon and Art Evans (both E-4s who work for Joe) into my office and asked them if they knew about the skeletons before this. They said yes. I asked them why they hadn't brought them to my attention. They said they didn't want to get their boss in trouble. Well, at least they were loyal.

But such was not the case with Jensen. As the day went on, she kept bringing me things--"Look at this mess"; "Can you believe he did (or didn't do) this"; "Chief, this has been laying in his in-basket for three weeks!" And on, and on, and on. Some of the things that Jensen uncovered were.

> An APR that was due that day had been sitting in Joe's in-basket for eight days. His people had to jump through their asses to get it to the Orderly Room on time. He received 17 notifications that decoration nominations had to be written by 21 December, and they still hadn't been distributed to the people who had to do the write-ups. They had been laying on his desk for seven days.
>
> I had assigned TSgt Jensen to help clean up the Awards and Decorations back-log on 23 December. As of the 29th, she hadn't worked a single one. Joe wouldn't allow it. Furthermore, he told her before he left for Seoul not to touch them while he was gone.

> When I signed Joe's leave request Monday, I told him he had to finish every important project I had given him before he took leave. He didn't do it.

I was emotionally torn. On the one hand, I hated Jensen for being a "nonny-nonny-boo-boo tattle tale", but on the other hand, if she hadn't brought these things to my attention, I'd still be in the dark. The fact that Joe refused to let her work the Awards and Decs back-log was the straw that broke the camel's back. I was furious and told Maj Weber that when Joe got back, I was going to give him an ultimatum. He would have one week to get his act together and, if he didn't, I'd have to fire his ass. That was the plan, but it got implemented a little earlier than I had anticipated. Here's how.

I told Jensen that I didn't care what kind of guidance Joe had given her, she was to pump as many write-ups as possible into the Command Section for final quality control, approval, and signature. I thought I was doing good. I wasn't.

TSgt Jensen went through that back-log like a fast burning forest fire, knocking out 25 packages in one day. And then she took them all to the Command Section *at one time* and dumped them. Lt Lane was upset to say the least. She called. I went to the Command Section. "How dare you take your back-log and turn it into my back-log", she stammered. "I'll have to work my people until midnight to get through that stack of write-ups."

I told her I was more than willing to feed her the back-log 2-3-5-7 packages at a time. But I reminded her that if I fed them to her piecemeal, the back-log might not be wiped out by the time the IG comes back. We were in the midst of working out an arrangement when Col Lucas came storming out of his office.

The Command Section was packed with people. Capt Henke, Capt Jacoby, and Maj Reardon were standing around waiting for a five o'clock appointment with the Colonel. TSgt Jensen was standing on the sidelines grinning like the cat that ate the canary. MSgt Earl Romano (budget guy) was working at his desk. The Command Section admin staff, Lt Lane, and a guy from Charlie Flight pulling clean-up detail were all just milling around. And with this audience looking on, Col Lucas got right in my face.

"Chief, I've got one question for you." His face was tomato red and inches from mine. "Where has that stack of Awards and Decs been until today?"

I had to be truthful. "In Joe Del Ricco's in-basket," I said.

"That's what I thought! I've been telling you all along that Joe Del Ricco was the problem and now I am going to remove that problem!" I backed up a little bit. I don't like people in my face. Makes me lose my temper and when I lose my temper, I do dumb, stupid things.

Col Lucas took a step forward so he could stay in my face. "If you and that gutless Major you work for don't have the balls to eliminate the problem," and at this point he started to pound his fore-finger into my chest, **"I'll (pound) eliminate the problem (pound) for you!!! (pound)"**, he screamed. Then he turned on his heel, stomped into his office, and slammed the door so hard that it knocked a picture off the wall.

Every fiber of my being screamed to knock that door off its hinges, go into his office, and kick his fucking face in. Instead, I slinked out of the Command Section like a whipped dog while the audience marveled at the spectacle. I went back to my office, destroyed an IBM Selectric typewriter, put on my parka and cap, and headed for the SKIVVY NINE Lounge. Maj Weber asked me what the hell had happened as I was going out the door, but I couldn't talk. I was afraid I'd cry.

I sat in one corner of the Lounge and pounded down three beers real fast. Usually, when I come in, it's "Hey Chief! How's it going, Chief; what's up?", that kind of thing. But Tuesday night, nobody said anything to me and no one came to talk to me in the corner. I guess my non-verbals are as strong as some folks say they are. In any case, there wasn't a soul in the Lounge that didn't know I was *PISSED.*

About 20 minutes later, Maj Weber came wandering in. He had the guts to join me and I was cooled down enough to tell him what happened. He's been sick all week (got hold of some bad fish in a restaurant) and he really looks washed out. But as I told him the horror story, his face got even more pale.

Although we had discussed what to do about the Joe Del Ricco situation earlier in the day, we decided that my one-way discussion with the Colonel had removed that option. We agreed that, no matter how much we hated to do it, Joe had to be fired and I was the one to do the dirty deed.

Wednesday morning dawned dark and gloomy. I hardly slept at all Tuesday night, dreading what I had to do to Del Ricco the next day. When I got to work, the phone was ringing. It was Lt Lane. She said the Colonel wanted to see Maj Weber in his office *NOW*. The Major wasn't in yet. She said she didn't care, the Colonel wanted to see him *NOW*! I called the Major in his quarters and he was suffering from diarrhea from both ends. He was really sick. But he crawled in by 6:30, white as a sheet with big beads of sweat standing out on his bald head. He looked bad!

The Major disappeared into Col Lucas' office for 15 minutes. When he came out, he looked a hellava lot worse than when he went in. The Colonel had chewed his ass BIG TIME. He didn't *order* the Major to fire Joe, but he made it perfectly clear that if he wasn't gone by the end of the day, it would be "career threatening" for the Major. My course of action was clear.

As soon as Joe came to work, I called him into my office and had him close the door. I told him what I had found the day before, about my "discussion" with the Colonel, and that I was going to have to let him go. While I was talking, big tears began rolling down his face. I had one hellava time getting through what I had to say. But I did it. Barely.

As he was leaving, I told Joe to take the rest of the day off and get in touch with SMSgt Robert Tolbert (the unit Director of Administration) the next day to find where he would work next. I waited a few minutes after he had gone, then went outside, found a good hiding place, and cried my guts out. I hated me.

When I got back to the office, I called Tolbert. I told him what I had done and added that I wanted him to find a meaningful job for Joe outside of SKIVVY NINE. He assured me he would do that (he has lots of connections in the Admin world). When the Major talked with Col Lucas earlier that morning, the Colonel had said he wanted Joe fired to one of the Branches in the Ops Division, which would mean a Master Sergeant doing Staff Sergeant work. I couldn't do that--it would be adding insult to injury. I wanted Joe out of the 6903rd, not because he was a bad guy, but because I didn't want him to suffer the humiliation of having to look unit people in the eye every day with them knowing he'd been fired. I wanted so desperately to leave him with at least a shred of self respect and dignity.

I checked in with Tolbert that afternoon and he said he had called all over Korea to find there just weren't any openings for Master Sergeant Admin types. He said for John to work in a Master Sergeant slot, he will probably have to leave Korea and go back to the States. John (and especially his Korean wife) don't want to do that, but it looks like I've nuked them right out of the country.

So Joe Del Ricco is gone. He's been replaced by SSgt Ruby (The Viper) Irons. She'll get everything straightened out, Col Lucas will be happy, and I'll always remember how I trashed a man's career. I can't wait until I get out of this fucking hell-hole. Why is my shit always so ragged? All I want to do is what's right. Why can't I?

♦♦♦♦♦♦♦♦♦♦

After the morning I had Wednesday, I didn't think my day could get much worse. It could.

Wednesday is major clean-up time in our Day Shops. What with all the emphasis Col Lucas has placed on cleanliness in the workplace, Wednesday clean-up has become one of my top priorities. My policy is that at 4:30 p.m., everybody in the Day Shop puts their chair on top of their desk and goes home. That allows the clean-up crew to get in and do their job without having to mop around people trying to work.

At 4:35, the guy in charge of the work detail stuck his head in my office door and complained that the people in the Exploitation Management shop refused to leave--too much work to do. I went out there and told MSgt DAL Lawler he and his people were going to have to clear out. He wasn't happy. "What you're saying, Chief, is that clean-up is more important than the mission." I didn't dignify his snide remark with an answer. I just told him to get the hell out and went back to my office.

At 4:45, DAL showed up in front of my desk. He wanted to know why his office was being forced to leave while my Ops Admin people were allowed to stay. He was right. It wasn't fair. So I shooed all my people out and went to the SKIVVY NINE Lounge to drown my sorrows.

I hadn't been there long when Maj Weber walked in. He looked totally washed out and his forehead was sweating profusely. This was beginning to be the normal look for my Ops Officer. He got me off in a corner and told me Col Lucas had chewed his ass *AGAIN*! I asked what on earth for.

The Major said he was driving to his quarters when he got a call on his radio to report to Lucas' office immediately. When he got there, the Colonel was in a rage. How dare Maj Weber release his admin people while the Command Section admin people were still sweating over the Awards and Decs back-log we had dumped on them the day before!!! The Major took all the heat. He didn't tell Col Lucas it was me who ran our people off.

The Major tried to argue that he was in a no-win situation. On one hand, the Colonel demanded the place be squeaky clean on Thursday mornings while, on the other hand, he didn't want people to leave so the clean-up crew could get the job done. The Colonel wanted to hear none of it and Maj Weber's shit was in the street again. So his day ended the same way it began--with a merciless ass chewing.

Thursday, it didn't get any better. Things were still tense, but they got even more tense during the weekly Commander's Staff Meeting. The Late APR slide was clean again (which helped the Major's and my feelings), but Col Lucas reversed his field again on the Orderly Room granting extensions on late APRs. When he came out with his no extensions/no excuses policy the first time, I thought Maj Weber and I had turned him around. Since then, things have been running smoothly, I've only had to ask for an extension once, and there haven't been any late APRs. And through it all, Capt Oakley and Jimbo have cooperated to the fullest.

As soon as the slide came off the screen, Col Lucas said the lack of late APRs on the slide wasn't a true picture of the health of the APR program in Operations. In order to get a true picture, he was reinstating his no extensions/no excuses policy. The announcement was like getting a hatchet planted right between my eyebrows.

Jimbo was sitting next to me. He passed me a note that said, "What the hell was that all about?" I scribbled one back, "The vindictive son-of-a-bitch wants to make sure the Major and I fail." Jimbo read the note and nodded his head knowingly.

Capt Oakley, Jimbo, the Major, and I got together after the Staff Meeting. They were as disappointed and downcast as the Major and me. We had been working so well together, but now Lucas had tied their hands to help us. We were on our own. I thought things couldn't get any worse. They could.

APRs on Staff Sergeants Ted Parker and Terry Shipp went to the Command Section Thursday morning for the Colonel's signature. They were due to the Orderly Room not later than close of business Thursday afternoon. Around noon, I went to the Command Section to see what their status was.

The APRs were on Sgt Della Loftus' desk. I told her I had to have them back by the end of the day or they would be late to the Orderly Room. The insubordinate bitch looked me straight in the eye and said, "Chief, those APRs are on the bottom of things I have to do today. They may or may not work their way to the top. If they don't, now that's just too bad, isn't it."

I exercised more self control than I ever thought I had. What I wanted to do was reach across that desk, tie the bitch's tits in a knot, break every bone in her crotch, then remind the impertinent cunt that she's talking to a Chief and would damn well do so accordingly. What I actually did was tuck my tail between my legs and go to Lt Lane to ask for help.

She acted sympathetic and said she would do everything she could to get the APRs to us on time. Later in the day, Ruby The

Viper went to the Command Section on another matter. While she was there, Loftus got her off to one side and told her in no uncertain terms that she was damned well tired of "that Chief" going over her head to the Lieutenant. Loftus told Ruby that if I did it again, I'd be sorry.

Ruby delivered this little tidbit of information to me with a great deal of glee. I guess everybody likes to see a Chief slam-dunked by a three striper. And Loftus made good on her threat; those APRs never did come out of the Command Section that day. So next Thursday, they'll show up on the Orderly Room's Late APR slide at the Commander's Staff Meeting. After that, the Major and I will be standing tall in front of Col Lucas' desk for another ass chewing. Oh well.

♦♦♦♦♦♦♦♦♦

Toward the end of the day Thursday, I was bemoaning my fate to MSgt Earl Romano. Although Earl works in the Command Section, he's the budget guy and doesn't get involved in the APR fiasco. He's also the only person in the Command Section that I can trust and talk to. Good guy. When I got to the part where Maj Weber had been chewed out for releasing Ops Admin "early" Wednesday night, Earl's eyes lit up.

He had been at his desk at five o'clock Wednesday when TSgt Jensen (remember her--the bitch who blew the whistle on Joe Del Ricco) came in. She announced to everyone within earshot that she had been kicked out of her duty section because of clean-up. How was she supposed to work on the Awards and Decs back-log if she couldn't work overtime to get the job done? Col Lucas overheard the tirade and my Major paid the price.

I decided right then that I was going to have a large chunk of TSgt Jensen's abundant ass. I told Earl my intentions and asked him to keep his eye peeled for Jensen coming to the Command Section.

I figured with her total lack of loyalty, she'd run straight to Col Lucas about her "mistreatment" after I talked to her. Earl agreed to be my trusted agent and confidant (spy) in the Command Section. Can you believe all this skullduggery, chicanery, and palace intrigue? It's hard for me to comprehend.

I went back to my office and called Sergeant Jensen in for a little heart-to-heart talk. I told her that, in the first place, she had stabbed Joe Del Ricco in the back. I said Joe's shit was weak and something needed to be done, but I didn't know how she could sleep at night knowing she had ruined a Master Sergeant's 20-year career. She tried to defend herself, but I told her to shut up--in those words--"Shut up!"

I continued by saying she may have dicked Del Rico away, but she wasn't going to do the same to my Major. She didn't know what I was talking about--Right! I told her what I had found out about what happened Wednesday night, and what the result had been. "Oh, I was only making conversation. I didn't know it would get the Major in trouble." BULLSHIT!

I said she knew full well what she was doing, just like she knew exactly what would happen when she dumped the Awards and Decs backlog on the Command Section.

I reminded her now that Joe was gone, she worked directly for me. All I wanted from her was the backlog wiped out and her total loyalty. I also said I was tired of her shit stirring and I wouldn't tolerate it anymore. And I told her I had eyes and ears in the Command Section. If she squealed to Lucas, I would stomp a mud hole in her ass and wade it dry. I concluded that if she didn't get her act together, I'd send her broad ass back to San Antonio in a heartbeat. And then I told her to get the fuck out of my sight!

After all that had gone on during the week, I hardly felt like doing any big time celebrating on New Years Eve. But there was a meeting of the 69th CTG that night at Boomer's place and I felt obliged to attend.

It was hard for me to disguise the fact that I was one down cowboy. I'm afraid I wasn't very good company but, even though I couldn't tell them why I was in such a rotten mood, the CTG and invited guests seemed to understand and pretty much left me alone. I grabbed a beer and hoisted my butt onto the edge of the kitchen sink to watch the proceedings and sulk. That wasn't a hellava lot of fun, so around 10 o'clock, I eased out, caught a Blue Goose back to the base, and was asleep before midnight. Happy New Year.

Wednesday, January 6th

It's 9:00 p.m. and I just got off work. We're talking 15 hour days here. Trying to get an award, decoration, OER, or APR through the Command Section quality control mechanism is like trying to stuff a wet noodle up a wild-cat's ass. It can't be done!

We've had six late APRs in the last four days, and all of the suspenses expired while the document laid in Sgt Lofton's in-basket. But we keep trying--that's why I'm so late getting home tonight. I wonder how long the bitch will hold the ones we finished today.

As a result of the late APRs, Maj Weber is summoned to Col Lucas' office at least daily for a sound ass chewing, but (thank God) the Colonel hasn't made good on his threat to nail the Major with a formal Letter of Reprimand. Yet.

Things aren't looking up a whole lot, but my spirits are. I'm learning to roll with the punches; nothing bothers me anymore. I remind me of the air-filled plastic dolls with the weighted bottom that were popular toys a few years ago. You know the ones--hit them with your fist and they fall over, but they keep popping back upright like they were begging for more. That's me. I take a blow in the chops, fall over, come back up, take another, and come back up again with a big grin on my face. "Like to try that again?" I keep getting knocked over and I just keep bouncing back. They can't hurt me. I'm ten feet tall and bulletproof.

♦♦♦♦♦♦♦♦♦

Joe Del Ricco refuses to die. He called me Monday morning and said he needed to talk. I met him in the SKIVVY NINE Lounge at 10:00 a.m. (when it's empty) and asked him what he wanted to talk about. He wanted his job back. I told him I couldn't do that. He cried.

I advised him to turn loose and forget about his old job and press on to find a new one. He said he couldn't. Every place Tolbert takes him for an interview, Col Lucas has already called ahead, telling them not to hire Joe. That low life scum-bag.

So it looks like Joe will have to leave Osan, either to another base here in Korea or out of the country. I asked him for a list of places he would like to go (if he had to) and told him I would work with the assignments people at headquarters and the Military Personnel Center to get him a decent assignment. I've been doing that, but so far, no luck. But I'll keep trying. That's the least I can do.

♦♦♦♦♦♦♦♦♦

Yesterday was the Recognition Breakfast. During the ceremony, Col Lucas was awarded the Legion of Merit for his good deeds at the Headquarters. CMSgt Kevin Novak (the guy I replaced as Ops Supe, remember?) came down from the U.S. - Korean Liaison Office in Seoul with a whole bunch of his troops to witness the grand occasion. After the breakfast, everyone went back to the compound and I got Ken off to one side and told him what had been transpiring over the past couple of weeks. I think he thought I was exaggerating a little.

On his way back to Seoul, he stopped by the Command Section just to say "hiddy". While he was there, Lt Lane gave him a note in a sealed envelope marked "EYES ONLY". It was a poison pen letter from Col Lucas. Ken had allowed one of his people to put in a leave request for the same time frame the IG Team will be doing the re-inspection. How dare he! The note was *very* nasty, so Kevin went into Lucas' office to challenge him, not on content, but the tone of the note.

Col Lucas wasted no time in putting Kevin at a brace and chewing his ass up one side and down the other. About 30 seconds into the ass chewing, Kevin interrupted, "Do you mind of I close the door, Colonel? I don't want the whole damned Command Section to hear this like they did with Chief Beal."

While Kevin closed the door, the Colonel went insane! When he was finished with the verbal abuse, Kevin asked if he could offer his side of the story. "No," Lucas said. "This is a one-way conversation. You are dismissed."

Kevin saluted smartly and left. Then he looked me up and told me what had happened. I just grinned and said, "See?" He rolled his eyes and nodded his head. Now he understands.

Sunday, January 11th

Boy! It sure is tired out. Really been bustin' my buns lately and was looking forward to a laid back Sunday to get rested up. I should have known better.

Went on one hellava Bean Run last night that, at one point during the proceedings, had to have over 100 people in attendance. The 69th CTG and its Commander were the centers of attraction. Danny Zeller is leaving the 15th headed for Goodfellow Air Force Base, Texas and last night was his last "hoo-rah".

The Bean Run itinerary was carefully planned so it only hit clubs that allowed carrier landings. Every time "Danger Zone" blasted out, dozens of people (not just CTG members) lined up to get the "go ahead" from Boomer Marshall, the Landing Deck Officer. When Boomer dropped his flags, they would charge ahead, dive onto the dance floor, and skid to the other side accompanied by roars of approval from the crowd.

And this Bean Run was also the occasion for the premiere performance of Chief Beal's SKIVVY NINE Acapella Choir, Jug Band, and Soul Rock Review. We only know one tune: "The Perfect Country and Western Song" by David Allen Coe. When it comes on the sound system, the CTG huddles up in the middle of the dance floor and sings along. We kinda mumble our way through the first few verses, but we've got the last one down pat and, when we get to that part, we really belt it out.

"I was drunk the day my Mom got out of prison,
And I went to pick her up in the rain.
But before I could get to the station in my pick-up truck,
She got runned over by a damned old train.

"Oh, I'll hang around as long as you will let me,
And I never minded standing in the rain.
You don't have to call me Darlin', Darlin'.
But I wonder why you don't call me
Yes I wonder why you don't call me
Why don't you ever call me by my fuckin' name?"

Pure poetry. It must have been, because we got a standing ovation at the end every time we did it.

♦♦♦♦♦♦♦♦♦♦

SKIVVY NINE!

Last night was one of the best times I've had since I've been here. But the Bean Run began to fall apart around one o'clock, so I headed back to the base and crashed around 1:30 a.m. At 5:00 a.m., my beeper went off. RECALL!! AGAIN!!

And this time, Colonel Lucas wasn't playing around. It was a 13 hour ball buster with three hours straight in gas masks. Fortunately for me, the Exercise Evaluation Team Chief, SMSgt Andy Powell (who wrote the exercise scenario) wrote a heart attack into the exercise for me.

About 10 minutes before the masks went on for the three hour mother fucker, one of the evaluators strolled up to me and handed me a 2 X 3 inch card. It read, "Don't say anything. Act normal. In three minutes, fall to the floor and simulate having a heart attack." I did.

I simulated the attack so well that SMSgt Brian Decker and TSgt Ted Fishburn (the two guys closest to me) thought it was real. Scared the living shit out of them is what it did. But they swung right into action. Ted was just about to give me CPR when I raised up and yelled, "EXERCISE! EXERCISE!". I didn't want that ugly mother's mouth on mine.

For exercise purposes, Ted and Brian did all the right things but I died anyway. That, in effect, put me out of the exercise, so I didn't have to wear that damned mask for three hours. But I didn't get to come back to my room for some much needed sleep, either. Exercise casualties became evaluators, which is almost as bad as playing in the exercise. But at least I didn't have to wear that damned mask. You can't know how much I hate that thing. The exercise was *finally* over at 6:00 p.m., so I went to the NCO Club for some breakfast/lunch/supper (I hadn't eaten all day. After I ate, it was back to the barracks to make this entry.)

Chapter Fourteen

THE IG'S COMING--*AGAIN!!*

Wednesday, January 14th

The IG Team will be back for the reinspection in three days, which is the reason for all the long hours I've been working. I, and the Admin Staff, have been putting in 12-14 hours a day to get the Awards and Decorations back-log knocked out. When TSgt Jensen came into the office to become the Awards and Decs Tsar, we had a back-log of 53. Our original goal was to have them to the Orderly Room by the 19th, the day the IG reinspection actually begins. We were moving right along and it looked like we would make our goal, then last Thursday (January 8th), Maj Weber changed the rules.

He decided he wanted the entire back-log completed and in the mail to Headquarters by the 14th. That meant getting them written, typed, quality controlled, into the Command Section for signature (the *real* son-of-a-bitch), down to the Orderly Room for processing, over to the Personnel office for more processing, back to my Admin People to be wrapped, and then to the Directorate of Administration to be placed in courier channels *in six days.* I told the Major it couldn't be done. He insisted it could.

I can understand his concern. It's his ass (and career) on the line if the IG comes back and finds that back-log again. So I mobilized all the Admin people in the Ops Division and gave them their marching orders. We worked 15 hours Thursday, 14 hours Friday, and 14 hours Saturday.

About four o'clock Saturday afternoon, it became painfully obvious to Maj Weber that it really couldn't be done. I convinced him that what we needed to do was prioritize the packages. Some of the awards were as much as a year over due, while others were written on people who haven't even left Osan yet (and therefore, weren't late). We were working those write-ups just as hard as we were the old ones.

So I gathered up the packages (by this time there were only 41 of them left) and put a big number 1, 2, 3, or 4 on the outside cover. Priority 1 is an award that should have been sent out in September or earlier. Priority 2 is October and November, Priority 3 is December and January (if the person is already gone), and Priority 4 is for write-ups on people who haven't left yet.

Using this system, we'll be able to get out all the Priority 1's, will probably ship all the Priority 2's, might get to some of the threes, and won't even worry about the Priority 4's. But even with this system, we'll still have to work at least 16 hours a day to meet the 16 January deadline.

We also made some headway in the Command Section Saturday. Until then, my people were knocking themselves out to get the job done and then the write-ups would go into the Command Section and stagnate on Sgt Loftus' desk.

Finally, Maj Weber had a heart-to-heart talk with Lt Lane. He told her that she and Sgt Loftus *had* to turn those packages around quicker if we were going to wipe out the back-log. She wasn't too sympathetic until the Major reminded her that, not only would his ass be in a sling when the IG Team gets here, but Col Lucas will get his lunch ate, too. Now, that got her attention.

But she was still adamant that she and Sgt Loftus couldn't get the awards back to us any sooner. They just had too much to do. After all, they had to prepare for the IG too. Then the Major made a bold suggestion. He would send someone from Operations to edit/QC the write-ups and free up Lane and Loftus for IG prep. He guaranteed the Ops person would play by Command Section rules and be just as tough on QC as they were. She couldn't give the OK, but she would take up the proposal with Col Lucas. The Colonel bought it.

So Saturday morning, we sent Sgt Jenny Burnell (remember the pregnant sergeant?) to the Command Section to be the QCer/editor. In one day, she got rid of all the Priority 1's, Priority 2's, and most of the Priority 3's. She's playing by Command Section rules, but she's not making ridiculous corrections like Lane and Loftus. With her working nothing but Awards and Decs and not sending write-ups back for needless corrections, we may make it through this thing yet.

Through all this, Maj Weber is starting to get a little punchy and awfully bleary eyed. Friday, I wrote a message to the Ops Officer and Director of Personnel at Headquarters demanding they send us some 207X1's. We're really short on 207's right now, and if we don't get some relief soon, we'll have to go on frozen shifts (no time off).

By the time I got to the last paragraph of the message, I was feeling a little feisty, so I finished it off in real rock 'em, sock 'em style. "If there is any way 207X1 assignments to SKIVVY NINE can be accelerated, it must be done now. If not, we will continue to bite the bullet, hold off the Godless heathen to the north, and keep the morning calm despite this crippling manning shortage."

I thought the Major would see the tongue-in-cheek paragraph when he reviewed the message, get a little chuckle out of it, and take it out. He didn't. Instead, he signed it and sent it unchanged! I figure the message will get one of two reactions at the headquarters: they'll think we really are desperate enough to write a stupid message like that and send us some 207X1 help right away. Or--they'll think we're the biggest bunch of dipshits that ever came down the pike and fart us off altogether. Oh well, we'll see.

♦♦♦♦♦♦♦♦♦

I'm still working hard to get Joe Del Rico a good assignment. Col Lucas has really pissed in his well here at Osan, so I called the headquarters to see if they could find him something somewhere else. When I talked to the Admin Resource Manager back there, he said, "Oh yeah, I've heard his name mentioned around here before. I think he's on some kind of IG "hit list" or something. Hold on. I'll ask my boss."

He came back on the phone a couple of minutes later and said, "Sorry, we don't have anything for him."

So the plot thickens. The IG Team identified Joe as a dirt bag along with our cop, Pat Aiken, when they were here and wanted him fired even though his Branch was rated SATISFACTORY. That would explain Col Lucas' insistence on getting rid of him. Well, the IG Team got their way.

After I got off the phone with Headquarters, I called the Admin Resource Manager at the Military Personnel Center at Randolph Air Force Base, Texas. Turns out he's an old Adminer himself with many years experience in ESC and knows Joe well. I explained the situation and asked for help. He gave me the names and phone numbers of some people in Seoul who might hire Joe and, failing that, assured me he could get him an assignment to Nellis Air Force Base, Nevada or in the D.C. area. Both of those were on Joe's "wish list". Maybe things will turn out OK after all. I sure hope so.

Saturday, January 17th

Joe Del Ricco has found a job. Tolbert finally convinced someone at 7th Air Force Logistics and Maintenance that he was worth salvaging so he won't have to go back to the States. I'm sure glad someone on this base had the cajones to go against Lucas. This'll make Joe's wife happy. I see him around the base every now and then. He still waves and sez "Hi", so I guess he doesn't hate my guts too much.

SSgt Ruby "The Viper" Irons is working out very nicely as the new Noncommissioned Officer in charge of Operations Administration. She's so damned efficient. I just wish she didn't have a personality like a buck-toothed cobra.

BEEPER NEWS: I've got one again. And, yes, it did take a call to BGen Heffner from Col Lucas to get it. Can you believe that? The Commander of the Comm Group had to give up his personal beeper so I could have one. I just can't believe they're *that* scarce. But I don't care where it came from. I gave Maj Reardon his beeper back, I've got my own and a truck, so I'm happy.

PARENTHETICAL COMMENT: SSgt "Henk" Henkendorf (bless his heart) used my truck yesterday and, since the IG is coming, he stopped by the motor pool and washed it for me. Don't want the Chief driving around in a dirty truck with the IG on the yard. I know he had the best of intentions, but when I went to get in it last night after work, the damn doors were frozen shut! I had to walk home and, if we had a recall or real world emergency last night, I'd have been afoot. Fortunately, it warmed up to about 35 degrees today, so I was able to get into the truck and now I'm back in business. Only to me!

Sunday, January 18th

My system to get the Awards and Decs back-log knocked out has been torpedoed again. Last Monday morning, the rules were changed by Col Lucas. He called Maj Weber into his office and chewed his ass again (sounds soooooo familiar). He told the Major that if those Awards and Decs didn't get out of this unit before the IG arrived, it would be the Major's ass (and career). Well, those marching orders were pretty plain, so our work was cut out for us.

We called the Admin folks together again and laid the bad news on them. I told them it would require some super-human effort and long hours, but it had to be done. They seemed to understand and pressed off in a flurry of activity.

Around 12:30 p.m., Ruby "The Viper" came to me and said she was getting corrected write-ups in from all the branches but Flight Operations. She said she had kicked five awards back for correction around eight o'clock that morning, but they hadn't come back yet. I called B.O. O'Banion and asked him what the hell was going on. He said his Admin type (SSgt Rick Meyers) had taken an "early lunch" and hadn't returned yet. I asked how early and why. He said Rick had left around ten o'clock so he could watch the NFL play-off game between the 49ers and Vikings.

Say what?? Here we were up to our asses in work and Rick has the balls to ask for time off to watch a football game. Even more amazing, B.O. gave it to him. I told B.O. to get Rick's ass back to work *now.* I checked back with him at one o'clock and Rick still wasn't back. B.O. said he called the dorm several times, but no one answered the hallway phone. I suggested he go to the dorm and get the boy himself.

When B.O. got to Rick's room, he knocked several times and, when there was no answer, he tried the door. It wasn't locked, so he walked in and there was Rick sprawled on his bunk--asleep. When B.O. and Rick got back to work, I called them into the office and had a little of both their asses. When I finished, Maj Weber had a go at it. Their only comeback was, "No excuse, Sir. No excuse, Sir." I can't remember when I've been that angry.

Around 5:30 p.m., it became obvious that we weren't going to be getting off any time soon, so I had Ruby start cutting the help loose one or two at a time to grab a bite to eat. I told her to give everyone an hour and tell them to be back sooner if possible.

Almost every one was cooperative. Most only took 35-40 minutes and came right back and hit it again. But at around 8:30, Ruby reported that two of her people, SSgt Cheniqua Wilson-Peters and Sgt Sylbethia Blue, had been gone for two hours and weren't back yet. I came unglued. At nine o'clock, they came drag-assing in and I had them into my office for a little chat.

To my absolute and total amazement, the stupid bitches had taken a taxi off base and ate at a restaurant down town. And when they were finished eating, Cheniqua went home to turn her lights on (she didn't want her house to be dark when she got home later that night), and Sylbethia ran an "errand" (not further explained). When I told them how stupid, inconsiderate, and selfish their actions were, they couldn't understand why I was so upset. What they did seemed perfectly logical to them. Never the less, I laid a Letter of Counseling on them outlining what I expected of them and promising a Letter of Reprimand if they erred again.

At 1:30 a.m. the next morning, I decided it was time to knock off for the day. Everyone was getting punchy and the work was getting sloppy because they were so tired. Got into bed around two o'clock and was up at five and back in to work for another tough day. My frustration level was "maxed out" all day long. We just couldn't get *anything* through the Command Section.

Sgt Jenny Burnell had been relieved of duty for being "too soft" on her quality control procedures and Sgt Loftus and Lt Lane were having a field day. Three examples of reasons they were kicking write-ups back for correction come immediately to mind:

> One write-up mentioned that the individual had planned and participated in the unit's chili cook off. They sent it back for correction because (they said) cook off was one word (cookoff)

> Another was sent back because they wanted a "d" after the 6903 in "6903 Electronic Security Group". Less than an hour later, they kicked one back for us to take the "d" out after the 6903 in "6903d Electronic Security Group". Go figure.
>
> Another write-up was rejected because "world wide" is supposed to be "world-wide".

I could fill a page with examples, but I think these three are enough to demonstrate the magnitude of the errors we were letting slip through our QC process. But I know better than to challenge Loftus or Lane, so we just make the changes and press on.

Even as I'm making this entry, I just got a call on my beeper. It was Col Lucas saying he needed 10 bodies *now* (the reader must remember that *now* is 10:00 a.m. on Sunday morning) to help move furniture into Dorm 475. I'm already furnishing 10 people a day on Friday, Saturday, today, and tomorrow to move furniture. But the Colonel sez that ain't enough. The job's not getting done fast enough.

So onto the phone to call the flight on duty. They could only spring two people. Then I called MSgt Johnny Samuels, the Chief of the Training Branch, at home and asked how many trainees he could dig up. He said four and I told him to roust them out and send them to Dorm 475. He's supposed to call me back at 10:30 with a progress report on how he's doing finding people. If he can't find them, I'll have to come up with another plan.

I still needed four more bodies, so I walked down the hall to SMSgt Brian Decker's room, got him out of bed (Boy, *that* made him happy), and broke the bad news to him: come up with four people to help move furniture or else. He's out right now trying to scare them up. I've got to quit writing and (beeper just went off: Samuels found three and is going to pull the detail himself to meet his quota of four) get up to the dorm to make sure enough people show up. Will get back to this entry later (I hope).

It's 3:00 p.m. and I'm back. All ten of my people showed up and were they ever pissed. Can't say I blame them. All the furniture had already been moved except half the first floor. I knew it would go faster if I pitched in, so I did. We just finished up. Now I've got ten guys and gals reporting for the detail tomorrow morning and there's not going to be anything for them to do. Soon as I finish this entry, I've got to try and contact them to tell them not to show up tomorrow. Don't know how much luck I'll have, but I've got to give it a try.

And now back to the Awards and Decs fiasco I was writing about when I was so rudely interrupted. We continued to endure the Loftus/Lane edit team the rest of the day and, every now and then, a package would finally make its way through to Col Lucas' desk for signature.

When about half the packages were finished around noon, I personally took them to the Orderly Room and waited for TSgt Greene to process them. From the Orderly Room, I took them to the Personnel Office where I waited again while all the data was entered into a computer. The people in the Personnel Office didn't want to give me "while you wait" service, but Chief Webb Rawlins (an old acquaintance from when we were both stationed in the headquarters) came to my rescue and "encouraged" his folks to give me good service. Then back to the Orderly Room for TSgt Greene to work some more administrivia magic, then to Ruby for her people to wrap the packages for shipment. From there it was over to Hill 170 where I turned the whole mess over to the Directorate of Administration for them to be placed in courier channels. Whew!!

It took almost two hours for me to do all that and when I returned to the office around two o'clock, Ruby gleefully laid another problem on me. Cheniqua Wilson-Peters and Sylbethia

Blue had gone to lunch at 11:30 and still hadn't returned. I couldn't believe they would do something that stupid, but I kept my cool and calmly went to my office and started writing two Letters of Reprimand.

When Cheniqua and Sylbethia got back to work at 2:30, I called them in and said, "Here's what I promised you," and handed them the letters. They tried to explain where they had been, but I was in no mood to listen. I told them to get their asses out of my sight and back to work. I still don't know what their excuse was. I don't care.

When supper time came around, I decided we would dine in. Maj Weber and I went to the Commissary Deli and got the makings for sandwiches: garlic balogna, ham, turkey, roast beef, and (at the Major's insistence) pastrami. Then we got mustard, mayonnaise, bread, lettuce, tomatoes, and pickles and took everything back to work. We spread it all out on our conference table and everyone lined up and made themselves a sandwich. Ruby broke out a big bag of potato chips she had stashed in her desk and SMSgt Sammy Velanti bought sodas for everyone and we just had ourselves a little picnic. Believe it or not, we all enjoyed it tremendously. The Major and I split the cost--only $10 each.

Went back to work after supper and stayed at it until midnight. The Command Section finally yelled "calf rope" and said they were going home. Yes, they worked the same hours we did. I've got to give them credit for that. And as the hours drug on, the insanity of their editing eased up. I guess we "out tired-ed" them.

Back in the next morning at 6:00 a.m. and by this time we were coming down the home stretch. We got Col Lucas' signature on the last award around nine o'clock that morning. I took the stack and repeated the Orderly Room, Personnel Office, Orderly Room routine again. By noon, the only thing left to do was wrap the stuff to be placed in courier channels and deliver everything to the Directorate of Administration.

Without going into a lot of detail, I'll just say that wrapping for courier isn't all that easy. It's very meticulous and time consuming work. At five o'clock, Ruby said there were still 20 packages to be wrapped. If three people worked overtime, they should be able to finish up by midnight and she could let the rest of her Adminers go home. I said I had just the right people for the job: SSgt Rick Meyers, SSgt Cheniqua Wilson-Peters, and Sgt Sylbethia Blue. Ruby sprung everyone else and we left the three of them mumbling, grumbling, and wrapping Awards and Decorations write-ups.

♦♦♦♦♦♦♦♦♦♦

Hurried back to my room to change into my mess dress and go to the 7th Air Force Airman/NCO/Senior NCO of the year banquet. It was all I could do to keep from going face down in my potato soup, but I somehow managed to stay awake and endure the ordeal.

♦♦♦♦♦♦♦♦♦♦

After seven good hours of sleep Wednesday night, I felt great Thursday morning. Got in to work at 6:00 a.m. and my phone was ringing. It was Lt Lane saying that Col Lucas wanted to see me in his office at eight o'clock. Oh, shit! I had no idea what I had done now, but I expected the worst. I wished there was such a thing as iron-assed jockey shorts. I lined up all the things I was going to say in my mind and decided that, if it got too bad, I was going to demand that Col Lucas fire me and get me the hell out of here.

I went to The Man's office at the appointed hour (he did not keep me waiting as he normally does) and formally reported in. "Sir, Chief Master Sergeant Beal reporting as ordered, Sir."

I hadn't done that in years, but that's exactly where our relationship is. The Colonel didn't have any difficulty picking up on my mood. He said things didn't have to be so formal between us and, when I came into his office, I should just sit down and be comfortable like any other Chief entering a Colonel's office. I told him I'd like to do that, but I didn't think our relationship called for that type behavior. He said, "That's what I want to talk to you about."

He offered me a chair, then came from behind his desk (a power position he normally uses when I talk to him) and sat down on the sofa across from me. Then he apologized for chewing my ass in the middle of the Command Section with an audience. I accepted his apology. Then he said my non-verbal communication was extremely strong and he had picked up on the fact that I had been "rolling over and playing dead" recently. I asked him what he expected, considering the treatment he'd been giving me. Then he apologized again.

He said he needed my help to run the unit and told me to give him feedback when there was something on my mind that was troubling me. I reminded him that every time I tried to do just that, he unloaded on me. He said that he wouldn't always agree on everything, but when he disagreed with me, I shouldn't just back off and let him have his way. We should "discuss" things.

I told him I could handle that, but I couldn't handle the "you enlisted swine--me Colonel" bullshit he was always laying on me. I reminded him of Beal's Chief Rule Number One: "When Chiefs and Colonels fight, Chiefs lose." I said I was willing to work with him, but I wasn't willing to fight him. As long as he comes on like a charging bull, I'll back off. And I'll keep backing off 'till I back right out of this unit. He seemed to understand that and said he wouldn't come on so strong in the future.

Next, I turned to the Joe Del Ricco affair. I told him I didn't need his prodding to deal with Del Ricco and related my plan when I found out how bad things really were in Ops Admin. He asked why I didn't tell him that before, and I said it would have sounded like an excuse. He agreed. Then I told him that I thought it was a cheap, underhanded shot for him to call everybody on base and telling them not to hire Joe.

"He finally got hired on at another unit, didn't he?" he said lamely.

"Yes he did," I replied, "but it was no thanks to you."

And then I brought up the matter of Sgt Della Loftus and her blatant disrespect for me. I told him if any other E-4 treated me like she does, I would reach down their throat, hook my finger through their asshole, and yank them inside-out. He asked me why I allowed her to be disrespectful and I told him it was a simple case of a three striper hiding behind his eagles. I knew if I reprimanded her, I would have to deal with him. It just wasn't worth it.

Col Lucas seemed genuinely surprised by this revelation. He said that no matter what else we might disagree on, we did agree on proper respect for rank and position. I told him now that we understood each other, the next time Sgt Loftus gave me flack, I was going to stomp an mud-hole in her ass and wade it dry. The Colonel's response to that was, "I'm sure you'll do whatever's right, Chief."

Our discussion ended with Col Lucas assuring me I was a key player in the unit and that the unit couldn't survive without my participation. And then he stuck out his hand for a shake and apologized again. I left his office feeling pretty good (but not cocky). As I walked past Della Loftus, I thought to myself, "Try me one more time, Bitch. One more time."

I have mixed emotions about my meeting with Lucas. On the one hand, I got some satisfaction, he ate a little crow, and hopefully our relationship will improve and tensions will ease. On the other hand, I feel uneasy about the timing of the talk. Was he motivated to "mend the fence" with me because he was sincerely sorry about all that's been going on to cause a rift between us, or was he afraid I would approach the IG about how bad the situation has become at SKIVVY NINE under his leadership? I certainly hope it wasn't he latter. I want the unit to pass the re-inspection as much as he does (maybe more), and I certainly wouldn't do anything to jeopardize our chances.

So that's where I stand with Lucas. I sure do hope things improve. I don't think I could make it to the end of my tour under conditions like the last couple of weeks.

♦♦♦♦♦♦♦♦♦♦

I got my first opportunity to test my new-found favorable relationship with the Colonel Friday. I had two disagreements with the First Shirt that we couldn't iron out (the boy is getting more like Duckworth every day) on our own, so I took them to Col Lucas for resolution.

The first flap centered on SSgt Len Shardursky and (in the First Sergeant's words) his "defacing of Government property". At Commander's Call last week, the Orderly Room folks passed out locator cards instead of the normal attendance slips. They figured that, since everybody had to attend Commander's Call anyway, it would be a great opportunity to update locator cards. Only trouble was, they didn't inform people what they were doing, so some folks didn't realize the importance of what they were filling out. Especially Len Shardursky.

When he filled out his card, the only thing in English was his name. Everything else was in Chinese. I guess he thought it would be cute to show the guys in the Orderly Room how good a 208 he was. They were not impressed. And in addition to filling out the card in Chinese, Len "doodled" on it, too. Heaven forbid! What could he possibly be thinking of?

Jimbo called me at around 10:00 a.m. and told me to send Shardursky to his office to receive a Letter of Reprimand. I asked what for. He told me. I didn't believe it. I drove to the Orderly Room to take a look at the offending locator card. I told Jimbo that unless some of that Chinese writing said, "The First Sergeant sucks donkey dicks", a Letter of Reprimand was much too severe. He disagreed. We talked. He still disagreed. He was adamant that Shardursky needed to be taught a lesson and a Letter of Reprimand was just the medicine he needed. I decided it was time for Col Lucas to get involved.

On the way to the Colonel's office, I ran into TSgt Chuck Flannigan in the compound parking lot. Chuck is a roly-poly little guy who's weight hovers right on the borderline of the maximum allowable weight (MAW) and he had a sad story for me. The Orderly Room had been conducting a week-long weigh-in in preparation for the IG visit. When Chuck weighed in, he was a full inch shorter than he has been in the past. One inch equals five pounds less on the MAW chart and that put Chuck two pounds over weight.

The guy who was conducting the weigh-in said everybody had been complaining about losing height (including me--I came in at 5'8" instead of my normal 5'10"), but Chuck was the first guy who had busted his weight limit because of it. So the weigh-in guy got a tape measure and measured Chuck against the wall. He came out a full inch taller, which meant he was three pounds under the MAW. The guy conducting the weigh-in was only a two striper, and didn't want to make the decision on whether or not to put Chuck on the program. So he went to Jimbo and told him the story.

Jimbo went to the weigh-in area and measured himself using both the scale and the tape measure. Sure enough, he came out an inch shorter on the scale. With that kind of proof, Chuck figured he wouldn't be placed on the weight management program. He was wrong. Jimbo said he had to go on the program anyway.

Needless to say, Chuck was more than just a little pissed. He protested furiously, but Jimbo refused to back off.

Right there in the middle of the parking lot, Chuck asked me to intercede on his behalf and see if I could do something about getting this thing ironed out. I went back to the Orderly Room (never did make it to the Colonel's office) and told Jimbo that something was obviously out of kilter here. I told him that I had measured two inches shorter on that scale, but I wasn't worried because I wasn't near my MAW. But in Chuck Flannigan's case (and anyone else who went over the MAW due to "shrinkage"), he should check out the scales before putting him on the weight management program. Jimbo wouldn't agree to that. I said "that's bullshit".

So he offered to take me to the hospital and check me out on their super calibrated equipment "if you've got the guts". I had the guts. At the hospital, I measured out at five nine and a half and weighed 184. We went straight back to the unit scale where I measured five eight and weighed 184. "OK, Jimbo, there you go. Your scales are measuring short. You can't put Chuck Flannigan on the weight management program."

He thought about that one for a minute and came to the obvious conclusion. His scale was wrong, but Chuck Flannigan still needed to go on the program. Here was his reasoning:

He didn't have time to re-weigh and re-measure everyone in the unit before the IG arrived. It wouldn't be fair to give Chuck special dispensation just because he went over MAW on a bad scale. Everyone needed to be weighed using the same standard. The fact that Chuck Flannigan would have to suffer an injustice because of the inaccurate scale didn't bother Jimbo at all. "Anybody that close to the max deserves what they get. Everybody should be at least 10 percent under their max."

I raised the bullshit flag. There's a Reg, it says how much you can weigh at which height, and that's the standard. No ifs, ands, or buts.

I headed back to see Col Lucas. Lt Lane allowed me into his office without having to wait (that's refreshing) and I told him about the locator card incident and the inaccurate scale. I asked for his support. He gave it to me.

Lucas called Capt Oakley and told him that Len Shardursky would not get a Letter of Reprimand. A verbal counseling may be more appropriate. Then he directed Oakley not to put Chuck Flannigan on the weight management program and to re-measure and weigh everyone who was within five pounds of the MAW before the IG arrives, this time using an accurate scale.

During an inspection, the IG weighs everyone who's within five pounds of the MAW, so the Colonel wanted only those people weighed. No use making everybody suffer through a weigh-in--just the ones who need it. Good on him.

♦♦♦♦♦♦♦♦♦♦

Yesterday was a normal duty day. It's been so long since I've had a day off, I can't remember what it's like. I thought today was going to be it, but as you already know, the furniture moving detail put the ki-bosh on that.

We dedicated yesterday to IG prep and Ruby the Viper and her crew painted the Major's and my office. I did a follow-up inspection based on the one I did last week. When I inspected the first time, I wrote everything down and put out a letter to all Branches telling them to get things fixed.

SKIVVY NINE!

During the follow-up inspection yesterday, everything looked great. They had all done everything I had asked, everyone, that is, except SSgt "Henk" Henkendorf. Ops Supply was in an absolute shambles. I told Henk he *would not* leave last night until the place was spic and span. I haven't been back to check it out yet, but I'll do that tonight. If it's not done, I'll track Henk down and make sure he does it tomorrow cuz the day after that, the reinspection starts. Can't let the IG see that place in the condition it was in.

Chapter Fifteen

THEY'RE HERE! ***AGAIN!!***

Sunday, January 24th

I often marvel that the APRs, Awards, and Decorations are Job One at the 6903rd (or 6903d, depending on who's doing the editing). Since Col Lucas' arrival, our entire priority system has been turned upside-down. SKIVVY NINE has one of the hottest missions in Electronic Security Command, but in the past few months, it's taken a back seat to administrivia. Just don't make sense.

But I must admit that, when I came here, APRs, OERs, Awards, and Decs were in sad shape. They shouldn't be top priority, but they shouldn't be ignored, either, And they were back then. At one time in May, Maj Weber alone had almost 20 overdue write-ups, a couple over six months late. Something needed to be done, but, B-Jesus, I do think we're overreacted just a little. There's got to be a middle ground somewhere. In any case, we've got the problem fixed (at least for the time being) and Ruby the Viper rides over the program like Attila the Hun, so it should stay fixed. God, do I hope it stays fixed.

And speaking of Ruby--I sure am glad to have her around. God knows the bitch is efficient and she has everything running smoothly. Even her personality is perking up a little bit. She doesn't growl at me when I say good morning any more. She doesn't return the greeting, but she doesn't snarl, either. Bless her heart.

Our two Reservists Admin types left Friday. TSgt Jensen and SSgt Best definitely left their marks on SKIVVY NINE. But they were certainly different marks.

Jensen almost single handedly destroyed a Master Sergeant's career and did maybe 15 minutes work during the total time she was here. All she was good for was stirring up shit. Unfortunately, I won't have an opportunity to write an APR on her. Reservist's APRs aren't written by the unit of assignment (here), but instead are written by the unit of attachment (in this case, the Headquarters.) But I will have an input. I've already made a couple of phone calls to Chief Joe Crain, the head beagle in Reserve Affairs at the Headquarters. He said he had hoped Jensen would work out better than she has on other assignments, but apparently, she hadn't. So he wants me to put some stuff in writing and he'll make sure it's included in her next APR.

The other Reservist, on the other hand, worked out just great. SSgt Millie Best was probably the sole reason the Orderly Room was ready for the re-inspection. They would never have gotten their shit together before the IG's arrival if it hadn't been for her. She did such a good job that Jimbo is going to recommend her for an Air Force Commendation Medal. That's almost unheard of for a Reservist. And she so impressed Col Lucas that he wants to hire her on as his secretary. Ingred McCall finally got enough of the Command Section and quit with only two weeks notice back in December. She's been Secretary to the Commander of SKIVVY NINE for almost 15 years, but she just couldn't take this one and bailed out. So the Colonel wants Millie to come back over here in her civilian capacity and be his secretary.

Monday was a holiday, but at SKIVVY NINE, we don't do holidays. I took a wee sleep-in and went in at 9:00 a.m. and worked until around three o'clock. Did a lot of last minute touching up in preparation for the IG Team who were scheduled to begin the re-inspection the next morning. Mostly, I spent the whole day making sure the place was clean. Lord! How I hate doing that. I remember the old gray-haired farts who were Ops Supes with I was a two-striper and what I thought of them. And I know what these kids must think of me. "He doesn't give a rat's ass about the mission. All he cares about is clean floors." I wish it didn't have to be that way, but it is.

♦♦♦♦♦♦♦♦♦

Got out of bed Tuesday morning bright eyed and bushy tailed, ready to meet the IG Team head-on. And then the recall sirens went off! The 51st Tactical Fighter Wing Commander had kicked off a base-wide recall and hadn't told Col Lucas it was going to happen. Based on Col Lucas' policy of, "We're going to be completely involved in base activities including exercises", I threw on a uniform, grabbed my fear gear, and headed for the door.

Before I made it outside, my beeper went off. It was the Mission Supe telling me to call him immediately. I did. The Mission Supe said the Colonel had decided we were *not* going to play in the exercise. We were too busy with the IG Team. So he back-slid again. But I was thankful; while the rest of the base was wearing gas masks, flak vests, and chemical gear all week, SKIVVY NINErs would have the run of the base like nothing was going on.

The IG in-brief kicked off at 8:00 a.m. Col Lucas gave our portion of the briefing himself and (I almost hate to say this but give the Devil his due) absolutely knocked their sox off. The man is one hellava speaker. Lt Col Brogan gave the IG portion of the program and stepped all over his crank--mumbled, stumbled, missed slide change cues, and generally scrod up everything. I loved it! With a start like that, we definitely had them on the defensive.

Operations people hardly knew there was an inspection going on. Since we did so well the first time around, no one messed with us except the Computer Resource Management Branch. The inspectors gave them a hard look-see, but SMSgt Sammy Valtani has had those boys humping every since I assigned him down there and they came out smelling like a rose.

As a matter of fact, everyone who was re-inspected did well. Orderly Room; Budget; Maintenance and Logistics; Disaster Preparedness; Emergency Destruction; Safety; they all watered their eyes. But the biggie was there were no late APRs, OERs, Awards, or Decorations. And believe me, they were looked at hard. Bottom line: we were in good shape everywhere they looked, but they didn't look everywhere.

A couple of months ago, I went to Col Lucas and told him that all the exercises he was having to get ready for the re-visit were unnecessary since the IG wouldn't have an exercise while they were here. Our exercise had been rated SATISFACTORY on the initial inspection and I knew from personal experience on the Team that the IG does not re-inspect anything rated SAT or above. It's just not done.

But the hard-headed bastard wouldn't listen to me and kept pressing right on with exercise after exercise, running the unit right into the ground in the process. When the Team got here, he asked when they planned to have their exercise. Their response was, "What exercise?"

Col Lucas *demanded* they have one, but Col Bergman (the IG) held his ground. They hadn't brought along the exercise inspection check list (or inspectors) and they damn well didn't intend to have an exercise. But Lucas persisted; he wanted to show them what his people could do. No good. Bergman finally told the boy to get out of his face. *"THERE WILL BE NO EXERCISE!"*

So we didn't have one and every two and three striper in the unit was asking, "Why did *he* do *that* to *me*? Why have we been jumping through our assholes getting ready for an IG exercise we didn't have?" Good question. The same question was asked by a lot of other people who came out SATISFACTORY (or better) on the first inspection but were forced to bust their asses getting ready for the re-look. A lot of damn hard work was done for no reason.

The out-brief is next Thursday with a "Kick the IG out of Town" party at the Lounge immediately thereafter. By regulation, a unit can't be rated higher than SAT on a re-inspect, but from the way things went, I'm sure the words in the briefing will have EXCELLENT and OUTSTANDING written all over them. Should be one hellava party.

♦♦♦♦♦♦♦♦♦

Thursday, the Staff Sergeant promotion list was released by Col Lucas. The list was releasable to the promotees at midnight and Col Lucas decided he wanted to notify each individual personally. Nothing unusual there; all commanders take great pleasure in telling their people they just got promoted.

But sane commanders do it during the first duty hour on the day the list is released. Not Lucas! He wanted to do it immediately after midnight. He decided to go to the promotee's place of residence (both in the dorms and off base), bang on their door, wake them up, and present them with the good news.

There were 33 people on the list and to notify each and every one would take at least four to five hours. That meant no sleep at all Thursday night/Friday morning. That's all well and good if the Colonel intended to make the notifications alone, but that wasn't the case. He wanted all the key people in the unit to go along with him: Capt Oakley, Jimbo, Capt Jacoby, Bob Estep, Maj Reardon, Maj Weber, Lt Lane, and me. Boy! What a dumb-shit idea.

Col Lucas called a meeting of all concerned at 5:00 p.m. to plan transportation arrangements and decide where we were going to meet up. He was excited as a little kid about the whole thing, but it was obvious from looking at the faces around the conference table that the rest of the group did not share his enthusiasm. I wanted to tell him what a dumb-shit idea it was, but I didn't dare; "Yes Sir, No Sir. Three bags full." So I sat there fuming while he babbled on about what a fun night we were going to have.

Finally, someone had the balls to speak up. Jimbo said, "Colonel, I've got a hard day with the IG Team ahead of me tomorrow. I can't see staying up all night to tell folks they made Staff and then bleed my ass off all day while I'm trying to put my best foot forward with the IG. I'm not going."

There was a long moment of uncomfortable silence while everybody's asshole puckered. Others (including me) had been so bold as to not go along with the Colonel in the past and regretted it. To disagree with the Colonel meant you were not a team player. I fully expected him to fire off on Jimbo big time. But he didn't. He simply said, "You don't have to go if you don't want to, First Sergeant. This is a voluntary thing; nobody has to go if they don't want to."

"Then count me out." It was Bob Estep. Then I told him I couldn't make it either. The three top enlisted men in the unit had taken the lead and the officers followed them like rats off a sinking ship. One by one, they suggested that maybe notifying the folks during the first duty hour was the way to go. That left the Colonel and Lt Lane to make the notifications by themselves.

Then Lane came up with a novel idea that was sure to save the day. We'd all come in at 3:30 a.m. and kick off a recall to get all the promotees to work. Then we'd tell them that the IG Team had directed a random urinalysis test and they were to report to the Commander's office immediately for further instructions. Then when they got to the Commanders office, Earl Romano would have them fill out lab slips, give them a "pee cup", and tell them to go to the Conference Room where the tests were being conducted. Then when they came into the Conference Room, there would be Col Lucas with a set of Staff Sergeant stripes in his hand and he would say, "I'll swap these stripes for that cup in your hand." And they would be surprised, and Maj Reardon would take a picture, and everybody would have a big laugh. *BAAAAAAARRRRRRRRRRRFF!!!*

Col Lucas bought the idea, lock, stock, and insanity. I didn't think the plan could get much more Mickey Mouse than it already was, but the next morning when I showed up at three thirty, I found it could. There was Col Lucas in a green operating room get-up complete with a mask over his face. We kicked off the recall and the first one showed up around 4:00 a.m. His only reaction when he came into the Conference Room was, "You have got to be shitting me."

I thought, "No, young man. We are not shitting you, but I bet you wish we were."

The promotees straggled in all the way up until around seven o'clock. None of them were "fooled"; you'd have to be an idiot not to figure out there was something wrong with this picture. They all knew the Staff list was going to be released that day. They also knew full well that you don't go to the Commander's Office for a urinalysis test. Those things are done at the hospital and they all know that. But they endured the goat rope, just happy to know they had been promoted.

And then to add insult to injury, once they reported to the Conference Room and got the news, they weren't allowed to leave until the last promotee reported in. Didn't want to take the chance that one of them might tell his buddy and ruin the "surprise" for him. So that first guy who came in at four o'clock ended up sitting in a holding tank twiddling his thumbs until that last one wandered in at seven. In short, a relatively pleasant experience had been reduced to a "piss off the troops" event. I know Col Lucas' heart is in the right place on this thing, but--Sweet Jesus--where's the sanity?

♦♦♦♦♦♦♦♦♦

I've ranted and raved throughout this epistle about how difficult it is to get anything through the Command Section; everything in writing is "edited' by Lane and Loftus and sent back for correction. Well, a couple of letters came out of the Command Section last week that will give the reader some idea of the hypocrisy of it all. The letters appear on the next two pages.

The first letter is from Lt Lane to MSgt Greg Guthier concerning the quality of the Airman/NCO/Senior NCO of the Quarter write-ups he submitted to be forwarded to Pacific Electronic Security Division for their consideration. I didn't see the packages; knowing Greg, they may well have been dog shit. That's not the point.

The tone of the letter highlights Lane's "holier than thou" attitude. The other thing the reader might want to look at is the writing itself. Paragraph two bears special notice. It looks like it was written by an illiterate; and that same illiterate is the one who kicks my writing back two, three, four, or more times because it's not good enough for the Commander's signature. And then there's ".....making them a product of your responsibility....." *Give me a break*!!

Letter number two is an even larger faux pas. MSgt Bob Hansen is the Chairman of the Morale Action Committee of the Senior NCO Council. A couple of weeks ago, he had a committee meeting and forwarded the minutes to Col Lucas so he would know what the committee was up to. The Colonel jotted down the answers to Bob's questions, intending them to go back to Bob and Bob *only*. Instead, the answers were placed in this letter and sent to the entire unit. When you read this letter, it's like playing

"JEOPARDY"; you've got the answers, but you don't know what the questions were.

The letter worked its way through the distribution system and when it reached the Operations Branches, my phone began to ring. The Branch Chiefs wanted to know what the hell the letter was all about. I hadn't even seen it yet; it was buried deep in the bowels of my in basket. When I dug it out and read it, it was relatively easy to discern what had happened. I took it to Lane for an explanation. "Well, gosh, Chief. That's a mistake anyone could make." Bullshit! But I didn't gloat. I didn't dare.

DEPARTMENT OF THE AIR FORCE
HEADQUARTERS 6903D ELECTRONIC SECURITY GROUP
APO SAN FRANCISCO 96570-6375

MSgt Guthier *19 January*

These quarterly award packages should have never made it up this far. As OPR for this program, it is.....or should be your responsibility to proof all these packages, standardize and ensure professional, well-written packages are submitted on our people.

Not only should the justification be at its strongest, but the biography, fact sheet, and cover letter should be as sharp as they can be. In my mind these packages <u>have</u> been reviewed by you making them the product of your responsibility. Please take the time to do a good job, the best job, the first time through---the better all of us will feel. You'll be proud of your program, and I won't frown when receiving the submissions for the commander's review 'cause I know about the PAST submission conditions.....LOUSY!!!

I understand that proofing and editing is very time consuming, but believe me, a little more effort on your part will go a long way for all of us.

If the next submission packages are submitted to the commander in this condition, I will send them back immediately.

LORETTA M. LANE, 1Lt, USAF *Cy: CC*
Executive Officer *DO*

DEPARTMENT OF THE AIR FORCE
HEADQUARTERS 6903D ELECTRONIC SECURITY GROUP
APO SAN FRANCISCO 96570-6375

FROM: CC *20 January*
SUBJ: Morale Action Committee Agenda Items
TO: Morale Action Committee

1. Contacted Promotions and Testing on this problem. Special order T-030 dated 17 November authorized payment to qualified 208's. Copy of orders sent to each individual. Message dated 18/0800Z Nov sent to USAF Finance Center in Denver identifying qualified 208's. Contacted Accounting and Finance on this problem. They are in receipt of a message from USAF Finance Center dated 24/1326Z Nov that authorizes payment to qualified 208's effective 15 Dec payday.

2. CCQ has been tasked to come up with policy letter for separate rations. With the new dining hall we will have to start people on separate rations. We are working with base and should have policy letter soon.

3. Do I ever understand what you are talking about on lack of total involvement in committees. Agree we can publish minutes which help a great deal in keeping people informed of status of programs and projects. We'll start.

JASON L. LUCAS, Colonel, USAF
Commander

Wednesday, January 27th

Went to the Base Airman/NCO/Senior NCO of the Year banquet Monday night. The guest speaker was Col Jim Michaud, the 51st Tac Fighter Wing Commander. He's even more of an egomaniac than Lucas. Only difference is, Michaud will probably make Brigadier General--Lucas won't.

His speech was centered around January 25, 1950. That's the day (at least according to the good Colonel) that the yellow hoard to the north invaded the helpless South Korea. He just kept hammering on "the fact" that, on the exact anniversary of this very night, the cause of democracy was put to its most severe test and not only survived, but flourished. And that's why we're here in the Republic of Korea today; to make sure those Godless heathens don't try it again. That's what this banquet was all about--to prevent a recurrence of 25 January 1950.

I don't know how many people in the audience knew it (everyone in the SKIVVY NINE delegation sure as hell did), but the Colonel had one *BIG* flaw in his presentation. The North Koreans didn't invade on 25 January; they invaded on 25 June. The boy made a complete ass of himself. The speech writer (probably some poor staff officer) probably died a slow, agonizing death the next morning when Michaud discovered the error.

And then just to pour salt in the wound, Col Michaud closed his talk with a slide and music show. There were pictures of Old Glory flowing gently in the breeze; the space shuttle taking off; bombs bursting in air; the Thunderbirds in close acrobatic maneuvers; fighter aircraft dropping napalm on those nasty Viet Cong; and fireworks over the Statue of Liberty. The only thing missing was a picture of Mom's apple pie.

While all that was flashing on the screen, music designed to stir the soul and tug at the heartstrings played in the background. Every so often the music was punctuated by a deep, resonate voice saying, "I am the spirit of the Air Force"; "I am the spirit of the Air Force"; "I am the spirit of the Air Force". And then came the Grand Finale.

The last slide was a picture of Col Michaud hisself in the cockpit of an F-16 fighter, a true depiction of a gallant warrior astride his noble steed. And just as that slide came on the screen, the deep, resonate voice rang out one final time, "I am the spirit of the Air Force!". Everyone at our table just kinda looked at each other like, "You have *got* to be bullshitting me!!" I don't want to overuse the word, but this passage cries out for it, so I must use it again: *BAAAAAAARRRRRRRRRRRFF!!!*

As a minor aside to the night's festivities, the 03rd didn't win anything--again. It's been over five years since one of our people won anything at the base level. I can't believe our people are that dumb. I've got to believe the deck may be stacked ever so slightly.

♦♦♦♦♦♦♦♦♦

Tomorrow is the big day. The IG Team does the final outbrief, but everyone knows we done good. There won't be any surprises.

Ever since we started preparing for the re-inspect six months ago, Col Lucas has been dangling one big carrot in front of the troops to keep them going. Immediately after the outbrief, everyone would go directly from the theater to the SKIVVY NINE Lounge for one hellava blow-out. Since the party would undoubtedly last far into the night, the next day would be a down day.

Well, now it's time to put up or shut up. It's time to give the troops a break, and Col Lucas has reneged. The briefing takes place at 10:00 a.m. and should be over by 11:00. But the Colonel won't let the party begin until 5:00 p.m.; got too much work to do to start a party before noon. And Friday as a down day? Completely out of the question--entirely too many man-hours lost.

The word has already gotten out and everyone is crushed. All the ones I've talked to say they intend to boycott the party. So I guess it'll be the Command Section, Col Lucas, me, and Maj Weber (we don't *dare* boycott). Sure sounds like fun, huh.

Sunday, January 31st

The IG outbrief went as expected Thursday morning--we were rated SATISFACTORY overall. The only surprise was the MARGINAL in one small area of Safety. Milt Joskey snuck that one in without telling the guy he was inspecting. Dirty pool--not like Milt at all, but like I've said before, the attitude of the Team has really changed since I was on it.

The outbrief itself was kind of a bummer. I've never heard anything so bland and ho-hum. Nothing like the lavish extravaganzas we put on when I was on the Team. Col Lucas had requested a full blown outbrief, complete with pictures of unit people doing their jobs and words that said how we *really* did. He knew we couldn't be rated higher than SATISFACTORY on a re-look, but after running the entire unit into the ground, he wanted the words to say EXCELLENT or OUTSTANDING even if the "official" rating couldn't. He wanted the good words as a reward for him and his people, and the good words just were not there. They were "SAT words" and the Colonel was pissed.

And there were no pictures of unit people--just word slides. The IG Team didn't even bring a camera with them. Col Lucas has seen enough outbriefs to know that there's always a "people show" made up of left-over slides the Team doesn't use in the outbrief. But since they didn't make any slides for the outbrief, there obviously wouldn't be any left-overs for a people show.

So Monday, the Colonel tasked the unit Public Affairs Representative to start taking flicks of people; lots of flicks. And the PA Rep (A1C Sammi Sue Woody) done good and burned up a ton of film. Everyone in SKIVVY NINE had that camera stuck in their faces at least once.

From the pictures Sammi Sue made, Lucas and Lane *personally* put together a people show. I've got to hand it to them; they did a jam-up job. The IG Team could have taken a few lessons for when they put their own people show together. The order of the slides was just right, the pictures of aircraft interspersed every now and then, and the music seemed to always fit what was on the screen. There was a whole series showing the Emergency Destruction Team setting off explosive devices as a demonstration for the IG Team. The music: "Danger Zone", the theme from "Top Gun". Like I said, very well done.

The only detractor from the show was at its end. There were lots of pictures of Mt Rushmore, the Golden Gate Bridge, Statue of Liberty, Grand Canyon, the Alamo, the Lincoln Memorial, etc, etc, etc while Ray Charles belted out "America the Beautiful". And the last slide was of Col Lucas saluting the flag during a retreat ceremony. Wonder where he got the idea for that?

And then as the screen slowly faded to black and the music tailed off, Bob Estep, who was sitting next to me, sprang to his feet and began slapping his hands together. He whispered, "Get up! Get up!"

I said, "For what?"

And he said, "Just do what I tell you." So I stood up and started applauding; couldn't let a fellow Chief down. Since we were the only two people in the whole damned theater doing it, I felt like an absolute idiot. But the audience was pretty savvy; they caught on after a while and stood up and began applauding too.

I was more than a little pissed at Bob. While the standing ovation continued, I asked why he did what he did. He said the move was prearranged by Col Lucas. He figured the two Chiefs in the unit should "take the lead" in showing the unit's appreciation for the people show. Oh well.

Then came the outbrief. After that, the unit staged it's own "Professional Performer" recognition ceremony. That's something else Col Lucas had asked Col Bergman to do; identify those people who did a super job during the inspection and recognize them at the outbrief as Professional Performers. Once again, the IG explained that's something that's done after inspections, not re-inspections. Lucas insisted, but Bergman held his ground, "We've never had Professional Performers on re-looks and we're not going to start now." So Col Lucas did it himself.

There was a noticeable lack of Operations people in the Professional Performer line-up, and that fact wasn't lost on the troops in the trenches. On the way out of the theater after the whole thing was over, I was walking behind a couple of young Airmen. One of them was brand new to the unit, so he wasn't here when we were inspected the first time. He asked his buddy why there were no Ops people identified as Professional Performers.

"Because we weren't re-inspected," the other Airman said. "Those people you saw on stage today flunked the initial inspection and now they're being recognized for fixing the fuck-ups they had the first time around. The *real* Professional Performers are in Ops--we passed inspection the first time." Hear, hear!!

After the Professional Performer program, Col Bergman said a few words. He was followed by BGen Heffner (7th Air Force Vice Commander), and then Lt Gen Reynolds (7th Air Force Commander) gave a pitch. Their talks were all different, but each one had a single central theme: In June, SKIVVY NINE was in the toilet, not worth the powder to blow us to hell. But since then, we have grabbed our bootstraps and pulled ourselves back up to our former greatness.

God! How I wanted to leap to my feet and yell, "Wait a minute, Fellas! What about Operations? We make up three quarters of the unit and we came within a gnat's eyelash of being rated EXCELLENT the first time around. We haven't had to pull ourselves back up by anything. We were in good shape then; we're in good shape now." But naturally, I didn't. I (along with everyone else in Ops) just sat there and took the rap for the sins of the rest of the unit. Shit!

After the IG and the Generals said their piece, they left and Col Lucas had us to himself to say a few words. He, too, congratulated us on our fine showing and said he realized how much hard work had gone into making it happen. He said he knew that people were strung out pretty tight, nerves were on edge, and physical/ mental fatigue were rampant. "But if you think you've been working hard getting ready for the IG, you ain't seen nothin' yet! We've been in high gear since I got here in August. Monday morning, we're going into overdrive. Now that we're through doing the nit-noy crap required by the IG, we're going to get back to what we're really here for--killing Commies!

"It's going to take a lot of work and some long hours. There's nothing wrong with hard work and long hours; that's what the Air Force is all about. And if you don't like the hard work and long hours, just remember this: the Air Force is an all voluntary service. You volunteered to be here and if you don't like being here, get out of my Air Force and go back to sacking groceries where the work isn't so hard and the hours aren't so long."

The talk smacked of the old "good news-bad news" routine: the good news was we're not going to have to work 14 hour days, six days a week. The bad news was we're going to work 18 hour days, seven days a week!

Col Lucas' talk covered the audience like a wet blanket. People were visibly sinking lower and lower in their seats with each word. And then he got to the punch line. "I know you people need some time to unwind. So I've reversed my decision not to have a down day tomorrow. All non-mission essential people will have tomorrow off, and I won't put out any tasking that has to be done over the weekend. That's three days to rest up, and you better use them to rest up. Come Monday morning, you're going to need all the stamina you can muster."

So the IG outbrief, which was supposed to pump new life into the unit, wasn't an "upper" at all. Instead, it was a very definite "downer". I left the theater and went back to work, but not a whole hellava lot went on the rest of the day. Col Lucas accompanied the entourage that took the IG Team to Seoul for their return flight to San Antonio. As is the case with most leaders of his type, when he's not around, people tend to get in as much screw-off time as possible. So everyone kinda marked time until 4:30 when we took off and headed for the Lounge for the "party".

For a Kick the IG Out of Town celebration to accomplish what it's supposed to, it needs to take place immediately after the outbrief, during duty hours, so people feel like they're getting a "bennie". This one started at five o'clock and, after the downer outbrief, attendance was just a little thin. And then there was the Operations boycott. Ops people stayed away in droves. But LG and the Orderly Room and the other folks who were re-inspected were there to party hearty. I felt good for them; they've been under a lot of pressure and needed a chance to blow off some steam. But it was a "controlled" blow-off, not a spontaneous rip-roar. By nine o'clock, the thin crown was even thinner and things were winding down. I left, went back to my room, and went to bed.

Slept in for the first time in a long time Friday morning and then *tried* to get some breakfast at the NCO Club. On my way over, I ran into Col Lucas (in uniform, as always) coming out of the Orderly Room. He reminded me that there was a going away luncheon for Sgt Jenny Burnell (she's *finally* getting out of here) at the Oriental House at noon. And then don't forget the NCO Prep Course graduation at three o'clock. "See you there, Chief (in uniform implied)," sez Col Lucas.

"Yes sir," sez I.

Well, so much for the down day. Since I was going to Jenny's luncheon in less than two hours, I farted off breakfast and went back to my room to shower and get into uniform.

♦♦♦♦♦♦♦♦♦♦

I didn't feel like running the 'ville Friday night, so I went to the SKIVVY NINE Lounge to watch movies and totally relax.

Since it was Friday night, most of SKIVVY NINE *was* running the 'ville, so the Lounge was virtually empty. Since it was, I asked the bartender if I could choose the next movie to be shown. She polled the clientele (six people) and they didn't mind, so I went through the tape catalogue and picked out "The Sting". I've seen bits and pieces of the flick over the years, but had never sat through it from beginning to end. The plot is so complicated that you have to see it uninterrupted from the beginning to appreciate it. So the barkeep threw the tape on the VCR and we settled back to enjoy it.

About half way through the movie, the door of the Lounge flew open and Col Lucas came swooping in. He was hyper. "Hey, Guys! SKIVVY NINE's playing a basketball game and there's nobody there to watch the game. Come on! Lets go cheer them on to victory!"

There was some mumbling and grumbling, but nobody moved. Then SSgt Karl Hampton, who was in the middle of the video game, said, "Colonel, the gym is all the way at the other end of the base and it's eight degrees outside. I can't see walking all the way down there to watch a basketball game."

"That's OK," bubbled the Colonel. "I've got my staff car outside and I know we can cram all you guys in. I'll give you a ride down there and back." Well, there goes that excuse.

Still mumbling and grumbling, everyone started putting on their parkas and heading for the door. Everyone except me. Through the entire scene, I had sat with my eyes glued to the TV screen, trying to be transparent. It didn't work. Lucas zeroed in on me. "Come on, Chief. We need some spectator support. Lets go!"

I never took my eyes off the TV screen while I answered Col Lucas. "Sorry, Colonel. It's not that I'm not an athletic supporter. I've been to every softball and football game SKIVVY NINE has played since I've been here. I like softball and football--I absolutely detest basketball. So I'm sure that, just this one time, you won't mind if I beg off doing unit business and just kick back and relax with a movie."

I braced myself for a verbal beating with the central themes being my disloyalty to the unit and not being a team player. It didn't happen. "That's OK. Maybe you'll change your mind and join us later. OK guys--lets go get 'em!"

And then he swooped out the door with his captive spectators in tow, leaving the bartender and me in an empty Lounge to enjoy "The Sting".

Chapter Sixteen

IT WAS THE BEST OF TIMES

Sunday, February 7th

Absolutely nothing has been happening around here lately and that suits me just fine. Col Lucas hasn't done anything stupid; the Orderly Room hasn't pissed me off; Maj Weber's staying up with his paperwork; Ruby the Viper has Ops Admin humming like a well-oiled machine; and I've been working reasonable hours (6:00 a.m. to 5:00 p.m.). The ho-hum life is great on my nerves, but it sure makes for piss poor journal entries.

About the only thing worth mention was the Monthly Recognition Breakfast last Monday. I had all the Admin folks who worked on the awards and decs project recognized as Professional Performers--all, that is, except Rick Meyers, Sylbethia Blue, and Cheniqua Wilson-Peters.

Professional Performers get a nice certificate, a letter of appreciation from Col Lucas, and a three day pass. The Adminers who reaped those bennies Monday really appreciated the recognition and they deserve it. The kicker was that all three of the above mentioned slugs came into my office after the breakfast and demanded to know why I hadn't put them in for the award. I threw them out. Sometimes, people amaze me.

♦♦♦♦♦♦♦♦♦

MSgt Greg Guthier went to Col Lucas to protest the triteness, tackiness, and tone of a letter he had received from Lt Lane. You can guess the outcome of the meeting. Greg didn't gain any satisfaction and lost a large chuck of his ass in the bargain. The

Colonel backs the Lieutenant and her help one hundred percent; right, wrong, or indifferent. It's not right, but that's the way it is.

Sgt Loftus gave me some shit last Thursday, and I gave her the "You E-4 Sergeant, me Chief Master Sergeant, and don't you fuckin' forget it any time soon, Bitch" routine. Finally--sweet revenge. When I got back to my office, the phone was ringing. The Colonel didn't even have his Executive Officer call me. He called direct. "Chief, I know I told you not to allow Sgt Loftus to be disrespectful, but you didn't have to rip her liver out. My staff has a tough enough time dealing with me. They don't need to worry about a Chief taking swipes at them. Take it easy!" Click.

Even Maj Reardon can't do anything with those two. They treat him the same way they treat everyone else--like dog doo doo. In the Command Section, it's the Lucas/Lane/Loftus show and Reardon is the odd man out. And it's not just because his name begins with an "R" instead of an "L". His only recourse is to come to my office, slam the door, and dump his guts on Maj Weber and me. That shows you just how much power those two ladies have.

Wednesday, February 10th

My improved relationship with Col Lucas seems to be holding. When I walked in the door at work this morning at 6 a.m., my phone was ringing. It was Col Lucas. He'd been calling since five o'clock. From what I understand, he gets to work around four, but I've never been here to witness that myself. Anyway, I've sold him on my plan to consolidate Flight Operations and Operations Production (one hellava job) and he wanted an update on what I had done so far. After I briefed him on my progress, he came from behind his desk, offered me a cup of coffee (say what??), and sat on the sofa across from me.

He started to chit-chat and then said he needed my personal view (from an enlisted perspective, of course) on the three officers who work for him; Majors Loren Winkler, Weber, and Reardon. I haven't mentioned Winkler before because he's the Detachment 1 Commander and I don't have many dealings with him. Thank God! He is the most pompous, sanctimonious, holier-than-thou, verbose, condescending, back-stabbing son-of-a-bitch I've ever seen. I wish I could think of some more adjectives to describe how I really feel about this whiffle ball, but I guess those will have to do. And they're the same ones I used to describe him to Col Lucas. I wasn't too surprised when the Colonel agreed with my assessment of the Major.

I told him Maj Reardon was a nice guy, well respected by the troops, but tended to "shoot from the hip" when making decisions. He agreed and asked if I thought he would make a good unit commander some day. I said yes and he said he would pass my recommendation on to MGen Mather when he comes in from the Headquarters to visit next week. (Are you believing this? I was stunned!)

And then we got around to Maj Weber. I told Col Lucas he was the most knowledgeable Operations Officer I've seen in 26 years in the Air Force. Once again, he agreed. I also said that of all the people I've ever worked for, I put him in the top two; only Maj Ward Fox (from my time on the IG Team) was better. The Colonel said, "I know Ward Fox. He's hard to beat. Good man." Then he asked if Maj Weber would make a good unit commander at some later date. I said, "Yes, as long as he doesn't have to work for someone like you."

That statement brought a raised eyebrow and a barely detectable flinch, but his only verbal response was, "Why?"

"Well, here's your chance, Big Boy," I thought. "Stay cool; be as objective as you can; don't blow it."

I leaned forward in my chair and looked Col Lucas straight in the eye. I told him how the Major and I have been reduced to eunuchs by Loftus and Lane; those two hide behind his eagles and he needs to take care of that. I said the Major wanted to protest, but was afraid of retribution. I told him Maj Weber (or anyone else) would shrivel up and die on the vine if they had a boss they were afraid to communicate with.

That got his attention. We spent the next 30 minutes *discussing* what had been going on over the past three or four months. He said he didn't really know the extent of what had been going on in the front office. In any case, he actually listened to me; he didn't get defensive; he actually gave me positive feedback. Our talk was a real eye-opener for both of us.

When it was all over, he stood up and stuck out his hand and said, "Chief, I wish you had come to me with this before."

I replied that with the atmosphere he had created, it was impossible for me to talk candidly with him on such a delicate subject. He *seemed* to understand. I don't know if our talk did any good, but I had a spring in my step as I walked out of that office. As I passed Loftus and Lane, I flashed my biggest, brightest smile and said, "Good morning, Ladies!"

Sunday, February 14th

I wrote a message for Col Lucas' signature Thursday on our manning situation. It's really bleak; we're down to 66 percent manned in 208s and 70 percent in 207s. The only AFSC that's "fat" is 202s, which bodes badly for them. They end up pulling all the not-shit details because we can't afford to spring any 207s and 208s. Anyway, I put together an eleven page message to ESC and the National Security Agency telling them the situation and saying we were not going to try to do more with less, which has always been the ESC philosophy in the past. Instead, we're going to stop doing all the nice-to-do things and do only that part of the mission that's absolutely essential.

The message was a political bombshell with no punches pulled. When I finished it, I sent it to the Command Section where I fully expected Lt Lane to rip it apart before she sent it in for the Colonel's signature. But she didn't change a single comma, period, or word, and neither did the Colonel. When it comes to something as politically sensitive as cutting back on the mission, they trust me explicitly. But if it's a not-shit APR, they hack it to pieces. Go figure.

♦♦♦♦♦♦♦♦♦♦

The 69th Carrier Task Group went on another operational mission last night and fun and frivolity ran rampant. We've started to draw crowds. Since we only frequent bars where our antics are tolerated/appreciated, "Danger Zone" usually cranks up the minute we walk in the door. And shortly after it comes on, the clientele start to whoop and holler. Last night was no different.

When we would line up for our carrier landings, we were joined by just about everybody in the place. There are only eleven "core" members of the CTG, but to watch the landings, you would think we have 50 members.

And the Jug Band has added another song (that makes two) to it's repertoire. It was given to me by DAL Lawler (who's been at SKIVVY NINE most of his adult life) over a few beers in the Lounge last week. DAL said that, years ago, the "SKIVVY NINE Fight Song" was sung in every bar on every bean run but, for some reason, it had fallen out of favor. He asked me if the Jug Band would bring it back. I said I wouldn't know until I heard it. He performed it for me right there at the bar and, when I heard it, I told DAL the Jug Band would be honored to resurrect the rousing tune.

I got the gang together in my room to teach them the song the next night and we performed it in public for the first time last night. The first place we went in, we did "The Perfect Country and Western Song". When it was over, Boomer motioned for the DJ to hold up a minute and I stepped to the front of the Jug Band to lead them in their first performance of the "SKIVVY NINE Fight Song" in front of an audience.

"We're a bunch of dirty bastards,
Scum of the earth.
Born in a whorehouse,
Shit on, pissed on, kicked around the universe.

"Of all the dirty bastards,
We are the worst.
We are from SKIVVY NINE,
The asshole of the earth"

It brought the house down.

<u>Sunday, February 21st</u>

Well folks, we've got ourselves a real block buster here. The possibility that there's a little more than a professional relationship between Lt Lane and Col Lucas is finally out in the open. I haven't mentioned the possibility before now because I didn't want to sound trite and trashy when relating my trials and tribulations with the Command Section. But I've always had my suspicions and Majors Weber, Reardon, and I have talked about the possibility many times.

The appearances have certainly been there. Col Lucas never goes *anywhere* without Lt Lane by his side. I understand that an Executive Officer and Commander have to be close. The Exec is the Commander's flunky and must be available to do little things the Commander wants done. But with Lane and Lucas, it's borderline ridiculous! They go *everywhere* together. It's obvious even to the two stripers. They call her "Lieutenant Shadow" and "The Lieutenant Colonel". If there is anything going on between them, it would certainly explain the overly protective attitude he has shown toward her.

The event that brought the whole mess to a head was a visit by Mrs Col Lucas. When she came over here, most folks thought it was just another tennis shoe run, but this past week, the real reason for the trip bubbled up to the surface. The Lucases (sans Lt Lane, of course--she doesn't seem nearly as indispensable with the Colonel's wife around) and the Reardons went to a reception at the Officer's Club Wednesday night. Col Lucas excused himself to go to the men's room and, while he was gone, Major and Mrs Reardon were doing small talk with Mrs Col Lucas.

Mrs Reardon asked her how long she planned to stay over here and she said, "As long as it takes to save my marriage." **WHAM-O!!** Right on the line--just like that. The Reardons stammered and stuttered and tried to change the subject, but Mrs Col Lucas continued to dump. She said it was all over the Headquarters in San Antonio that her hubby and his Exec had a thing going. She also said she wasn't about to give up her 24-yer marriage without a fight. When the Colonel returned, the conversation (naturally) changed to other, more pleasant, avenues. But the cat was out of the bag.

Maj Reardon was in my and Maj Weber's office first thing Thursday morning to tell the sordid story. Even though we had had suspicions, Maj Reardon's revelations still came as one hellava shock.

Later that day, Maj Reardon showed up at our door again. His wife had just called him with more developments in the Lucas/Lane affair. Mrs Reardon is on the planning committee for some kind of function the Officer's Wives Club (OWC) is having. At a committee meeting that very morning, one of the other members (a

Colonel's wife) told Mrs Reardon that the Lucas/Lane thing was the talk of the OWC and Lt Gen Reynold's wife was seriously considering having her hubby get involved. Shiiiiiiit!!! If the three star gets involved, we're talking some big time dirty doo doo.

To throw even more shit into the game, MGen Mather is due in Thursday for a four-day visit. If this Lucas/Lane fiasco is the talk of the Headquarters like Mrs Col Lucas said, the General has got to know what's going on. And if he knows, what's he going to do about it? Ah yes, the plot does thicken.

Things could get pretty dicey around here over the next week or so. Majors Reardon and Weber and I have decided our best move is to lay low and not get hit by the shrapnel. If an explosion doesn't come, at least maybe the events of the past few days has gotten Col Lucas' attention and he'll back off where the protection of his Exec is concerned. If that happens, the lives of two Majors and one old gray haired Chief will get a little easier. Anyway, that's where things stand now. How 'bout them apples.

I think the surfacing of a possible situation between the Commander and his Exec is already starting to have the desired effect. Went to a luncheon Thursday to celebrate the tenth anniversary of employment for five Korean Ministry of National Defense civilians who work closely with us. I must go to these kinds of things all the time and this one was much like the others. But there was one major difference: Lt Lane wasn't sitting at the head table by Col Lucas.

That has been a real sore point for a lot of people in the past. The price of the meal for one of these things is always inflated to cover the price of meals for all the people at the head table. That's expected, and most folks don't mind picking up the tab for the Commander's and honored guest's meal; paying for the Exec's meal really stuck in a lot of craws.

For this ceremony, the Lieutenant was seated way in the back of the room, just about as far away form the head table as she could get. Maj Weber and I agreed that the Colonel was putting about as much distance between himself and his Executive Officer as he possibly could.

♦♦♦♦♦♦♦♦♦♦

The Fred McNair saga continues. You remember old Fred; he's the guy who walked off with half the classified material in Operations and got Court Martialed and sent to jail for his efforts. Well, this story isn't over.

The fact that Fred's wife was preggy is the one thing that got him a light sentence at his Court Martial. Well, his wife came due back in January and Fred wanted to be at the hospital for the blessed event. But since he was still in jail, he had to have someone escort him from Camp Humphries (where the jail is) to Seoul (where the hospital is).

He got in touch with two of his buddies (yes, he still has some) and asked them to do him this favor. Sergeants Mark Lynch and Charlie Cohen got a briefing from Jimbo Gambill on their duties and responsibilities as prisoner escorts and they headed out for Camp Humphries to pick Fred up and take him to Seoul.

There's a minor detail that needs to be highlighted at this point in the story. Charlie was appointed as the guard and Mark was the designated driver. Therefore, when they got to the warden's office, Charlie was the only one who had to sign the paperwork accepting custody of the prisoner. They got Fred to Seoul in time to be with his wife when the baby was born, but while he was in the delivery room, Mark and Charlie left the hospital for something to eat. The prisoner was left unguarded.

While Mark and Charlie were gone, Fred's wife had the baby and he went with her and the newborn back to her room. When Mark and Charlie returned to the delivery room--no Fred. They began looking for him but, before they could find him, Fred decided he'd had enough time with his family and, since his ride was nowhere to be found, he went to the bus station, bought a ticket, and headed back to Camp Humphries!

When Fred showed up at the warden's office (sans escorts) to be reincarcerated, the warden was not a happy lady. Meanwhile, Mark and Charlie reported back to Jimbo in the Orderly Room with the sad news that they'd lost their prisoner. Jimbo went ballistic.

By the time everything got sorted out, Col Lucas decided he was going to lay an Article 15 on both of them. The Colonel had Cohen dead to rights; he had been the designated guard and had signed for the custody of the prisoner. He got a $500 fine, busted to A1C, and one month of extra duty.

Mark Lynch, on the other hand, was another matter. He contended he hadn't signed for shit; he was only the driver and therefore, wasn't responsible for the prisoner. When Jimbo and Capt Oakley checked with the Legal Office, they were told that Lynch was right. Going strictly by the book, he had done absolutely nothing wrong.

But Col Lucas insisted that, at least by the *spirit* of the law (if not the letter), he was just as responsible as Charlie Cohen. He decided to apply pressure on Mark to accept the Article 15.

I've got to hand it to Lynch. He stood his ground, didn't knuckle under to the pressure, and refused to sign the Article 15. That meant the Colonel's only alternative was to Court Martial him. Only problem was, he *knew* he couldn't get a conviction. So Jimbo, Capt Oakley, and Col Lucas applied even more pressure. Same result; Lynch refused. So they gave him a Letter of Reprimand.

Last week when his APR hit the Orderly Room with top ratings, Capt Oakley called me and demanded that I apply pressure on his supervisor to mark him down on the APR. I couldn't do that. I told the Captain that, legally, Lynch hadn't done anything wrong and I wasn't going to do anything to punish him. The Captain didn't like it, but he finally sent Mark's APR on to the Personnel Office with the ratings remaining the same.

I don't know if I did the right thing on this one or not. Lynch was guilty as sin for leaving McNair unattended in Seoul and his buddy paid for it. But, technically, he wasn't in the wrong. I guess sometimes there really are shades of gray.

♦♦♦♦♦♦♦♦♦

Col Lucas has raised the "Battle Dress Uniform Picture" issue again. A couple of months ago, he wanted a unit picture with everyone decked out in BDUs to send to MGen Mather to show him how gung-ho SKIVVY NINErs were under his strong leadership. Well, only a little over 40 people showed up for his picture. That really pissed the Colonel off, but he dropped the idea until recently.

Since MGen Mather is coming out here next week, Lucas has decided that he wants to present him that picture personally. He had tried to get the flick himself and failed, so he gave the project to me. Although I loathed and detested the entire picture project, I decided to do the best job I could.

The first thing I did was analyze what went wrong the first time and do exactly the opposite this time. I considered the following factors:

TIME: The first picture was taken at 10 o'clock on a Saturday morning. A person has to be pretty damned motivated and dedicated to fall out for something like that on a Saturday morning. So I set this one up for 3:00 p.m. on Friday afternoon. People, especially day whores, will show up for just about anything if they're getting out of work to do it.

LOCATION: The first attempt was done on the flight line for two reasons. First, the flight line has plenty of room to hold a mob (although a mob didn't materialize). Second, for a picture with a lot of people in it, the photographer needs to shoot down on them and the control tower allowed for that. Problem: the flight line is a long way from anywhere. Not too many people are going to walk all that distance just to get their picture taken.

So I changed the location. This time, the picture was taken in front of the Orderly Room which is centrally located, easy to get to, and it's next door to the SKIVVY NINE Lounge (where the beer is). To get the altitude the photographer needed, I called the Chief in the Comm Group and got him to lend me one of their trucks they use to work on phone lines. The bucket on the back of the truck is capable of carrying a passenger to a height of 40 feet.

To get the space needed for a large crowd, I called CMSgt Larry Westinghouse (currently the head beagle in the Security Police Squadron, but formally one of my students at the Senior NCO Academy) and had him block off the street in front of the Orderly Room. A whole street would be enough to handle any crowd.

THE CONFUSION FACTOR: The first time the picture was attempted, Col Lucas couldn't seem to decide on an exact date and time. He wanted to be in the picture, but he kept trying to change the crowd's schedule to fit his schedule--and his schedule kept changing. Right up to the day before the picture, people weren't sure if it was on or off.

ADVERTISING: It was lacking (non-existent) the first time out. This time, in addition to the letter I sent, I flooded the entire unit with fliers and posters telling folks what was happening, when, and where.

BILLING: The first picture was billed as "BDU Picture", insinuating that if you didn't have BDUs, you weren't welcome in the picture. I played this one up as a "Unit Picture"; BDUs encouraged, but not required. If they didn't have BDUs (and I used myself as the example), they should come on out anyway. They could borrow a BDU field jacket from a buddy or, failing that, stand on the back row where no one could tell if BDUs were being worn or not.

With all those things taken care of, I was relatively sure of a good turn-out. Then Friday morning at the Commander's Staff Meeting, Col Lucas ensured the success of the project. He announced the picture to his entire staff and followed that up by saying, "Tell your folks to be sure and turn out. I'd hate to reduce Chief Beal to Senior Master Sergeant because he failed to get the picture I want." I didn't say anything--I just sat there and smoldered.

Later that day, during the Ops Officer's Staff Meeting, I told the Branch Chiefs what the Colonel had said and to be sure to pass his very words on to the troops. I said I full well realized no Colonel can demote a Chief Master Sergeant (that's an honor reserved for General Officers only), especially for not getting the picture he wanted. All that said, I wanted the best turn-out possible just so I could stuff his threat up his ass. The result was dramatic.

At 3:00 p.m., there were at least 150 SKIVVY NINErs standing tall in front of the Orderly Room. Col Lucas was literally beaming--

I thought he was going to have an orgasm. Off to one side so no one could hear, I said, "Well, Colonel, I guess this means I can keep my Chief stripes."

The snide remark went right over his head. He just kept smiling and nodded his head "yes".

Everything went off without a hitch. When the photographer was finished, the Colonel stepped to the front of the assembled multitude and made some announcements, one of which was the basketball game that night. He expected each and every one to be out there and give the team their support. Not one word of appreciation; not one word of thanks.

He dismissed them, but I went to the front of the crowd and stopped them in their tracks with one of my patented whistles. After I got them stopped. I gave them a few words on SKIVVY NINE pride, then ended it by saying, "I want to thank each and every one of you for coming out here this afternoon and making this picture happen for El Jefe'."

I was watching the Colonel when I said the words "for El Jefe'" and he had a look on his face like I had pissed in his well. Jesus--did he think they had done it for *him*? In any case, he has his picture now so I hope he's satisfied.

♦♦♦♦♦♦♦♦♦

SKIVVY NINE manning over the past couple of months has really been in the toilet. Our manning lives and dies on how many people extend their tours. Everyone comes over here on a one year tour, but a lot end up staying three, four, even five years. That's the only thing that keeps the manning at a sufficient level to get the job done.

Right now, we're down to as low as 60 percent manned in some AFSCs because people just haven't been extending. This problem has been causing ripples all the way back to the National Security Agency and the Headquarters and they want to know why the extension rate is so poor.

To answer the question, Col Lucas directed a survey be conducted asking people why they extend, why they don't, and how things should be better so more people would extend. When he gets "Here's why our people extend and here's how you can get more of them to do the same."

All the surveys came through me before going to SSgt Kerry Weaver to compile. I've been reading them just for grins and it seems that the main reason people aren't extending is Col Lucas himself. Morale is lower than whale shit. You can see an example of what I've been seeing below. It's obvious this young lady (I'm assuming it's a young lady from the look of the handwriting) has a definite opinion about what ails the 6903rd. And that ailment is Colonel Jason L. Lucas.

FROM: DOW *8 February*
SUBJ: Extension of Tour Survey
TO: Unit Members

1. To encourage extensions at SKIVVY NINE, management needs to identify what motivates your decisions to extend or to leave at normal rotation. This information is extremely critical to retention of our people in the Unit, especially now. Please give some careful consideration to the questions below and help us by offering your suggestions to improve extension rates. Please be objective and constructive.

- *If you have extended, what was it that motivated you to extend?*

  ____

  ____

- *If you aren't extending, give some reasons for your decision.*
  I hate this fucking place! Everyone here is out to screw everyone else. Attitudes are pissy! Morale sucks! No one here gives a damn! This is really a damned stupid question. Look around. Wake up and smell the coffee.

- *What can we do to improve the quality of life and the extension rate? (Here's where to remember the objectivity and constructiveness of your suggestions. Remember that some actions will take a lot of time to get approved and others would require greater authority than we have here at the local level. Use reverse side if additional space is necessary.)*
  It would take a fucking miracle. It won't happen! There's nothing here to extend for.

2. Thanks for your careful consideration. We hope to improve the "Quality of Life" here at SKIVVY NINE by implementing some of them. Please forward your completed surveys to your Branch Chief. I will collect the completed surveys by noon 18 February.

3. Name (Optional)________________ Grade: SSgt__ AFSC: 20250__

KERRY K. WEAVER, SSGT, USAF

After seeing the results of the survey and the timeframe the extensions started to drop (the day he arrived), I seriously doubt if he'll forward the results. The tone of the surveys gives one some idea what the atmosphere in SKIVVY NINE really is.

Wednesday, February 24th

Since Col Lucas arrived and went on his rampage, people don't want to stay here anymore. It is not a pleasant place to work and live. This thing is *serious*. So serious that I picked up four 207X1s at the air terminal today who were shipped in from the Philippines for a 90-day stay with us. Sunday, we've got 12 Korean linguists coming in from Okinawa for another 90 days and next Monday, we'll have nine Chinese 208s step off the Freedom Bird. They're coming in all the way from NSA, also for 90 days. All this is costing the Air Force MEGABUCKS in travel and per diem--all because one Colonel and his Lieutenant turned the place into a hellhole.

Col Lucas refuses to believe the extension rate has gone down all that much over the past few months. He asked the manpower folks in the Programs and Resources Division to conduct a study comparing how many people were serving on extensions when he arrived and how many are on extensions now. The results of the study were dramatic, graphic, and startling.

As you can see from Ken Price's letter below, there's a definite correlation between Col Lucas' arrival (10 August) and the drop in tour extensions.

From: PR (Sgt Price) *11 February*
Subj: 6903ESG Extension Statistics
To: CC

The information that you requested (Ref blue slip control number CC-0349) is proving to be nearly impossible to get. I have been able to come up with some figures that go back at least six months and I think you will find them useful. As of 10 Aug last year, there were 120 (of 339 authorized, and 315 assigned, not including officers) 6903ESG Operations personnel serving on extensions for a percentage of 35.4%. As of 10 Feb this year (exactly six months later) there are 40 (of 339 authorized, and 265 assigned, not including officers) 6903ESG Operations personnel serving on extensions for an overall percentage of 15.1%. The following charts give a further breakdown:

<u>10 August Last Year</u>

AFSC	AUTH	ASGD	ON EXT	PCT
202X0	70	65	22	33.3
205X0	15	17	1	5.8
207X1	38	31	8	25.8
208X4A	35	28	8	28.5
208X4G	171	165	81	49.9
209X0	10	10	0	0
TOTALS:	339	315	120	35.4

<u>10 February This Year</u>

AFSC	AUTH	ASGD	ON EXT	PCT
202X0	70	67	5	7.4
205X0	15	15	1	6.6
207X1	38	30	3	10
208X4A	35	27	0	0
208X4G	171	115	31	26.9

209X0	*10*	*9*	*0*	*0*
TOTALS:	*339*	*265*	*40*	*15.*

The 202 AFSC was down 26.4 percent; 205s only had one on extension then and they have one now. The reason their percentage went up was they have fewer people assigned now. The 207s had a 15.9 percent drop; the 208X4As (Chinese) had the most dramatic downturn at 28.5 percent; and the Koreans (208X4Gs) were almost as bad off at 22.14 percent. 209s didn't extend then and they don't now (they never have).

I don't know how Col Lucas plans to use this information, but I'm sure as hell he won't show it to MGen Mather. He'd have to be an idiot. But on the positive side, maybe the survey results will open his eyes and he'll change his ways. Yeah...Right. Figure the odds.

Sunday, February 28th

The MGen Mather/CMSgt Showalter (ESC Senior Enlisted Advisor) visit went well--for the most part. There wasn't a whole hellava lot to it. Just the normal walking around and skinning and grinning with the troops, briefings out the wazoo, and all the pomp and circumstance that always accompanies a General's visit. God, do I ever hate that shit!

I guess the biggest negative during the visit was Jimbo Gambill's handling of Billy Showalter's schedule. Jimbo was Billy's official host and, as such, was responsible for coming up with an agenda and then holding his hand and guiding him through it. Thursday night, the SKIVVY NINE Chiefs (Bob Estep, Sammy Veltani (a soon-to-be Chief), yours truly) and the First Sergeant were supposed to have supper at the Down Town Restaurant at 6:30. Sammy Veltani and I were there at 6:25 and waited outside for Showalter, Gambill, and Estep to arrive.

At 6:45, they still hadn't arrived, so Sammy and I got tired of standing around in the cold waiting, went inside, and ordered our meal. At seven o'clock, they came strolling in and, since Sammy and I were at a table for two, sat down at a table across the room. Jimbo came over and asked us to join them. We were right in the middle of the meal and I wasn't about to pick up my plate, silverware, drink, and coat and do a balancing act across a restaurant just to sit with them. When we did finish, we went over and sat with them while they ate. By the way, there was no apology and no explanation as to why they were late.

Friday night was supper at the Tai Lo Chinese Restaurant at 6:00. Once again, I was there on time, but this time, there was no Sammy Velanti. I didn't bother to stand outside and wait, but went right in and ordered my usual fried noodles and a beer.

By the time I got my food and ate it, it was seven o'clock and the entourage still hadn't showed up. I paid my bill, left the joint, and was on my way back to the base when I ran into them. Once again, no apology or explanation, but they did invite me to go back to the restaurant and watch them eat. I did. Sammy never did show up. Guess he's a little quicker on the up-take than I am.

Last night I was supposed to have cocktails and dinner with the gang at the Afterburner Club, but I decided I didn't need that aggravation, so I just didn't show up. I guess I may have burned a bridge with Bobby Showalter, but I just got tired of being treated like a bastard step-child.

MGen Mather and CMSgt Showalter left this morning. I think the visit was a good one; if it was, Col Lucas will be happy and, when he's happy, everybody's happy. If it didn't go well, I hate to think what the next weeks here are going to be like

♦♦♦♦♦♦♦♦♦

And then there's the straaaaaaange story of Sgt Lyla Garber. She's a 207X1 on Charlie Flight and, before she showed up at my office door last Thursday, I had never seen her before. She's the "fade into the woodwork" kind of person.

The saga began when Sgt Garber went to see the First Sergeant Thursday morning to protest the ratings on her APR. Although the APR isn't even written in final form yet, she had been snooping around Capt Henke's office on a mid shift and found the draft. She had been rated an overall seven (tops is nine) and she thought a nine would be more appropriate. So she went to see Jimbo to cry on his shoulder. He was busy babysitting Showalter, so he palmed her off on me. I gave her a 30 minute appointment for 2:30 and she ended up talking for an hour and a half.

To go into the minute details of her story would take a ream of paper, but the general gist was this:

She's been here six months, and from the moment she got off the plane, SSgt Vic Webster had been making passes at her, trying to get her to go out with him. To make matters worse, when she was assigned to Charlie Flight, Webster was assigned as her trainer. She was in close contact with him almost every hour of the working day. He applied big time pressure for her to go out with him, and told all the guys on Flight that she was his girl and to stay away from her. A classic case of sexual harassment.

She finally had enough and asked her supervisor (SSgt Joe Long) to assign her another trainer. He did, but Webster continued to harass her, not only at work, but also off-duty. Because of this, she was in a terrible state of mind when she took her initial job qualification test. She failed miserably.

Sgt Garber went into remedial training for a re-test, but the situation with Webster got worse, causing her to do poorly in training. She finally took her problem to the Mission Supervisor, MSgt Mitch Burrell. Mitch had a meeting of all the principles--himself, Webster, Garber, and Joe Long. He gave Webster a lawful order to stay away from Garber and then (according to Garber) launched into a verbal attack on her. He accused her of enticing Webster and told her, "Young lady, if you don't get your head together, I'll do everything I can to get your clearance revoked."

This unprovoked, undeserved verbal abuse caused Garber to lose all hope. She completely withdrew; she wouldn't look at or speak to anyone on Flight unless she was spoken to first, and even then, her replies were one syllable answers whenever possible. She said everyone on Charlie Flight hated her and were out to get her. It was in that frame of mind that she took her second job qual re-test and failed again. She admitted Long and Burrell had given her words of encouragement before the test, but she was sure they were not sincere and, in fact, Burrell secretly wanted her to fail. So she obliged him.

When someone fails the job qual test the second time, they must meet a Special Review Panel. The panel is chaired by Maj Weber and it's their job to determine what the problem is, if it's correctable, and whether the person is trainable and should retain their AFSC.

When Garber went before the panel, she was very defensive, downright surly, and, at one point in the proceedings, was insubordinate to Maj Weber. The Major was taken completely aback, but he kept his cool and the panel decided to allow Garber to take the test a third time. If she failed, her 207X1 AFSC would be taken away and she would be involuntarily retrained. Maj Weber had her, Long, and Burrell into his office the next day for a private counseling session where he chewed her ass for her insubordination the pervious day.

Sgt Garber went into remedial training again and did much better because, according to her, Webster had left for Chicksands,

England and she didn't have the added pressure of having him harassing her all the time. But she continued to be withdrawn and anti-social because Burrell, Long, and everyone else on Charlie Flight hated her. But when she took the test for the third time, she passed--barely.

And now Long is leaving too and, before he goes, he has to write an APR on Garber. He marked her down in Bearing and Behavior (insubordination to Maj Weber); Job Performance (the job she does can't be done without communicating with other people); Interpersonal Relations (surly and withdrawn); and Training (after all, she did fail two tests). It all added up to a seven rating instead of a nine.

I asked Garber what she wanted me to do. She replied that, because of her special situation, there were good reasons for her behavior, and I should call Long in and force him to re-accomplish her APR. I said I couldn't do that. I offered to get with Burrell and Long, tell them her story, see if their side jived with hers, and ask them to reconsider the ratings.

When she left, I called Burrell and Long (fortunately they were working a swing shift) and they came right over to my office. Since Capt Henke was filling in as Flight Commander on Charlie Flight, she came along, too.

I told them the Lyla Garber story in great detail just as she had told it to me. As I went along, I couldn't help notice the trio's looks of disbelief. They were especially upset with the part where Burrell threatened to suspend her clearances. Both he and Long swore that most of the story was half-truth and exaggeration, but that part of it was a downright lie.

After getting the rest of the story from Long, Burrell, and Henke, we all agreed that, although she had been wronged by Webster, they had taken care of that problem early. For her to completely withdraw, in their opinion, was a gross overreaction. We also decided she may be suffering from a persecution complex ("everybody hates me and are out to get me") and might benefit from a psychiatric evaluation. Also, Long refused to re-do her APR.

I didn't know how to go about getting Garber entered into a mental health program. Jimbo handles that kind of stuff. It was getting close to time for my meeting with Showalter, so I told Long, Burrell, and Henke I would discuss the situation with Jimbo that night during dinner and ask for his help.

I did, but Jimbo's reaction was one that I did not expect. He said he was very reluctant to give Garber a psych eval because he had corroborating evidence that her story was true. I was bumfuzzled. I asked him who his sources were and he gave me three names--all black guys.

I struggled like crazy to keep the thought from even entering my mind, but it did. Jimbo, Webster, and Garber are all black; the three sources are black; Burrell, Long, and Henke are white. So do we have a case of black folk sticking together in a fight against white folk or vise versa? The plot thickened even more Friday morning.

Jimbo took time out from his busy schedule with Showalter and gave me a call. He said he had discussed the "Garber case" (his words) with Capt Oakley and the Captain wanted to see me, Long, Burrell, and Henke later that morning to discuss the situation. Charlie Flight was on Swing/Mid break, but I got hold of everyone and we went to see Capt Oakley at 11:00 a.m.

Capt Oakley was very defensive during the discussion. He said he was reluctant to question Sgt Garber's sanity when, in his opinion, her story was probably true. I said we weren't questioning her sanity. We just think she *may* be suffering from paranoia and needed help. The only way to get that help is to get her to a psych.

Capt Oakley said our story sounded good, but he had reason to believe we weren't sincere in our good intentions. He added that he wanted statements from each of us so he would have "written documentation" on what we were trying to do to Garber. He would make a determination whether to give Garber a psych eval after he had read our statements. By the way, Capt Oakley is black, too.

It may all be a coincidence that the two sides in this thing are divided along racial lines. God! I sure hope it's a coincidence. This is all I need with less than six weeks to go; the possibility of a sticky racial incident. I don't know how this thing is going to shake out, but I don't want to see anyone on either side get hurt.

Wednesday, March 2nd

Tuesday night, I went to the SKIVVY NINE Lounge to help Sammy Velanti celebrate his first day as a Chief Master Sergeant. He put $50 on the bar and when that was gone, he put up $50 more.

For some reason, the "chemistry" of the crowd was just right and, before anyone knew what was happening, there was one hellava party going on. No reason--nothing special--everybody just felt good. Even Col Lucas' arrival didn't kill things. Usually when he and Lt Lane come through the door, people clam up, stay a few more minutes, and leave. Not last night. I didn't get to bed until almost midnight which, for me, is unheard of on a work night.

♦♦♦♦♦♦♦♦

And speaking of the Colonel, his wife went home Monday. I don't know if she saved her marriage or went back to start divorce proceedings. All I know is it's a sticky situation. Since she left, Col Lucas and Lt Lane don't seem to keep near as much distance between themselves as they did with Mrs Col Lucas here.

♦♦♦♦♦♦♦♦♦♦

The Garber thing has cooled down a little. Capt Oakley looked at the statements from Henke, Burrell, Long, and me along with all the rest of the evidence and made the only decision he could make. Sgt Garber goes for her initial psych eval Friday and I'm sure it will show she's suffering with a bad case of paranoia.

Chapter Seventeen

THE WORM TURNS

Sunday, March 6th

The urinary Olympiad between Col Lucas and me has resumed--in spades. Due to an almost unbelievable series of happenstances, our relationship reached new depths last week.

Maj Weber was taking a well deserved, long overdue leave. Before he left, he submitted my APR (with recommended endorsements) to the Command Section. When it got there, Lt Lane sent it to Col Lucas for his review and approval/disapproval. She also included her thoughts on whether or not I deserved an APR that strong in the form of little yellow "stick-ons" attached to the write-up.

The package came back to the Ops Admin folks (as they always do) for correction; the write-up wasn't centered on the page. It was one space too far to the right (honest-to-God). Only problem was, either Lucas, Lane, or Loftus forgot to remove the "stickies" and Ruby the Viper found them. She took a great deal of pleasure showing the notes to me; got so excited, she damn near peed her pants.

When I read the notes, I got sick to my stomach and then I got real mad. (The notes written on the "stickies" can be seen on the next page. The italicized entries are Lt Lane's exact words; the bolded text is my interpretation of them so the reader can better understand what the illiterate Lieutenant was trying to say.) After I read them, I carefully removed the stickies from the APR, attached them to a piece of paper, and made copies. Then during lunch that day, I dropped the originals in the mail to my wife in San Antonio.

THE LANE "STICKIES": Each comment below was on an individual stick-on with an arrow drawn to specific portions of the APR write-up.

Jason,
No comment other than.....this is what disgusts me most about the system.
Jason??? And it "disgusts" her that the system would allow me to have such a strong APR.

You promised you would get him for me. This APR isn't getting him. It is a reward!
Oh, I see. This makes a lot of things clearer.

The truth is all that is asked for!!
I think here, she is implying that my APR write-up isn't the truth--in other words, a lie.

Affectionately Yours--
You Know Who
"Affectionately yours--you know who"? She might as well have signed it "Sugar Snookums". Not exactly what one would expect of correspondence from a Lieutenant to a Colonel.

At that point, Ruby and I were the only two people outside the Command Section who had seen the notes. I intended to keep it that way, but it just didn't work out. Before the week was over, I would be forced to use the note as a shield against the venomous rage of Col Lucas.

Before he went on leave, Maj Weber also wrote Capt McGranahan's OER at just about the same time he wrote my APR. Every time he sent it to the Command Section for Col Lucas' endorsement and signature, it came back with "stick-on" notes from Lt Lane plastered all over it directing changes that had to be made. Wednesday morning, it came back one more time.

This time it had a note on it that said, "This portion of the OER sounds just like the part in Block IV. Rewrite it!" Since the Major had been on leave, I had been making Lane's corrections for him, but this one was a little over my head. It required a complete rewrite, and Chiefs just don't write evaluation reports on Captains. So I put a "stick-on" note on it that read, "Maj Weber; Here's another nasty note from our favorite Lieutenant, but I'm afraid I can't handle this one. You'll have to fix it when you get back. Sorry. TWB" Then I dropped the package in the Major's in-basket.

When the Major came in on another matter later that day, he found the OER and my note, spent an hour or so making the correction the Lieutenant had directed, and gave the package to Ruby for re-typing. Then he left thinking everything was cool. It wasn't.

When Ruby made the correction, she sent it back to the Command Section for Lane's approval and Lucas' signature. AND SHE LEFT THE NOTE TO MAJOR WEBER ATTACHED TO IT!!! (Knowing Ruby, I'm not absolutely sure she didn't leave the note on the package on purpose.) Lt Lane found it, of course, and turned it over to Col Lucas for his action. The Colonel went frothing-at-the-mouth berserk. He called Maj Weber in off leave *again* (this time at 6:00 a.m., I might add) for another of his patented ass chewings.

He showed the Major my note and demanded to know what had been so "nasty" about Lane's note. Maj Weber had to admit that there really wasn't anything that "nasty" about the note. It was just frustrating and exasperating to have to keep making unnecessary corrections and that's what came out in the note.

According to Maj Weber when he recounted the exchange, that was the wrong answer. It sent Lucas into absolute conniption fits. He launched into a ten minute tirade about what an asshole I am and said he was going to have me in to relieve me of a couple pounds of my ass because of my attitude. Hell, he might even fire my ass and send me back to San Antonio with my tail between my legs. Since Sammy Velanti had made Chief, he had a ready replacement, so why not. It all depended on how repentant I was after he was finished with me. And then he dispatched the Major to fetch me for the slaughter.

Maj Weber showed up in front of my desk wearing the now-familiar post-ass chewing expression on his face. He told me what had happened and said the Colonel wanted my ass in his office right now. My stomach did a loop-the-loop as I reached way in the back of my right hand, bottom desk drawer and drew out a little piece of paper. I handed it to the Major.

"Sir, Ruby found this on a copy of my APR that was sent back for correction. I sent the original back to San Antonio after I made several copies." Maj Weber read the note as I talked.

"As you can see, Sir, if the Lieutenant wants to get into the 'lets compare notes' mode, I think she's got more to lose than me." When the Major finished the note, he held it to one side between his thumb and forefinger, whistled real low, and said, "Jesus!! This is hot!"

"Yes Sir, it is," I said. "If you would do it for me, Sir, I'd like for you to take that copy of the note to Col Lucas instead of me going to see him. Tell him that only three people outside the Command Section know about it; Ruby, me, and now, you. However, he should be informed that the original is safely back in San Antonio and I can get my hands on it quickly should the need arise.

"I also want you to tell him that if he still insists on chewing my ass or entertains the remotest thought he might want to fire me, I will stuff that note so far up his ass that he'll have to take it out through his nostrils. And I want him told in those exact words, or as close to it as you can get. Can you do that for me, Major?"

Maj Weber, for the first time in a long time, had that little boy, impish look he used to get sometimes before Lucas came. He kinda chuckled and said, "Chief, I would be honored to be your messenger."

"Thank you, Sir."

The Major walked out and I leaned back in my chair, stared at the ceiling, and waited for the phone to ring. It didn't. Five minutes drug by before the Major stuck his head in the door with a smile so big, his face almost couldn't hold it.

"Message delivered in your very words, Chief," he bubbled. "Message received and fully understood. I'm outta here--I've enjoyed about as much of this shit as I can stand." He gave me a "thumbs-up" and left to enjoy the remainder of his leave. I felt as though a gigantic weight had been lifted off his chest.

Wednesday, March 9th

Well, here I am making my Wednesday night entry on a Wednesday morning--*early* Wednesday morning. It's 3:00 a.m., and boy am I having fun! The mad Colonel has struck again.

We're in the middle of a week-long 51st Tac Fighter Wing exercise. True to his philosophy of participating in base activities (when it suits him), Col Lucas is into the exercise right up to his eyebrows. Under normal conditions, they are a monstrous pain in the ass. But the chicken shit we're being given in this exercise makes it the worst ever..

About the only plus to being in SKIVVY NINE during an exercise is that the building we work in is one big gas mask. During a chemical attack, the air is filtered so the inhabitants won't have to wear chemical gear. Therefore, we rarely wear gas masks during exercises unless we go outside. But for this exercise, the Mad Colonel decided we all needed a little torture time in the mask. So every two hours, he has the Exercise Evaluation Team simulate the building's air filters have broken and everyone goes into chem gear (to include the mask). Sometimes we stay in it 30 minutes, sometimes 45, and a couple of times, an hour. That ain't training; that's harassment.

Another piece of shit the Mad Colonel threw into the game for this exercise is the 24-hour duty day. The exercise kicked off at 5:00 a.m. yesterday morning and he waited until nine o'clock to decide that he wanted to go to 24 hour operations. Then he told the "B Team" to go back to their dorms and be back to work at 6:00 p.m. I'm on the "B Team" (Maj Weber is on the "A Team") so I left and went back to my dorm to try for some sleep. No luck. I had just had a good night's sleep, so I wasn't in the mood.

Came in to work at 6:00 p.m. and, except for putting on the gas mask every hour or so, have done absolutely nothing exercise related. I did clean out my in-basket where stuff had been accumulating all day because I wasn't at work.

The base don't play exercise at night; they're almost all home in bed where sane folks should be. But not SKIVVY NINE! We're sitting inside an air-tight, chemical proof, concrete reinforced bunker with eight foot thick walls wearing our gas masks, twiddling our thumbs because there's nothing to do, and wondering why the hell we're here at three o'clock in the morning!!!

Oh well, one good thing came from this fiasco. Maj Reardon (B Team Commander) walked into my office about an hour ago and a bullshit session broke out. We chit-chatted for a long time and then the subject got around to what it always does--the Mad Colonel. The topic of "the notes" came up: my note to Maj Weber that ended up in the Colonel's hands and Lane's note to the Colonel that ended up in my hands.

Maj Reardon said Col Lucas fully intended to fire me when he saw my note. But when he found out I had Lane's note, he admitted (in his words), "The son-of-a-bitch has me over a barrel with that note. If I fire him, he'll nail me with it." So he decided to allow me to finish my tour. How nice of him.

Chapter Eighteen

SLIDIN' ON OUT

<u>Sunday, April 3rd</u>

I'm somewhere over the Pacific, winging my way toward "The Land of the Big BX", courtesy of United Airlines. I've got myself a Wild Turkey on the rocks, the sweet sound of Country & Western blasting out of the headphones I'm wearing, and a perfect atmosphere for my last entry in this missive. So here we go, boys and girls.

It's over. It's finally over. My year at Osan could have been the crowning jewel in my career. Instead, I endured a massive security violation; a MARGINAL IG Inspection; a fired Commander; a new "John Wayne-type" Commander hell-bent on healing a sick unit; the humiliation of a public dressing down; scores of unnecessary exercises; an IG re-inspection; and finally, the skullduggery and intrigue I had to perpetrate to avoid being relieved of duty. Not exactly the way I envisioned it would go when I started out.

But the positive side of my Osan experience was the people--well *some* of the people. There were some damn good ones, and they made my last few days in Korea an absolute pleasure.

First, there were my Bean Runs. They were fantastic! You read right--multiple Bean Runs. The first was on 22 February and everyone (including me) thought that was it. But the next Monday morning, a new flier appeared announcing the first Run was actually a "practice" for the *real* one on Friday, the 28th of February. What class. Two Bean Runs for the old Chief.

They both began at O.B. Up (tradition is hard to kill), but from there the schedule was all C&W Bars in deference to my music preference. The CTG was in rare form, the Jug Band performed admirably, and frivolity ran absolutely rampant.

The night after the first Bean Run, Maj Weber organized a going away dinner at Greg Guthier's house. It was an intimate affair; the guest list was very small. Of course there was Greg, his wife, and the Major. Then there was Capt Jean Henke, Capt Ed Jacoby, MSgt DAL Lawler, MSgt Boomer Marshall, Capt Curt McGranahan, SMSgt B.O. O'Banion, Maj Phil Reardon, MSgt Earl Romano, CMSgt Sammy Velanti (my replacement), and Sea Sergeant Gerry Wise.

Greg whipped up some Italian grub accented with some superb Chianti. After dinner there was a little ceremony where the Major presented me with a clock he had especially made for the occasion.

It's actually a framed display that's about 18 inches wide and three feet high. The timepiece is at the top and the bottom has a representation of the Korean Peninsula with the U.S. flag on one side of it and the Korean flag on the other. Under that, there's the 6903rd Electronic Security Group shield flanked by two gold colored Oriental dragons. At the bottom of the display is a small plaque with this inscription:

> *Chief;*
>
> *We are proud to have served a tough year with you. You are made of the finest stuff we could want from our Chiefs...guts, brains, integrity, and commitment. You taught us a lot and never let us down. Thanks for being a priceless leader, counselor, and comrade-in-arms. Thanks just for being 'El Jefe'."*

When Maj Weber presented it and I read it, it brought a little tear to my eye. Only Major Weber can write like that. I said a few words of thanks, the party wound down quickly, and I went back to the base and my room early.

After the second Bean Run, I was sure that the festivities celebrating Chief Beal's departure from Osan Air Base was over. I was wrong.

Last night I was sitting in my room listening to my portable radio, reading a book and sipping on a beer when there was a knock on my door. I opened it to find Boomer Marshall and Waco Williams standing in the hallway with big grins on their faces. There was a meeting of the 69th Carrier Task Group in Air Force Village and my presence was required immediately.

The meeting was in Boomer's apartment and, as usual, it was obvious he was in charge. Also true to form, he cooked fajitas, and there were pinto beans, Mexican rice, and plenty of beer.

After we ate, everyone gaggled up in the living room, Sea Sergeant Gerry Wise presented me the Navy good conduct medal, which he pinned to the collar my sweater. That presentation was followed up by Boomer, who gave me a framed photo of the original CTG, which can be seen on the next page. The snorkel appeared from nowhere, I shot down the contents, and the ceremony was over--again. What a classy way to send the old Chief off.

Even though I didn't get to bed until two o'clock, I rolled out this morning at 6:00 a.m. Maj Weber had agreed to take me to the airport in Seoul and was scheduled to pick me up at eight. I was packed and ready by 7:45 and sipped on my coffee until the Major knocked on my door promptly at eight o'clock.

We were putting my luggage in the trunk of his Daiwu sedan

when Col Lucas appeared from out of nowhere. He was in uniform, even though it was 8:05 a.m. on Sunday morning, and he had his "brick" (radio) in his hand (just in case a war broke out). He did a lot of hemming and hawing before he stuck his right hand out and said, "Good luck, Chief. Have a safe trip."

We shook, he turned and started walking off toward the Orderly Room. Then he stopped and turned toward Maj Weber and me and said, "I was just out checking the area." Didn't want to leave the impression that he had come to see me off.

The Major got me to the airport with two hours to spare. Since we had some time to kill, we hit the bar and had a couple of Bloody Marys. Over our drinks, we rehashed the past year until an hour before departure time. We said our good-byes and I worked my way through the snarl of security arrangements toward the boarding area. At the least checkpoint, a little Korean guy rushed up to where I was standing.

"You Mr. Beal?" he asked.

"Yes."

"How come you not on that plane," he demanded, pointing to the Northwest Airlines Boeing 747 lifting off the runway on the other side of the plate glass window.

The little Korean guy proceeded to explain that Daylight Savings Time had become effective in the States that very day, and all the schedules had been set up one hour to meet connecting flights. My flight had taken off an hour early and I had missed it. Bat shit! Now what?

The little Korean guy escorted me to the bowels of the Northwest portion of the terminal. He said, "Wait here," and disappeared. Momentarily, he returned with an Army Specialist Fourth Class in tow. She turned out to be the Military Liaison for all of Kimpo Airport and wanted to know how she could help. I explained my situation to her and asked if there was anything she could do.

"No sweat, Chief," she chirped as she motioned me to follow her. "There's a United flight leaving in 30 minutes. I'll have you on it--guaranteed."

She worked her magic, I got a new boarding pass, and here I am. Of course, my luggage is on the Northwest flight (God knows if I'll ever see my clothes again), I'll never make my connections to San Antonio, and I'll probably end up spending the night in Chicago. The perfect ending to a perfect tour of duty!

Well, it's getting to be time to close out this entry and, I guess, the journal. The late hours I kept last night, the confusion at the air terminal, and the Wild Turkey I've consumed have combined to make me one sleepy puppy. So I'll just go to sleep now. I didn't write all this down for someone to read someday, but if you did, I hope you enjoyed it. Good night.

GLOSSARY OF TERMS

1. **Air Force Rank Structure:** Almost every character you'll encounter in SKIVVY NINE is a member of the military and will be referred to by their rank. The following table of Air Force ranks is provided for the reader who may not be familiar with our "pecking order"

ENLISTED

RANK	GRADE	ABBREVIATION
	Airmen	
Airman Basic	E-1	AB
Airman	E-2	AMN
Airman First Class	E-3	A1C
Senior Airman	E-4*	SrA
	Noncommissioned Officers (NCO)	
Sergeant	E-4*	Sgt
Staff Sergeant	E-5	SSgt
Technical Sergeant	E-6	TSgt
	Senior Noncommissioned Officers (SNCO)	
Master Sergeant	E-7	MSgt
Master Sergeant	E-8	SMSgt
Master Sergeant	E-9	CMSgt

* There are two ranks for the E-4 grade. A1C's are promoted to Senior Airman. After a year of "probation", SrA's are promoted to Sergeant and receive a pay raise. Outstanding Sra's may meet a board at the six month point, and if they are selected, are promoted "Below the Zone".

OFFICER

RANK	GRADE	ABBREVIATION
	Company Grade	
Second Lieutenant	O-1	2Lt
First Lieutenant	O-2	1Lt
Captain	O-3	Capt
	Field Grade	
Major	O-4	Maj
Lieutenant Colonel	O-5	LtCol
Colonel	O-6	Col
	General Grade	
Brigidear General	O-7	BGen
Major General	O-8	MGen
Lieutenant General	O-9	LGen
General	O-10	Gen

2. Shift Work: Shift work is a son-of-a-bitch and it wreaks havoc on the people who work it. First, the body clock is constantly out of whack, and most of the time, you feel like shit. Second, the shift worker gets screwed on off duty time. Their cycle is 14 days long followed by three days off. A day worker gets four days off every 14. A shift worker doesn't get holidays off (unless it coincidentally falls on a day of break). And a shift worker can't take time off in the middle of a Day Watch to take care of personal or official business. Hell, a shift worker don't even get time off to eat lunch.

Most people who don't work shifts have little or no empathy for those who do, so shift workers often feel like the bastard stepchildren of the unit. Therefore, they often develop a siege mentality and become intensely introverted and loyal to their Flight, the only people who really care about them.

3. Senior Enlisted Advisors (SEAs): A title given to Chief Master Sergeants who are selected to advise commanders on enlisted matters. Appointments are not necessarily made on merit, but are usually politically motivated.

As a group, SEAs are a glad-handing, back-slapping, brown-nosing lot who look down upon their fellow Chiefs as somehow inferior. Although most are assholes, there *are* some good ones. They maintain a rigid pecking order within their own ranks. A SEA's status is entirely dependent on the level and rank of the Commander they advise.

No commander below the rank of Colonel is authorized an SEA. Furthermore, SEAs are not authorized at organizations below the Wing Level, even if that organization is commanded by a Colonel. A good example is the 6903 Electronic Security *Group*, commanded by a Colonel.

Senior Enlisted Advisors assigned to Wings are "outranked' by those assigned at Divisions and Numbered Air Forces. Those SEAs are, in turn, "outranked" by those residing at Major Command (MAJCOM) level such as Strategic Air Command, Tactical Air Command, Military Airlift Command, Air Training Command, Electronic Security Command, etc, etc, etc.

Since all MAJCOMs are subordinate to Headquarters Air Force, one would think there would be parity among the SEAs at the MAJCOM level. One would be wrong. The Commander's rank and, to some extent, the mission of the Command determine status. SAC, TAC, MAC, and ATC are all commanded by four-star

Generals. But the SAC commander has bombers and missiles at his disposal that can destroy the world and civilization as we know it. He's number one, and his SEA milks it for all he's worth.

The TAC commander is pretty powerful, too. After all, those pesky little fighter aircraft can do a lot of damage.

The Commander of MAC holds sway over the lowly transport aircraft, commonly referred to as "trash haulers" by members of TAC and SAC. But even MAC comes before ATC in the pecking order--ATC doesn't fight. Its only mission is training.

If there is subordination among the SEAs who work for four-stars, you can imagine where the guys who work for the three- and two-stars fit into the overall scheme of things. By-the-bye, ESC is commanded by a two-star, so you can see where that puts our SEA.

And then there's the "Big Kahuna" of *all* the SEAs, the Chief Master of the Air Force. He, too, works for a four-star, but that four-star is the Chief of Staff of the Air Force. CMSAF is the ultimate enlisted position and the ultimate politician usually gets it.

Does all this sound a little silly, petty, and downright ridiculous to you? Well, it does to me, too. The best thing that could happen to SEA positions (except for the Chief Master Sergeant of the Air Force) would be elimination.

4. **Office Symbols:** Below are listed the Office symbols one can find at the 6903 Electronic Security Group.

OFFICE	ORGANIZATION/TITLE
CC	Commander
CD	Deputy Commander
CCQ	Orderly Room Commander
DA	Director of Administration
DP	Director of Personnel
LG	Logistics and Maintenance

SP	Security Police
XO	Executive Officer
XP	Plans and Programs

And then there's my gang:

DO	Director of Operations (always called the "Operations Officer")
SDO	Operations Superintendent
DOA	Exploitation Management
DOE	Ops Administration
DOF	Operations Production
DOFA/B/C/D	Able/Baker/Charlie/Dog Flights of Operations Production
DOI	Tactics Analysis
DOO	Mission Management
DOQ	Computer Resources
DOR	Airborne Operations
DORA/B/C/D	Able/Baker/Charlie/Dog Flights of Airborne Ops
DOS	Operations and Communications Security
DOT	Operations Training
DOV	Standardization and Evaluation

5. **Air Force Specialty Codes (AFSCs):** An AFSC consists of five digits with the first two representing a large, overall category of skills. The third digit is a specific skill within the overall category. The fourth number is the skill level (3=apprentice, 5=specialist, 7=technician, 9=manager) of the individual being identified by the AFSC. The final digit in an AFSC is a shredout to show that two AFSCs are very similar, but are somehow different. You'll see what we mean as we explain the Intelligence AFSCs.

INTELLIGENCE AFSCs

201X0:	General Intel Specialist (None assigned to ESC)
202X0:	Radio Communications Analyst
203X0:	Interrogator/Interpreter (None assigned to ESC)
204X0:	Photo/Imagery interpreter (None assigned to ESC)
205X0:	Electronic Intelligence (ELINT) Operator
206X0:	Intelligence Librarian (None assigned to ESC)
207X1:	Morse Systems Operator
207X2:	Non-Morse Systems Operator
208XX:	Cryptolinguist (Last digit used to indicate language)
209X0:	Communications Security Operator

As is often the case with military people, AFSCs have crept into our everyday vocabulary. We identify ourselves and others by using (usually) the first three digits of the AFSC. "I'm a 202 and my friend here is a 209."

The exceptions are the 207s and 208s. The 207s are referred to as simply X1s and X2s. The 208s almost always have their language precede their AFSC. "He's a Russian (or Korean, or Chinese, etc.) 208."

6. **Article 15:** Articles 15 are good and bad. The good part is, if you *know* you're innocent, you don't have to accept the Article 15. If you don't accept it, you've put the commander in a very ticklish position. He can recommend you for Court Marital, but if he does, he better have the evidence to convict. Therefore, most commanders are very reluctant to recommend Court Martial.

   On the bad side, if you do accept the Article 15, you're at the commander's mercy. There are few guidelines or rules to regulate punishment, so you could get off with a slap on the wrist from a wimp or hung from the highest yardarm by a hard-ass.

7. **Emergency Destruction Team**; There are two serious flaws in the EDT concept. First, the EDT is made of 202/5/7/8/9's who don't have a clue how to go about destroying massive amounts of paper and magnetic media. They get training and they practice, but they're still pencil pushing, computer jocks groping to do what's right. These people are entrusted with things that burn and explode and they sometimes hurt themselves and others.

   The second serious flaw is the probability of an ESC unit ever being attacked by an enemy force. At some units there *is* a possibility--here at Osan, Berlin, Crete, and definitely when we were in Viet Nam. But figure the odds at Chicksands, Endland, Misawa, Japan, San Vito dei Normanni, Italy, and Anchorage, Alaska. But the EDTs at these units practice and play the game just as hard as those with the "red menace" breathing down their neck.

8. **MAC Space-A:** Anyone connected with the military can walk into any air terminal in the world and request space available seating on a MAC aircraft. If there's a seat open, you get on the aircraft and go. However, there is a "pecking order" for MAC seats. First on the list is people on Permanent Change of Station orders, then come the people traveling to a Temporary Duty assignment, then the ones on emergency leave, and so forth until you get to the dependents of military personnel who "just need a ride". Space-A is "free" in terms of money, but the Space-A traveler pays dearly in grief, heartache, and raw harassment.

9. **Morale, Welfare, and Recreation (MWR):** The first question one might ask is where does MWR get the money to provide all these services. The Army and Air Force Exchange System (AAFES) operates the Post and Base Exchanges, the military version of a department store. They also run the service stations, auto repair shops, movie theater, snack bars, "roach coaches", book stores, liquor stores, and anything else on base that generates revenue.

The profits gleaned from these ventures are supposed to be pumped into MWR to pay for all their programs. However, not all the money AAFES makes finds its way into MWR's coffers. Over the past twenty years, there have been several scandals where people in high places have been caught with their hand in the cookie jar.

Until the early seventies, MWR services were provided to military members for free or next-to-nothing. Now, they charge people for everything. They're in the business more to make money than provide Morale, Welfare, and Recreation to our troops. And nobody seems to be âble to explain where that money goes.

To make matters worse, Air Force Regulations are gerrymandered so no one can compete with either AAFES or MWR. Can't allow money to be taken away from the organizations designated to funnel that money into goods and services for the troops. Well that's so much bullshit.

The hot dogs that Maj Weber and I *gave away* at an athletic event could be construed as "competing with" AAFES and MWR. And the SKIVVY NINE Lounge is definitely looked upon as competition so there's been a long, on-going campaign to shut the Lounge down and eliminate that competition.

10. **Dinings Out:** The dress for a dining out is formal (mess dress for men and evening gowns for ladies), the proceedings are formal, and there's usually a formal speech. There's a President of the Mess (always the Unit Commander) and a Vice President of the Mess (usually the lowest ranking officer in the unit, but enlisted folks are sometimes afforded this honor if they are especially glib.) But there the formality ends. Without going into a lot of excruciating detail, there is much frivolity at a dining out. One good example is the "Grog Bowl".

During cocktails, dinner, and the after dinner speeches, members of "the Mess" look for violations in decorum or dress by other members of the Mess. When one is found, the offense is brought to the attention of the Vice President of the Mess (referred to as Mister/Madam Vice). The offense could be something as trivial as wearing a non-regulation tie, using the wrong fork while eating your salad, medals worn crooked, that kind of thing. Mister Vice refers the matter to the President of the Mess who then sentences the offender to visit the Grog Bowl.

The Grog Bowl is a commode (unused, I think) filled with some manner of alcoholic libation. The offender proceeds to the Bowl, dips the ladle into the concoction, apologizes for his transgressions, offers a toast to the President of the Mess, and goes "bottoms up" with the ladle.

11. **Chief Suites:** Every base in the Air Force has quarters set aside for people who are on temporary duty to that base or are "just passing through". For most folks, these accommodations are "adequate"--a bed, a place to hang your clothes, a shower, a TV, and a clock radio (if you're lucky). Chief's suites are a little different.

    Chief's suites are borderline luxurious. They commonly have a living room, kitchen, bedroom, fully stocked wet bar, TV in both the living room and bedroom, stereo, coffee pot (with coffee), and beer in the fridge. I've stayed in a lot of Chief's suites and found that some are more luxurious than others, but they're *all* very nice.

12. **Chief's Rules:** There's a display hanging behind my desk that I try to read at least once a day. It says:

    "There's an old belief that a Chief has only two rules. Rule One: The Chief is never wrong. Rule Two: If the Chief is wrong, refer to rule one.

    At the chance of alienating the Mystical, Magical, Order of the Chiefdom, I would offer these as the *Real* Chief's Rules.

1. When Chiefs and Colonels fight, Chiefs lose.

2. When two Chiefs fight each other, it's like two elephants fighting. About the only thing that's accomplished is the grass gets crushed.

3. Don't ever try to "act like a Chief". Be yourself; that's what made you a Chief in the first place.

4. Lower enlisteds can't fuck with Chiefs; officers don't fuck with Chiefs; other *Chiefs* fuck with Chiefs.

5. A Chief is not God. God was *never* an Airman Basic."

13. **The BITCH BOX:** Bitch Boxes are actually complaint boxes where Joe Two Striper can scribble a complaint on a piece of paper, drop it in the box, and get an answer directly from "the Colonel". The answers are given in the form of the "Bitch Box Bulletin", which is published weekly.

Naturally, Col Lucas doesn't write the replies himself. He doesn't have the time or all the answers. He has his staff farm out the bitches to people who know the most about the subject and they write the answers. But they write them as though the Colonel himself were doing the writing. People would have to be pretty stupid to think the Colonel writes all those replies himself (sometimes as many as 50 a week), but that's the way he wants it, so that's the way it's done.